MANUAL OF
PRACTICAL
INSTRUMENTATION

MANUAL OF
PRACTICAL
INSTRUMENTATION

CHARLES-MARIE WIDOR

DOVER PUBLICATIONS, INC.
Mineola, New York

Bibliographical Note

This Dover edition, first published in 2005, is an unabridged republication of
the edition published by Joseph Williams, Limited, London, in 1946.

International Standard Book Number: 0-486-44269-1

Manufactured in the United States of America
Dover Publications, Inc., 31 East 2nd Street, Mineola, N.Y. 11501

—Revised and New Edition 1946—

THE
TECHNIQUE

OF THE

MODERN ORCHESTRA

A MANUAL

OF

Practical Instrumentation

by

CH.-M. WIDOR

—Translated by EDWARD SUDDARD *—*

With an Appendix
by
GORDON JACOB

Price 40/- net.

LONDON
JOSEPH WILLIAMS Limited
29, ENFORD STREET, MARYLEBONE
W.1.

PARIS
HENRY LEMOINE & CIE

NEW YORK
MILLS MUSIC INC.

Original title page

Order of Chapters

In the present work, the order in which the instruments are usually arranged in orchestral scores has been followed, beginning with the most acute-toned:

$$(CHAPTER\ I) \begin{cases} \text{FLUTES,} \quad \text{(Piccolo)} \\ \text{OBOES,} \quad \text{(Cor Anglais)} \\ \text{CLARINETS,} \quad \text{(Bass Clarinet)} \\ \text{BASSOONS,} \quad \text{(Double-Bassoon)} \\ \text{SARRUSOPHONE,} \end{cases}$$

Then, after a short *Theory of the tone-production of Brass Instruments*, the following are dealt with:

$$(CHAPTER\ II) \begin{cases} \text{HORNS,} \\ \text{TRUMPETS,} \quad \text{(Cornets à Pistons)} \\ \text{TROMBONES,} \\ \text{TUBAS,} \quad \text{(Saxhorns)} \end{cases}$$

Next come

(*CHAPTER III*)   The PERCUSSION INSTRUMENTS,

Then, so to speak, in parentheses,

$$(CHAPTER\ IV) \begin{cases} \text{The} \quad \text{SAXOPHONES,} \\ \text{The} \quad \text{HARP,} \\ \text{The} \quad \text{ORGAN,} \end{cases}$$

And lastly,

(*CHAPTER V*)   The   STRINGS.

VI

Contents.

APPENDIX TO CHAPTER IV.

APPENDIX
by
GORDON JACOB

CONTENTS

Characteristic features of the present book are the <u>Complete Lists of Shakes and Tremolos for the Woodwind</u>, and of <u>Double, Triple, and Quadruple Stops for the Strings.</u>   It has always seemed to us that these matters are dealt with in somewhat too summary a manner in most works on Instrumentation. We venture to think the lists contained in this manual will fully meet the requirements of the student, and may even occasionally be of service to the accomplished composer.

Memento.

The velocity of sound is about 1100 f⋅t per second.

The deepest tone we are able to perceive is produced by a 64 f⋅t pipe (Organs of S⋅t Louis, U. S. A., and Sydney, Australia, in which the low C=8 vibrations per second).

A	64 f⋅t pipe corresponds to	8	vibrations per second.		
—	32	—	—	16	—
—	16	—	—	32	—
An	8	—	—	64	—
A	4	—	—	129	—
—	2	—	—	258	—
—	1	—	—	517	—

The low C which the Double-bass ought to be able to produce (and which *can* be obtained on some recently constructed instruments) is equivalent to a 16 f⋅t pipe.

Double C on the Violoncello . . . . is equivalent to an 8 f⋅t pipe.

Tenor C on the Viola . . . . is equivalent to a 4 f⋅t pipe.

(Standard French Pitch [*Diapason Normal*] = 435 vibrations).

The most acute tones perceptible to the ear are produced by 15,000, 20,000, 30,000 vibrations, and even more.

Timbre (Quality or Color of Tone—*Klangfarbe*) depends on the manner in which the column of air is set in motion, rather than on the material of which the instrument is made. In the case of the brass instruments, the mouthpiece, to a great extent, determines the mode in which the air is set in motion. Compare the little *cup* which forms the mouthpiece of the Trumpet with that of the Horn; these two cups are, in respect of depth, as 1 : 2, and the shallower the cup of the Trumpet, the shriller the tone, as may be seen by the Cavalry Trumpet; the deeper the cup of the Horn, the mellower its *timbre*.

It is only possible to sound the various harmonics—high and low— on brass instruments, provided there is a suitable ratio between the diameter and the length of the tube. If the diameter is too small—the tube too narrow— it is impossibe to obtain the fundamental tone.

The subdivision of the column of air contained in a pipe into halves, thirds, fourths, fifths, sixths, etc... (harmonics), corresponds to the subdivision of a string into the same aliquot parts.

Chapter I.

— ✧ —

The Woodwind.

THE FLUTE.[‡]

(Ital., *Flauto.* Ger., *Flöte.* Fr., *Flûte.*)

1.— The three-octave chromatic scale of the Flute, embracing 37 degrees, extends from to .

Some players are able to sound a few still higher notes, even reaching E♭; this, however, is quite exceptional, and music should be written not for a few out of the way *virtuosi*, but for the ordinary run of performers.

The scale of the Flute is fairly even; the first 35 notes can be attacked and sustained *forte* or *piano* at will, without requiring the player to take any special care:

The 36th and 37th degrees can only be produced with some difficulty, and are inevitably harsh:

Impossible *piano*  excellent *forte.*

1st Remark: In case of need, the **36**th degree can be played *piano* by some performers, but this too is exceptional. As for the **37**th degree, it is perfectly impossible to obtain it *piano.*

2nd Remark: All intervals can be played *legato* on the Flute, save two:

Dangerous; *piano e legato* impossible. 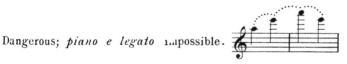 The E is harsh.

2.— By saying that this scale is fairly even, I mean that the composer may consider each of its degrees as being sufficiently in tune with the others, and need not trouble to think about the defects of a few of the notes.

3.— These defective notes are eight in number:

The three C's (N<u>os</u> 2, 6, 8) are somewhat too sharp, E♭ (N° 1), on the other hand, rather flat. D♭ (N° 3) requires special care in emission, and N<u>os</u> 4, 5, 7 are difficult to attack.

However, these defects hardly concern anyone but the performer, whose talent to a great extent corrects them.

4.— Although the Flute excels in the execution of florid passages, and its favorite keys are consequently those whose signatures contain few sharps or flats ✱, yet when called upon to

---

[‡] The Bœhm Flute with cylindrical bore, adopted nowadays by most performers, is alone referred to here.

✱ Avoid, however, the tonics D, E♭, E♮ as pivots of rapid arpeggios, the following intervals being difficult,

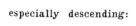 especially descending:

breathe forth a sweet, loving melody, no key suits it better than D♭. Of this several charming modern compositions afford sufficient proof. A♭ is likewise an excellent key, as may be seen by the following example, which also illustrates another point calling for comment.   We here see an *Andante* finishing on a C *pianissimo,* so sweet and pure that it would seem to be one of the best notes of the Flute, despite the remark made above (§3):

(By kind permission of Heugel et C⍳ᵉ, Editeurs-Propriétaires).

The reason is that this final C is not obtained in the usual manner. The performer in this case makes use of the *F* fingering (inferior twelfth), the pressure of the lips producing the third upper partial, like the finger on a violin-string.

5.— The only harmonics employed are the following:

the fundamentals being the first 14 degrees of the scale:

It is impossible to obtain any higher notes.

6.— As Gevaert very judiciously remarks in his *Treatise on Instrumentation:* "When a Flute doubles a melody assigned to a Soprano, or to a wind instrument of like pitch, its natural position is an octave above the voice."

When an organist wishes to brighten the tone of a group of 8ft. stops, he adds a 4ft. flute-stop, which merely strengthens the harmonics of the 8ft. stops, without at all creating the impression of a transposition in the octave.

Likewise, the office of the Flute in the orchestra frequently consists in reinforcing the first harmonic of the Oboe or the Clarinet. If, in a group of wind instruments, the Flutes doubling the upper parts in the octave be suddenly suppressed, everything will immediately become dull and gloomy, desperately poor and weak; yet on reading the score, the Flutes would seem to be perfectly needless luxury, mere filling-up.

Articulation.

7.—"Tonguing" is to wind instruments what bowing is to stringed instruments.

Flute-players make use of three kinds of tonguing, which they call *single, double,* and *triple articulation.*

Single-articulation is obtained by pronouncing the consonant *t* (as in "tut!"). It is with this species of tonguing that the maximum strength of tone and greatest intensity of color are obtained; it corresponds to detached bowing on the Violin:

Single-articulation:

However, great speed cannot be attained in this manner. In florid passages the performer has to make use of other, so to speak, mechanical means, allowing of neither the same intensity of tone, nor liberty of expression.

In such cases he resorts to *double-tonguing*, alternately articulating the consonants *t* and *k*, or to *triple-tonguing*, which involves the use of the three letters *t k t*, as in *t(ut)*, *c(ut)*, *t(ut)*, i. e. *t* and *k* are pronounced according to the phonetic system.

8.—As an instance of *double-tonguing*, let us take the Scherzo of Mendelssohn's *Midsummer Night's Dream*;

Single-articulation would not, considering the rate of movement, allow of producing the lower notes; so they are played as follows:

Double-tonguing:

The same remark applies to the solo in *Namouna* (Lalo):

Double-tonguing:

(J. Hamelle, Editeur-Propriétaire.)

Remark: Flute-players look upon both these examples with great apprehension, *staccato* passages being difficult to execute in the low register, but as they are possible and their effect delightful, what does it matter?

Double-tonguing also allows of easy and rapid iteration:

(By kind permission of A. Durand et Fils, Editeurs-Propriétaires.)   (Saint-Saëns, *Ascanio*)

9.—When ternary groups are in question, *triple-tonguing* is adopted, being nearly as rapid as *double-tonguing*, but with this kind of articulation there is always a slight risk of inequality of tone, on account of the natural tendency to accent the last of the three consonants.

Passages such as the following are quite easy, owing to the uniformity of the figure and the absence of any kind of melodic feeling; they are played quite mechanically:

But here is a much more difficult figure, the execution of which calls for the utmost care on the part of the performer:

(Gounod, *Ballet in Faust*)
(Choudens, Editeur-Propriétaire).

Speed of Articulation.

10.— With *single-articulation* the maximum speed attainable in the low register may be stated as ♩ = 112, and even then the passage must not be too long, on account of the fatigue experienced by the player, and the consequent heaviness of emission:

Single - articulation:

In the high register, the speed of articulation may, of course, increase; however, B♭ *in al-tissimo* can hardly be articulated in quicker *tempo* than ♩=120:

Single-articulation:

Double-tonguing allows of easily attaining ♩=144, at the expense, it must be confessed, of intensity and clearness:

Single-articulation:
(Difficult beyond ♩=116)

With *double-tonguing* ♩=160 could easily be reached.

11.— In the medium register, thanks to *double-tonguing,* Flutes can manage to compete with Strings in point of speed, being able to produce a true tremolo, as may be seen by Rimsky-Korsakow's *Grande Pâque Russe:*

A violinist's wrist could not act more swiftly, or produce a closer tremolo.

Length of Breath.

12.— The mouthpiece of the Flute making greater demands on the performer's breath than that of the Clarinet or the Oboe, the composer must beware of requiring tones to be sustained beyond certain limits, in slow *tempo*.

Easy breathing has not always been carefully attended to by composers, even in some celebrated works, e. g. the Trio of the "Young Ishmaelites" in Berlioz's *Enfance du Christ,* where the *Andante* requires such long wind that it is the terror of performers.

Shakes.

13.— All shakes are good from the lowest D to E *in alt.*

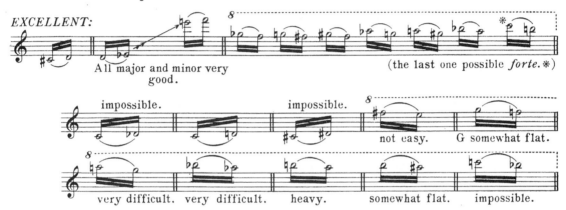

N. B. This shake is a very awkward one; if Wagner did not scruple to use it in the 'Ride of the Valkyries' (page 284), it was because he had it doubled by the Piccolo.

Complete List of Shakes and Tremolos.

(The cross means: *bad,* the double cross: *impossible.*)

14.—

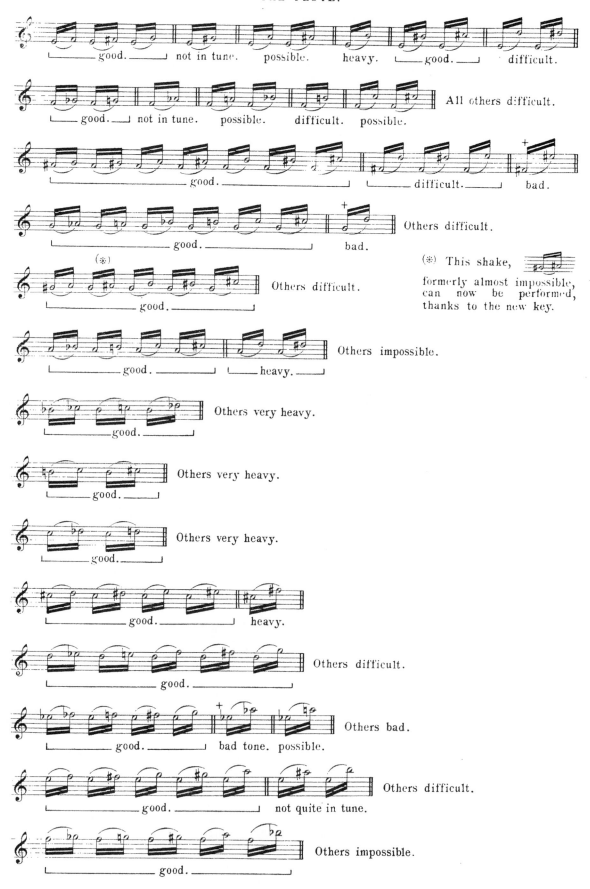

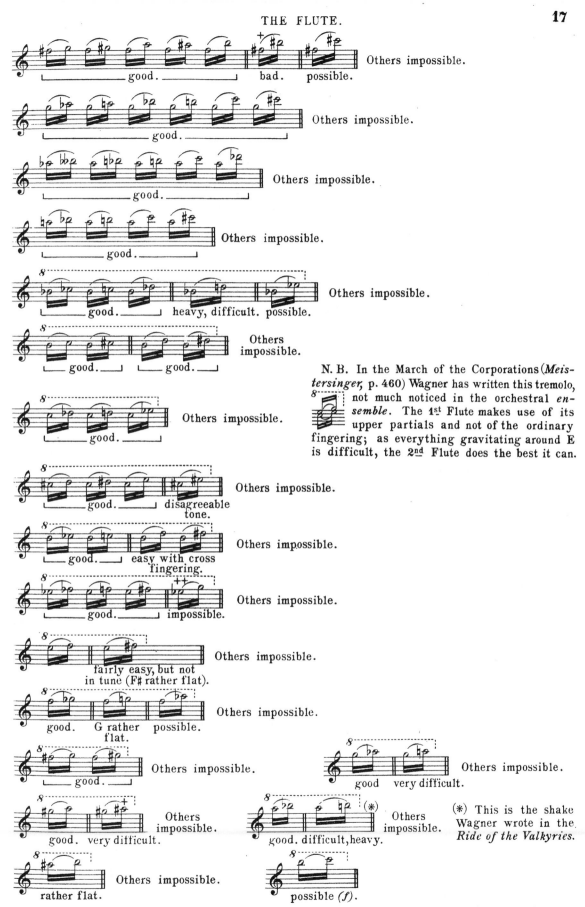

Others impossible.

Others impossible.

Others impossible.

Others impossible.

Others impossible.

Others impossible.

N. B. In the March of the Corporations (*Meistersinger*, p. 460) Wagner has written this tremolo, not much noticed in the orchestral *ensemble*. The 1st Flute makes use of its upper partials and not of the ordinary fingering; as everything gravitating around E is difficult, the 2nd Flute does the best it can.

Others impossible.

Others impossible.

Others impossible.

Others impossible.

Others impossible.

Others impossible.

Others impossible.

Others impossible.

Others impossible.

(∗) This is the shake Wagner wrote in the *Ride of the Valkyries.*

Others impossible.

N. B. All this section has been verified by Mr Barrère, Solo flute-player of the *Concerts Colonne.*

15.—Authors and Works to be studied: Bach (*Sonatas*), Händel (*Sonatas, Trios*), Mozart, Schubert, even Kuhlau, and a whole modern repertory: Reinecke's *Sonata*, Langer's *Concerto*, Andersen's *Concertos* and *Fantasias*, Peter Benoit's *Symphonic Poem*, Saint-Saëns's *Romance*, Fauré's *Fantasia*, Godard's and Widor's *Suites*.

Transposing Flutes.

16.—Flutes are made in several keys. At the Paris Exhibition (1900) was to be seen a Bass Flute, tuned an octave below the standard instrument, but, unfortunately, it was almost impossible for the lips to bring out the lower notes. There are also Flutes tuned in G, A, and Bb (below the normal pitch); the first of the three (in G) is excellent, and likely to figure in the orchestras of the future.

Among Flutes tuned above the normal pitch, the only one we now have left is the Flute in Eb, still in use, it is hard to see why, in military bands. In the time of Mozart the Flute in F was still used: for this instrument he wrote the *Entführung aus dem Serail*, played nowadays on the Piccolo.

Remark: The Flute is so weak-toned in its medium register, as compared with other wind instruments, that, when used in combination with them, it only begins to tell from G or A upwards. Written lower, it cannot be heard, and *what cannot be heard is harmful rather than otherwise*.

The only question we should venture to ask Weber would be about his Second Flutes, often an octave below his First Flutes, and consequently not sonorous, whereas the other instruments are always so admirably treated in his incomparable orchestra:

(*Oberon*, Rezia's Air.)

and again:

(*Oberon*)

I could give numberless instances; at every step we are filled with the same questioning wonder.

THE PICCOLO.

(Ital., *Flauto piccolo*. Ger., *Kleine Flöte*. Fr., *Petite Flûte*.)

1.— The Piccolo is written like the Flute, but sounds an octave higher. Note, however, that it has neither the lowest C nor the highest B♮ of the Flute.

Compass: from   to   (Sounding an octave higher.)

Remark: B♮ is impossible for most performers, but in case of need the C above may be written, being easier to produce:

(Sounding an octave higher.)

impossible.   possible *ff*

2.— The defect of the Piccolo is that it is not quite in tune. I remember a short-lived opera in which the composer had given it an important and ultra-sentimental part to play.

This Piccolo with its swooning tones, having a tendency to flatness, evoked the idea of some unfortunate wretch beginning to feel sea-sick.

3.— It is a mistake to write a melodic part for the Piccolo, or even to use it as a first Flute, as a soprano to the other two Flutes, unless its part is, so to speak, mechanical, as in the example already quoted (V. P. 14) from the *Pâque Russe*.

Berlioz always employed the Piccolo most effectively. See the *Damnation de Faust*, where it usually has *staccato* passages or rapid runs to play: *Valse des Sylphes, Evocation, Course à l'Abîme.*

4.— All the remarks made in the preceding section, concerning the fingering and articulation of the Flute, apply equally to the Piccolo.

All that was said about shakes and tremolos holds good also in the case of the Piccolo, with two exceptions, however. The two highest shakes on the Flute, one very difficult, the other only just possible,

Flute   very difficult.   possible *ff*

are absolutely impracticable on the Piccolo. If the first of these two shakes were written, it would be played in the lower octave — such is the practice of orchestral performers when a composer has been too daring; as for the second shake, the B♮ not existing, there is less risk of its being written.

5.— The Piccolo is usually made of wood; the modern Flute, on the other hand, of metal; most *virtuosi* having come to the conclusion that metal is more practical, less sensitive to changes of temperature, more sonorous, better adapted for producing contrasts of tone-color, besides being truer of intonation. A skilful performer on the metal Flute preserves all the best characteristics of the Flutes of yore, at the same time imparting to the instrument a richness of tone formerly unknown. In some parts of Europe wooden Flutes have already been discarded. In a few years, I suppose, a wooden Flute will be a great rarity.

Authors to be consulted: Berlioz, Wagner, Liszt, Meyerbeer, Rimsky-Korsakow, etc., in their scores. No special works have been written for the Piccolo.

THE OBOE.

(Ital., *Oboe.* Ger., *Oboe.* Fr., *Hautbois.*)

1.— In the time of Bach the scale of the Oboe extended from 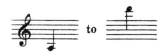 to

The Oboe used by the symphonists of last century, the one still to be found in most German, Russian, Italian, Dutch, and other orchestras — the Oboe of Beethoven, Weber, Schumann, and Wagner — has the following compass:

(Sometimes B♭ was written for the Oboe, and, in *Siegfried,* Wagner quite exceptionally requires G *in altissimo*).

This instrument is not perfect; some shakes are difficult, others impossible:

2.— The compass of the modern French Oboe is from 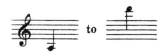 to

comprising 34 notes of tolerably homogeneous *timbre,* the lower ones being admirably intense, the whole of the medium register capable of expressing the human feelings in all their varying shades_ from joy to sorrow, from tragedy to idyll_the two highest degrees alone becoming thin and losing something of their *timbre:*

All the degrees (save two: C♯ and D *in alt*) are well in tune, flexible, clear, and as easy to attack as to sustain, either *piano* or *forte.*

Remark: The two notes referred to above (C♯ and D) are not inferior to the others in point of quality, but they are difficult to attack suddenly, as, for instance, in these two really very difficult tremolos:

(to be avoided)

Articulation.

3.— The Oboe differs from the Flute in not being capable of any great execution; it is a melodic instrument, the reed being slower of speech than the mouthpiece of the Flute. V. in the "Tristesse de Roméo" the very characteristic, pathetic wail, which, slowly rising, reaches its maximum intensity on the vibrating sonorous **E** *in alt:*

Larghetto espressivo.

(Berlioz, *Roméo et Juliette*, p. 36)

4.— The Oboe exclusively employs *single-articulation*, the letter *t* (as in "tut") being made use of. *Double-tonguing* is impossible for the Oboe; likewise *triple-tonguing,* and consequently any rapid iteration of the same note is beyond its power.

5.— It is advisable not to require the Oboe to articulate in quicker *tempo* than ♩= 120, in whichever register it may be playing:

(♩ = 120)

We now give a few examples from W. Ferling's *Etudes,* with metronomic rates fixed by Professor Georges Gillet for the use of his pupils at the Conservatoire:

(♩. = 72)

(♩ = 80)

(♩ = 108)

(♩ = 112)

(By kind permission of Costallat et Cie, Editeurs-Propriétaires.)

And here follow three examples of speeds exceeding ♩ = 120, which are possible, thanks to their alternately *legato* and *staccato* character, the difficulties of one bar being compensated for by the easy nature of the following bar:

The last bar, with its wide skips, is extremely difficult to play.

Slurred Notes.

6.— Ascending intervals are, generally speaking, more easily slurred than descending ones, the lips being more easily contracted than distended.

All octave skips can thus be slurred, from middle C to E, a tenth above.

The same slurs would be much more awkward descending, as in the following passage, which is dangerous beyond 120:

Or this one, impossible beyond 112:

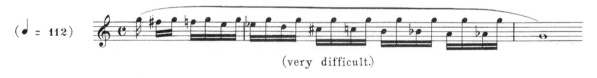

(very difficult.)

On the other hand, here is a perfectly practicable passage, with a very expressive concluding cadence. Despite the quick rate of movement, the difficulty of execution is here not very great, because this cadence allows the lips time to prepare for the wide skip:

Length of Breath.

7.— Superior in intensity and *timbre* to all the other woodwind instruments,   possessed of such carrying-power that it formerly constituted the main element in military bands, while if we once fix our attention on it in a modern orchestra we can finally hear nothing else, un- rivalled as regards the ease with which it can swell and diminish its tone, the Oboe more- over excels all its congeners in sustaining-power. Despite the strength of its vibrations, it comsumes far less wind than the Flute, for example. If a competition were started between ohoists and flautists, these latter players would soon be compelled to acknowledge them- selves defeated, their wind-supply being exhausted long before that of their rivals.

There are few examples more convincing, in this connection, than the *Largo* of Hän- del's *Second Concerto,* and the Prelude to the 3rd act of *Tannhäuser,* so difficult of per- formance, on account of the length of the phrase and the impossibility of taking breath. The Oboe alone, among the woodwind instruments,   is equal to the task.

Shakes and Tremolos.

8.— Nowadays all major and minor shakes can be executed on the French Oboe, from:

Every modern French Oboe allows of finishing off a shake on the lowest B♮, or on C   (a semitone above) with a turn, but this was formerly impossible:

Complete List of Shakes and Tremolos.

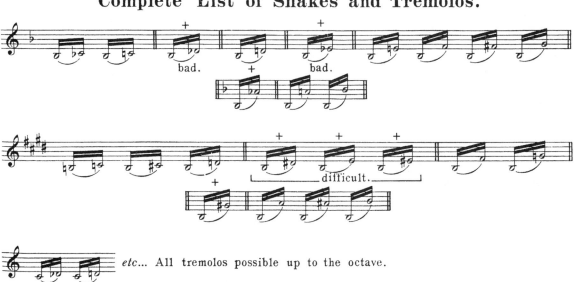

etc... All tremolos possible up to the octave.

etc... All tremolos possible up to the octave.

etc... All tremolos possible up to the octave.

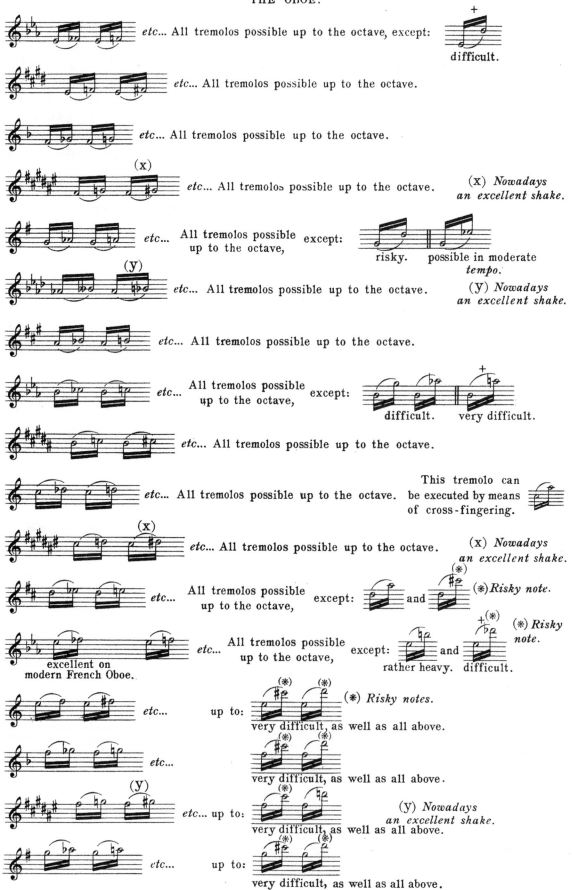

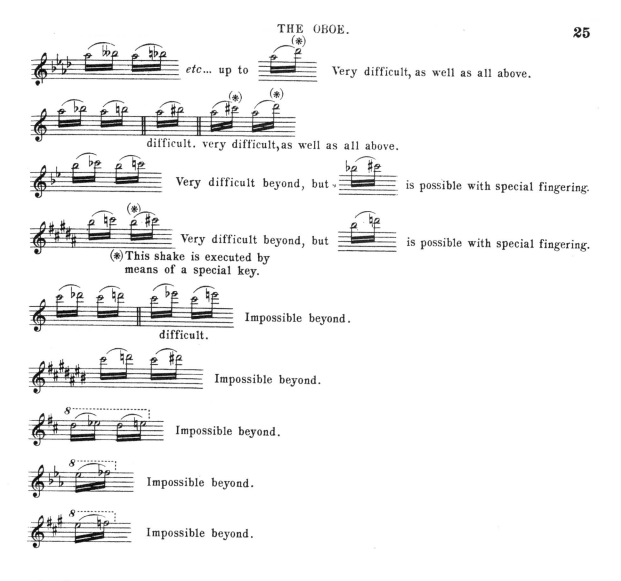

9.— Some sixty years ago, the Oboe was ingeniously perfected by Triébert (*of Paris*), working upon the suggestions of Barret, a soloist in the Covent Garden orchestra; despite all these improvements, however, many shakes were still impossible, and others not quite true of intonation. Our modern instrument, constructed in accordance with the views of Georges Gillet, is perfect as regards truth of intonation, and allows of executing all shakes, major and minor, throughout its entire compass, up to F, either *piano* or *forte*.

10.— AUTHORS AND WORKS TO BE CONSULTED: Bach (*Cantatas*); Mozart (*Quartet*); Händel (*Concertos, Trios, Sonata*); Beethoven (*Trio, Quintet*); Schumann, Dvořák (*Pieces*); Théodore Dubois (*Pièces en canon, Hautbois, Violoncelle*); *Pieces* by Paladilhe, Busser, Ferling, Vogt etc.

Transposing Oboes.

11.— To the Oboe family belong three transposing instruments: the Oboe d'amore, the Cor Anglais, and the Barytone Oboe. (*see Appendix*)

The Oboe d'amore.

12.— This instrument is a minor third lower in pitch than the standard instrument.   Its compass is from

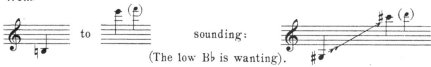

to   sounding:

(The low B♭ is wanting).

Remarkable as it is for its homogeneous quality, why is it not habitually used in our orchestras?   To the Oboe d'amore Bach assigns his most pathetic *cantilenas*; for *mezzoforte* effects nothing can equal the charm of the upper register:

(Actual sounds)

(Qui sedes. *Mass in B minor.*)

Each time the instrument skips by a sixth to the accented beat, in the last three bars of the example quoted above, the effect is truly exquisite.   See also, in the same Mass, the Bass air: *Et in spiritum sanctum*, accompanied by two Oboi d'amore.   In this connection too, the *Passion according to St. Matthew*, the *Christmas Oratorio*, the *Cantatas*, the *Magnificat*, etc. should be studied.

13.— The Oboe d'amore is played in the same manner as the ordinary Oboe; it has the same mechanism and can execute the same shakes, save two:

good.   impossible. very difficult.   All major and minor
                                                     shakes excellent, up to D *in alt.*

These two shakes (*x, y*) will be rendered possible by means of a special key, easily fitted on to the instrument, if ever it comes to be used in the orchestra.

The Cor Anglais.

14.— The Cor Anglais is simply the Alto of the Oboe — the old *Oboe da caccia*, so much used in former times — a fifth lower in pitch than the standard instrument, with the same relative compass as the Oboe d'amore (the B♭ being wanting as in the case of this latter instrument).

Compass: Sounding:

Lacking both the strength and the homogeneous quality of the Oboe d'amore, the Cor Anglais exhibits three distinct varieties of *timbre*.   The lower register is very powerful, the upper register weak and sickly.   The best register lies between

and   sounding:

All figures gravitating around the highest C♯ 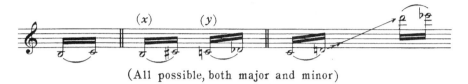 are very troublesome for the performer, this being one of the worst notes on the instrument.

15.— Formerly this shake 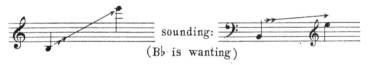 was impossible on the Cor Anglais; nowadays, thanks to a special key, all shakes from low B♮ to high D♮ can be executed:

(All possible, both major and minor)

Remark: The two shakes *x* and *y*, mentioned as being impracticable on the Oboe d'amore (see paragraph **13**), are quite easy on the Cor Anglais, because this latter instrument actually possesses the special key of which I spoke.

16.— Works to be studied: *Les Huguenots, Guillaume Tell, Lohengrin, Tristan und Isolde, Siegfried, Tannhäuser, Manfred, Le Carnaval Romain, La Prise de Troie, Henry VIII, Samson et Dalila, Sigurd, Salammbô, Le Cid, Thaïs,* etc.— Beethoven (*Trio for two Oboes and Cor Anglais*).

The Barytone Oboe.

17.— An octave below the standard instrument, with the following compass:

sounding: (B♭ is wanting)

The fingering and mechanism are those of the ordinary Oboe. The Barytone Oboe will form an admirable bass when all the instruments of the same family are concentrated into a focus of intense, almost bellicose quality, at the heart of the orchestra, in the immediate neighborhood of the Horns.

18.— I need hardly refer either to the *Musette* or to the *Pastoral Oboe* (in A♭), two varieties of the same kind of instrument, only differing in the reed, for neither is admitted into the orchestra. But I must mention the Soprano Oboe in E♭, used, together with the Small Clarinet in E♭, in military bands; this is a very sonorous instrument with an extremely piercing upper register, and would prove very useful if a complete family of Oboes were at any time required. Its compass is from

to sounding:

The fingering and mechanism are the same as for the other instruments of the Oboe family. So far, the Soprano has only been used once in the orchestra: by Vidal in *La Burgonde.*

19.— *Remark*:   The *timbre* of the Oboe is so characteristic and predominating that, when using it for holding-notes, for chords, or for background effects, care must be taken to employ the best register only, and to choose the most euphonic intervals, the very aggressive notes of the lower register being scrupulously avoided— in a word, the Oboe must never be "lost sight of."

If, for instance, the following common chord has to be written in four parts, the first of these two ways of scoring it is preferable:

In the conclusion of the *Allegro* of the *8th Symphony,* Beethoven leaves the Clarinets, Horns, Trumpets, and Bassoons in the background, bringing to the front the Flutes and Oboes, on which he alone relies:

If the Clarinet parts were given to the Oboes and the Oboe parts to the Clarinets, all elegance would forthwith vanish, and the harmonic mass appear to sink beneath its own weight, like a bird with shattered wings.

THE CLARINET.

(Ital., *Clarinetto.* Ger., *Klarinette.* Fr., *Clarinette.*)

1.— The compass of the Clarinet is 42 notes, from ♪ to ♪, and is consequently more extensive than that of the Flute or the Oboe.

It is always difficult to fix the extreme limit of any instrument, as some *virtuosi* can reach heights inaccessible to others. A *in altissimo* is here given as the upper limit of the scale, because such it proves to be in the case of the great majority of clarinet-players. In any case, C *in altissimo* ♪ is beyond the most persevering efforts of most performers, and in *piano* passages G ♪ should be considered the extreme limit.

Every degree of the Clarinet's extensive scale is excellent, but the *timbre* of the instrument varies considerably in the different registers, of which it may be said there are three:

Chalumeau. medium. high.

The dramatic intensity of the chalumeau, of which Weber's predecessors seem to have had no suspicion, was for the first time brought into notice by the Overture to *Frei-schütz.* The medium register has a much less characteristic *timbre,* and the high register is very piercing.

2.— When I say that all the degrees of the scale are excellent, I mean, as in the case of the Flute and the Oboe, that the composer need not stop to consider the defects of some few notes, relying, as he may, upon the talent of the performer to conceal these little imperfections.

These defective notes are three in number: ♪

They are inferior in point of intensity to the neighboring degrees of the scale, and should not be used as pivots for figures of any description, but apart from this, they need give the composer no further concern. The same remark applies to the difficult passage from A to B♮ ♪; when a shake on A is written, it has to be performed by means of a special kind of fingering.

3.— Next to the Flute, the Clarinet is the wind instrument capable of most execution. It shows to great advantage in scale passages (especially chromatic ones), and in arpeggios of the common chord, or of the chords of the dominant seventh and diminished seventh. However, when the Clarinet is required to play *bravura* passages, care must be taken not to increase the difficulty by writing in extreme keys — C, F, G, B♭ and their relative keys are excellent, because they are easy; with D major and E♭ major difficulties begin.

On perusing *Die Walküre,* I find only two instances of signatures with three or four sharps or flats, and then only for a few bars, but this is solely due to a sudden mod-ulation not allowing of a change of Clarinet just at that precise moment. Besides, Wag-ner very well knew that, in these particular cases, he was giving the player an extreme-ly simple, slow part to execute, involving no kind of risk or difficulty of fingering. At the first resting-place the composer indicates the change of Clarinet necessary, and the performer begins playing again in C, or in F, or in G.

When Mozart, for the first time, assigned arpeggios to the Clarinet in its lower register (*Trio dei Mascheri*), he chose the key of C. Beethoven used the key of F for a sim-ilar effect in the Finale of the *Eroica*.

4.— C Clarinets have disappeared, and nowadays Clarinets in B♭ and A are alone em-ployed. The former are more brilliant in tone; *virtuosi* have adopted them for their concert-pieces. The latter, lower by a semitone, not only possess an extremely rich and noble *timbre*, but are also able to descend as low as C♯ (an inestimable advantage),where-as the B♭ Clarinet stops at D.

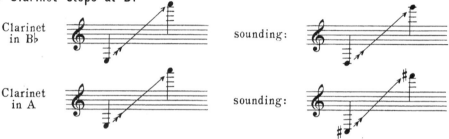

5.— Clarinet-players complain of composers who prefer involving them in a thorny bush of accidentals to changing the instrument. It is quite true that it is annoying to have to replace an instrument which has been gradually warming up in the performer's hands by another instrument, colder, and therefore less accurately in tune. But at the end of a few bars the new instrument will be found doing duty as properly and efficiently as the old one, and the performer is satisfied. It seems to rest his lips and give him new life.

Of course, I am now speaking of the theatrical orchestra and of long musical performan-ces; in symphonies, which are of relatively short duration, such substitutions are very sel-dom necessary. It is true that the use of the B♭ Clarinet is frequently prescribed in an *Allegro,* and that of the A Clarinet in the following *Adagio,* but no change is ever made in the course of a movement; the same remark applies to *bravura* pieces.

6.— Among the wood-wind instruments, the Clarinet alone is able to contrast a *piano* with a *forte* in such a marked manner that the former would really seem to be the echo of the latter:

The *pianissimo* of the Clarinets (in the low and medium registers) represents the minimum of sound obtainable from wind instruments. Compared with Clarinets, Flutes in their lower register seem as intense and metallic as Trumpets would be in a *mezzoforte*. It is hardly even a *pianissimo*; the instrument has almost lost its *timbre*: 'tis but a whiff of air.

7.— Another characteristic of the Clarinet is its neutral tone-color in the medium register, which allows of its blending with almost every group in the orchestra. While the Oboe can be mistaken for no other instrument, the Clarinet can, without attracting notice, take the place of a Second Flute, or of a Second Horn, or even of a Bassoon, its full, rich quality of tone possessing an unrivalled power of blending with that of any other instrument.

In his Piano *Concertos*, Mozart frequently wrote a single Flute part and two Clarinet parts, treating all three instruments in the same manner, as if they were three Flutes.

In the Overture to *Egmont*, Beethoven has ventured to assign the dissonant note of the chord to a single Clarinet, treated as if it were a second Horn, the only instance of want of balance in the whole of his orchestral writing, for this one *G♭* against one *E♭*, four *C's* and two *A♭*'s is really very weak:

Actual sounds.

Clarinets.

Bassoons.

Horns.

Egmont (Breitkopf & Härtel's edition)

All musicians must have noticed the "poetic Bassoon" effect produced by the Clarinet in the *Ballet des Sylphes*. A real Bassoon would have been ridiculously dry, and a Horn too heavy. The Clarinet thus marking the accented beats, beneath the harmonics of the Harp, sounds truly exquisite; it would seem to leave in its wake, as it were, a little spray of sound.

And what shall we say of the orchestral peroration to the duet in *Béatrice et Bénédict!*

Note the admirable effect produced by associating the tremolo of the Clarinets with the tremolo of the Violins:

Clarinet
(actual sounds).

Violins
(divisi).

Violas.

Celli.

Double-bass.

8.— All that has been said about the articulation of the Oboe (§§3, 4, 5) applies equally to the Clarinet.

As in the case of the Oboe, the maximum speed for articulated notes and *staccato* passages should hardly exceed ♩=120, in any one of the registers.

But, as in the case of the Oboe, numerous examples of passages exceeding this speed may be found in *Etudes* and Concert-pieces, e. g.

(Widor, *Introduction & Rondo.*)

(By kind permission of Heugel et Cie, Editeurs-Propriétaires.)

Many composers treat Clarinets as if they were Flutes, obliging them to articulate as rapidly as these latter instruments in very quick *tempo*, witness the opening of the *Italian Symphony:*

Clarinet-players admit that, in this passage, although they use their utmost endeavors to keep pace with the Flutes, their execution is not really satisfactory, and that if they stood in the foreground they would attract unfavorable notice.

9.— In the matter of sustaining-power, the Clarinet can rival the Oboe; in fact the two instruments may be considered on a par. Take, for instance, the return to A♭, after the phrase played by the Horn, in the Adagio of the *Septet:*

(Beethoven.)

a good clarinet - player does not take breath after the *crescendo* (marked +), but only two bars later, after the A.

Here is another example:

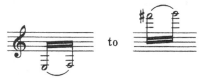

Professor Turban (of the Paris Conservatoire) and myself calculated that a holding-note could be sustained *piano,* in the medium register, for 40 or 45 seconds.

Shakes and Tremolos.

10.— Since Bœhm's system, perfected by Buffet, has been applied to the mechanism of the Clarinet, all major and minor shakes have become possible, from:

A few of these shakes are not very brilliant, others rather difficult, and consequently heavy:

possible with a special key.

N. B. The fingering of the Clarinet repeats itself in the twelfth, so that the special key which now allows of executing the shake B C♯ in the low register also renders the shake F♯ G♯ practicable in the upper register.

not very good. (G♯ somewhat flat.)

 This shake occurs in *Meistersinger.*

11.— As a matter of fact, all these shakes may be written, even the doubtful ones (especially when other simultaneous shakes more or less conceal their defects), up to:

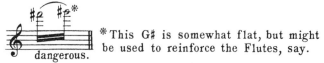

* This G♯ is somewhat flat, but might be used to reinforce the Flutes, say.

12.—We now give a complete list of shakes and tremolos:

Complete List of Shakes and Tremolos.

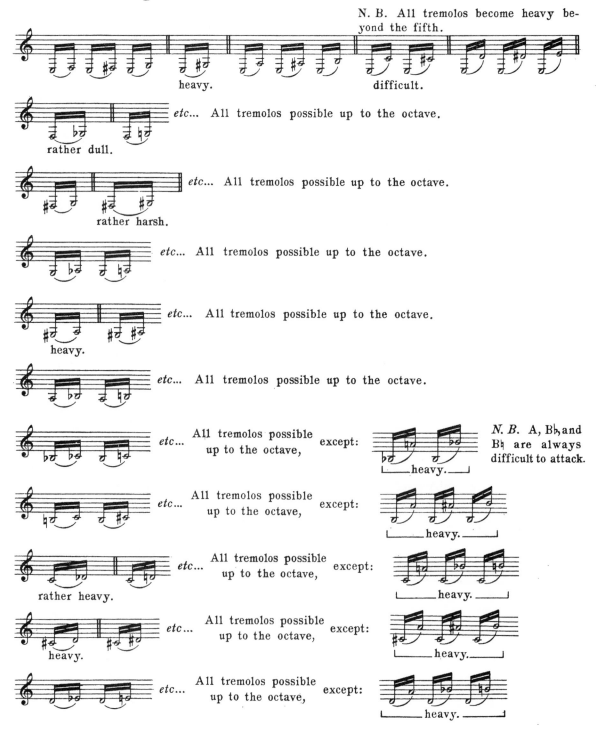

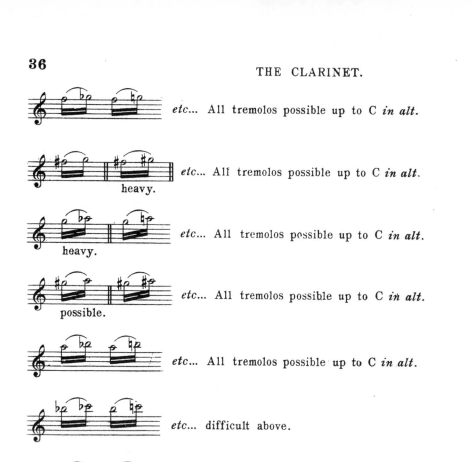

etc... All tremolos possible up to C *in alt.*

etc... All tremolos possible up to C *in alt.*

heavy.

etc... All tremolos possible up to C *in alt.*

heavy.

etc... All tremolos possible up to C *in alt.*

possible.

etc... All tremolos possible up to C *in alt.*

etc... difficult above.

etc... difficult above.

Higher tremolos should be avoided.

good, but D♮ is a trifle flat. difficult.

Higher tremolos should be avoided.

almost impossible. possible. difficult.

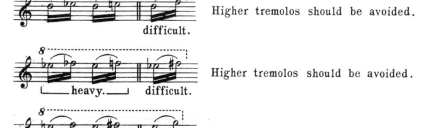

Higher tremolos should be avoided.

difficult.

Higher tremolos should be avoided.

heavy. difficult.

Higher tremolos should be avoided.

difficult.

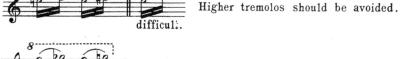

Higher tremolos should be avoided.

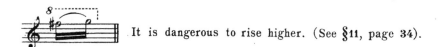

It is dangerous to rise higher. (See §11, page 34).

Transposing.

13.— We have already seen (§4) that the C Clarinet is no longer in use, modern composers writing exclusively for Clarinets in B♭ and in A.

All that has been said about either instrument applies equally to both, for they have the same mechanism, the same qualities, and the same little imperfections. The only difference lies in the *timbre*, the richness of tone, the sweetness and fulness of the A Clarinet, not to mention the valuable C♯ which the B♭ Clarinet is unable to sound in the lowest register.

The Alto Clarinet.

14.— The Alto Clarinet is tuned in F, a fourth below the standard instrument (if B♭ be considered the normal key). This member of the Clarinet family is not much in use nowadays. Its compass is from

No higher notes can be obtained.
Mendelssohn has written two Duets for Alto Clarinet and B♭ Clarinet.

The Small Clarinet.

15.— This, also, is an instrument rarely used, save in military bands, for which it is tuned in E♭; it sounds a minor third higher than written.

Berlioz has employed it in the *Nuit de Sabbat* of his *Symphonie Fantastique*, and Wagner in the Finale of the *Walküre*. In this latter work, the Small Clarinet is tuned in D, but the performer frequently transposes his part, playing on the ordinary instrument in E♭.

Clarinet in D.

ff (By kind permission of Schott & C°, Publishers-Proprietors.) (*Walküre*, p. 442.)

The Bass Clarinet.

16.— The Bass Clarinet is written like the B♭ or A Clarinet, but sounds an octave lower; its compass is from

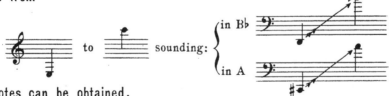

No higher notes can be obtained.

The lower register, which contains the richest and fullest notes, is, of course, the most valuable. The mechanism of the Bass Clarinet is identical with that of the standard instrument.

The Bass Clarinet is an admirable melodic instrument; Meyerbeer was the first composer to bring it into notice (in the *Huguenots* and the *Prophète*). Afterwards, Wagner used the Bass Clarinet as an almost constant bass to the other wind instruments, as an auxiliary to the Bassoons, and now and then also for melodic purposes. (See the 3rd act of *Tannhäuser*, the 2nd act of *Lohengrin*, Liszt's *Dante-Symphony* (Purgatory), the 2nd act of *Samson et Dalila*, etc.)

Note the effect produced by the holding-notes for Clarinets, Bass Clarinet, and Bassoons, that form the accompaniment to Elizabeth's prayer.

17.— The Bass Clarinet can pass from a *forte* to a *pianissimo* as easily as the standard instrument itself. If it were necessary to have a phrase repeated in slowly-dying echoes, the effect required could probably be obtained by employing the three following wind instruments in succession:

Here is an example, from the *Legend of the Loreley*:

(A. Bertelin.)

In this competition of comparative tone-qualities, the Clarinet would certainly take the *pianissimo* prize, by unanimous consent.

18.— Meyerbeer and Wagner have employed the same notation for the Bass Clarinet as for the standard instrument (treating it as a 16 ft. stop); such too is the French practice.

But from *Lohengrin* onwards, Wagner writes for the Bass Clarinet in the F Clef:

This gives rise to a serious misunderstanding, which it would be well to clear up. The Horns and Violoncellos call for an urgent reform in this respect; bewildered as they are by the various systems, they are never sure in which octave the composer means them to play. Would it not be worth while holding a congress to decide the matter?

To my mind, notation in the F clef is nearer the truth. To write in the G clef for a Bass-Clarinet playing in unison with a Bassoon in the F clef seems to me as illogical as the pronunciation of the words 'honorary and 'honorarium. Let us vote for the F clef.

19.— AUTHORS AND WORKS TO BE STUDIED: Mozart (*Concerto*); Weber (*2 Concertos, 1 Concertino, Variations, Quintet, Sonata*); Spohr (*Concerto*); Schumann (*Pieces*); Brahms (*2 Sonatas, Trio, Quintet*); *Etudes* for the Clarinet by Kalliwoda, Frédéric Beer, Klose, etc:

For instances of use of B♭ Clarinet, see, in *Tannhäuser*, the scene between Venus and Tannhäuser in the first act, the entrance of Tannhäuser and Wolfram in the second act, and Elizabeth's prayer in the third; for instance of use of A Clarinet, the whole beautiful scene of Andromache at Hector's tomb, in the *Prise de Troie*.

20.— *Remark:* One of the most frequent mistakes made by students who are beginning to orchestrate consists in taking the Flutes, Clarinets, or Bassoons as a groundwork on which they attempt to embroider the polyphony of the salient instruments, without duly considering the pitch at which they are writing the Woodwind. What is wanted is a neutral background, i. e. an unostentatious, veiled tone-color — a mere foil — a kind of far-off organ-music. If holding-notes for the Clarinets are written in the chalumeau, the dramatic effect of *Freischütz* is immediately produced, and the background becomes dark and threatening. If, on the other hand, holding-notes are written in the upper register, in spite of all efforts made to subdue their squeaking quality, the background is suddenly brought into undue prominence, completely eclipsing the instruments it had been intended to throw into relief.

The true neutral register of the Clarinet, which seems to continue the Flute, bridging over the distance between the latter instrument and the Bassoon, lies in the medium, between E and B♭

Even C   is much more sonorous.

When Robert Franz undertook to arrange the Organ part of Bach's Cantatas for concert-rooms not possessing an Organ, he was obliged to make use of Bassoons and Clarinets. The latter he wrote in the medium register, so as to imitate as closely as possible the almost anonymous sound of a Bourdon or Flute-stop playing in the medium. He could not do otherwise; nothing can be more dreary than a holding-note for the Clarinet written too low down.

THE BASSOON.

(Ital., *Fagotto.* Ger., *Fagott.* Fr., *Basson.*)

1.— The Bassoon has a compass of 37 notes, from ⟨notation⟩ to ⟨notation⟩

In writing for the orchestra, it is dangerous to exceed this upper limit, but in a *bravura* piece the performer may be required to play up to D, a third higher ⟨notation⟩

Wagner once even ventured to write E, but he was justified in doing so in that special case, firstly because his theme was of such a nature that the high E could not be dispensed with, and secondly because the intensity of the Violoncellos and Violas, playing in unison and doubling the Bassoon part, was likely to neutralize any mistake made at such a height.

Allegro. *ff*   (*Tannhäuser,* Overture, p. 25.)

In former times, the Bassoon was seldom required to descend lower than Gamut G ⟨notation⟩.

Later it became possible to obtain B♭, but neither B♮ nor C♯ could be produced, so that the scale was diatonic for the first few notes, only becoming chromatic from E♭ upwards:

diatonic. ⎍ chromatic.

Mozart, who wrote so admirably for the Bassoon, usually kept it within its old limits, between ⟨notation⟩ and ⟨notation⟩; it was only very rarely that he wrote lower notes, as, for instance, in the Overture to *Don Giovanni* (Double D) and in the Andante of the *Concerto in C minor* (Double C).

2.— In *forte* passages all the 37 notes of the Bassoon may be looked upon as equally good; not so in *piano* passages, the lowest B♮ and D being difficult to attack, E♭ in the medium register somewhat sharp, the four following degrees (E♮, F, F♯, and G) poor and thin in quality, A♭ in the highest register unsatisfactory; and the highest D requiring some preparation:

difficult to attack *piano*.   somewhat sharp.   ⎣poor and thin.⎦   bad.   requires preparation.

3.— In fact, the Bassoon, although it usually constitutes the sole bass of the entire Woodwind group, is an instrument of very uneven quality, its admirable low fifth ⟨notation⟩ being followed by a fairly good medium register ⟨notation⟩; then, after four weak notes, comes an exquisite seventh, with a *timbre* closely resembling that of the Horn ⟨notation⟩, and finally, after a bad A♭, a dull fourth produced by a tube constantly diminishing in diameter.

admirable.   fairly satisfactory.   poor and thin.

exquisite.   bad.   thin.   requires preparation.

The lowest fifth could vie with the Brass in point of tone-power; Bb might even form the bass of the Trombones. However, in that case, the strain on the lungs involved in the production of such intense sounds would need to be taken into account, and the part written in such a manner as not to completely exhaust the performer.

4.— Since Wagner, the Bassoon has often been required to play down to A; it could just as well be made to descend still lower by increasing the length of the tube. Doubtless in a few years all Bassoons will be able to sound this A, but for the present it is well not to write lower than Bb, this being the last note on the great majority of instruments.

Articulations.

5.— Like the Oboe and the Clarinet, the Bassoon employs only *single-articulation*. From the lowest Bb to the highest Bb, throughout a compass of three octaves, all notes can be repeated or detached, either *forte* or *piano*, almost as easily as on the Cello.

For instance, in the low register:

In the medium and high registers:

Of course, when effects of this kind are employed, all prolonging of the difficulties must be avoided, as the tongue soon falters, and the instrument must not be brought too conspicuously into the foreground.

6.— The lightness of articulation of a mass of wind instruments, even when they are required to play in very rapid *tempo,* is a matter for both surprise and admiration; instances abound in the scores of Wagner, Berlioz, Liszt, Brahms, Tschaikowsky, Glazounow, Borodine: since Beethoven there has hardly been a composer who has not thus contrasted the Wood-wind with the Strings, in very quick *tempo.*

If each member of the group were examined separately (with the exception of the Flutes, of course), the most astonishing timidity, heaviness, and even absolute inaccuracy of some of them would be discovered. When isolated they become nervous and frightened, but when playing all together they are the very image of assurance and self-confidence.

7.— The Bassoon, as we have already seen (§2), has several doubtful notes, not quite in tune, whose defects it requires all the performer's skill to conceal, but when these notes are doubled by the Violoncellos they seem excellent.

Here are four bars whose bass had been given by an inexperienced composer to a solo Bassoon:

Now, this bass, being in the register of the *fairly good medium* and of the *weak notes* (§3), sounded feeble and out of tune, not through any fault of the performer's, but because the *timbre* of the instrument was in itself unsatisfactory.

As soon as the composer had concealed these defective notes beneath the *pizzicato* of the Celli, the passage sounded quite different:

The instruments all blended in a pleasing *ensemble,* perfectly satisfactory as to truth of intonation.

7.— In the matter of slurred notes, the Bassoon like the Oboe and Clarinet, can rise more easily than it can descend:

However, descending slurs are practicable in slow *tempo,* and even in quick *tempo* when the intervals are small:

Staccato notes, skips of an octave, a tenth, a twelfth, a fifteenth, etc. can be played on the Bassoon with incredible ease and rapidity:

8.— *Descending slurs to be avoided:*

as well as all slurred intervals starting downwards from Gb, Eb, D, C#, and C♮ in the lowest register:

9.— In slow *tempo*, descending slurs can be played (always excepting the intervals mentioned above), provided they are used in an *ensemble*, and not in a solo:

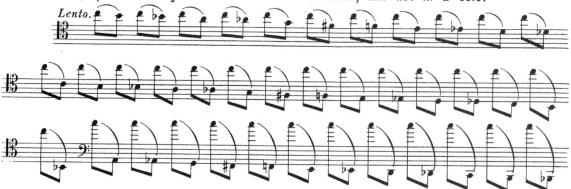

Taking any one of its notes as a fulcrum, the Bassoon can thus descend the scale chromatically, but this is somewhat dangerous, and speed is, of course, entirely precluded.

10.— Is it not astonishing that an instrument descending lower even than the Horn, and able to sound deep notes of such intensity, should also be capable of acrobatic feats which none of its neighbors can perform? What services it renders in the orchestra!

It is available for every combination; it blends with every group — Woodwind, Brass, and Strings alike;— it may be put to all kinds of work.

It can reinforce an accent of the Strings, without its presence being even so much as suspected:

(J. Hamelle, Editeur-Propriétaire.)

(Widor, *2nd Symphony,* p. 130.)

It may complete the Horn group, blending so perfectly that it cannot be distinguished from the Brass:

(Mendelssohn, *Sommernachtstraum*.)

Without the least weakness, it can bear upon its Atlas shoulders the whole weight of the harmony:

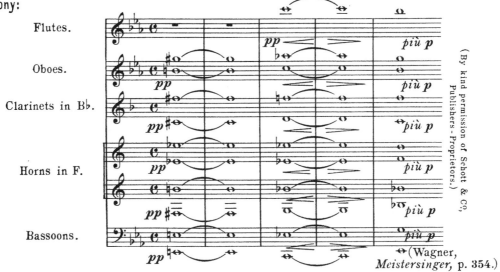

(By kind permission of Schott & Co., Publishers - Proprietors.)

(Wagner, *Meistersinger*, p. 354.)

Figures played by the Violoncellos and Double-basses, or even by the whole group of Strings, gain very much in energy and intensity when doubled by the Bassoon:

(Beethoven, *4th Symph.*)

The *staccato* of the Bassoon can, when necessary, be as light as the *pizzicato* of the Strings:

(Meyerbeer, *Struensee.*)

Is not this staccato of the Bassoon, in the Serenade of Mephistopheles, fully as supple as a *pizzicato?*

(Gounod, *Faust.*)

By combining the Bassoon with the Flute, at a distance of two octaves, Mozart obtained the sweetest and richest *timbre* in the orchestra. Sometimes he even writes the Bassoon two octaves below the Violin:

(*Il Flauto Magico*, Overture.)

(*Nozze di Figaro.*)

Any score, opened at random, will afford instances of the Bassoon's singular ability to serve all kinds of purposes with unrivalled facility and efficiency.

Length of Breath.

11.— General rule: *The lower the pitch of the instrument, the more breath is required to play it.*

The sustaining-power of a Bassoon, playing in the lower and upper registers, is limited— according to experiment made with the assistance of M!. Eugène Bourdeau, Professor at the Conservatoire — respectively as follows:

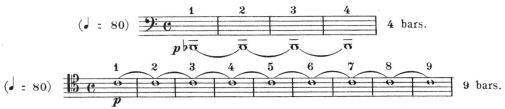

Even in the still higher register, this maximum is seldom exceeded, and, of course, when playing *forte*, it is considerably diminished, the duration of the sound being in inverse proportion to its intensity.

Shakes and Tremolos.

12.— From Double B♭ to Double F no shakes are possible, save the two following:

From Double F to B♭ in the Treble staff nearly all are possible, except:

Complete List of Shakes.

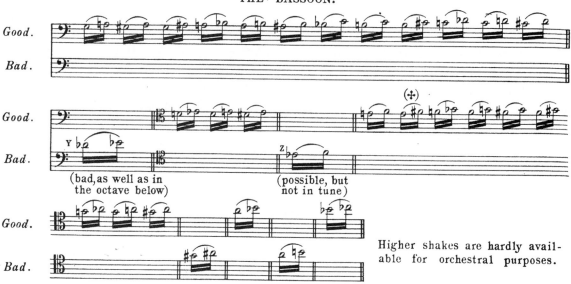

Higher shakes are hardly available for orchestral purposes.

⊕ *Remark:* The major shake on E (E F♯) was formerly reckoned one of the most awkward, but all the modern *virtuosi,* having carefully practised it since Bizet's time, can now execute this shake brilliantly.

(Choudens, Editeur-Propriétaire.) (*Carmen,* p. 177.)

13.— Tremolos are hardly practicable on deep-toned instruments like the Bassoon and Horn; it would be difficult to quote an instance of their employment in any of the works of the great masters. Below Tenor C the effect produced would hardly be satisfactory; from this C upwards thirds, or even greater intervals, are sometimes used, but the third itself is often impracticable, if not rising, at least falling.

* N.B. Beyond this point, tremolos become almost impossible.

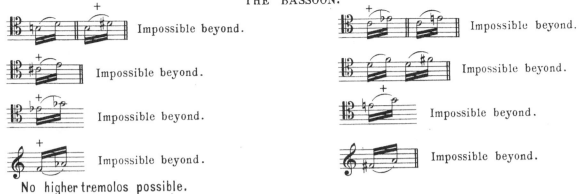

No higher tremolos possible.

WORKS AND AUTHORS TO BE STUDIED: Mozart (*Concerto, Serenades, Quintet*); Weber (*Concerto, Andante and Hungarian Rondo*); Beethoven (*Quintet, Octet, Trio* for Flute, Bassoon and Piano, *Septet,* etc.); Schubert (*Octet*); Rubinstein (*Quintet*); Reinecke (*Octet*); Thuille (*Sextet*); Raff (*Sinfoniette*); *Suites* by Ch. Lefèvre, Pierné, etc. *Etudes* by d'Ozi, Gambaro, Neukirchener, Milde, etc.

TRANSPOSING INSTRUMENTS.

The Basson-quinte.

14.—The Basson-quinte has not yet been made, but bassoon-players are calling for it. It would form the true bass of the Woodwind group, a fifth below the standand instrument, descending consequently to Eb, a semitone lower than the Double-bass:

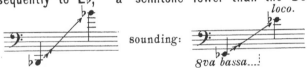

sounding:

The low A which Wagner wrote below Bb is admirably rich and full; 'then', say professionals, 'why not descend to Eb, with the same fingering and the same capabilities as the ordinary Bassoon?' We have already seen (§3) that the low fifth, from Double Bb to Double F, is sufficiently robust to bear any weight of sound; the "new" low fifth would be still more robust. The Basson-quinte is said to be easy of construction; we look to instrument-makers to provide us with it in the near future. (See C. Pierre, *La facture instrumen-tale à l'Exposition de 1889*).

The Double—Bassoon.

15.— The Double-Bassoon is pitched an octave below the standard instrument, but does not possess the lowest Bb and B♮. Its compass is

from 𝄢 to 𝄢 written: 𝄢

The Double-Bassoon is made either of wood or of brass. It is decidedly inferior to the Bassoon in point of *timbre*, especially in the register common to both instruments. Satisfactory in the first seventh, it begins to grow weaker from Double B♮ upwards, diminishes considerably in intensity in the neighborhood of F♯ 𝄢 — all higher notes being obtained by overblowing — and comes to a stop about 𝄢, with a nasal twang like that of a toy trumpet.

Actual sounds:

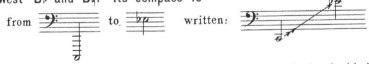

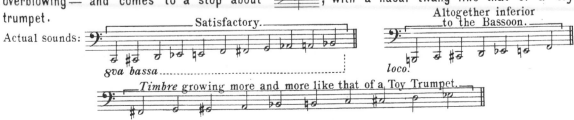

The first low octave is alone fairly satisfactory, when used in slow *tempo* to play deep pedal-notes sustaining the Woodwind, or even the Horns, but *staccato* notes are to be entirely eschewed. The manner in which the tone is produced is much the same as in the case of the Bassoon, but the reed, being larger, is slower to vibrate, so that florid and *staccato* passages are very ineffective on the Double-Bassoon. Beethoven, in the 9th Symphony, treats this instrument very carelessly, first making it rise to A, and then giving it rapid passages to play, which it cannot possibly execute in a satisfactory manner; they sound like *bravura* effects performed on a bad Harmonium:

These weak notes of the upper register and these florid passages, which would be difficult even for an ordinary Bassoon, are lost in a compact mass of sound, where the most experienced ear can distinguish nothing. Beethoven cared very little about details; besides he was deaf when he wrote his immortal work. I mention all this as a caution to young composers not to be too venturesome, unless they happen to have Beethoven's genius.

Here, on the other hand, is a fine effect produced by a Double-Bassoon brought into prominence; nothing can sound richer and deeper than its Double G beneath the low G of the Horns:

(Saint Saëns,
3rd Symph. p. 124)

(By kind permission of Messrs A. Durand et fils, Editeurs-Propriétaires.)

Robust lungs are needed to play the Double-Bassoon; the low notes, especially, consume a deal of breath. The maximum duration of a low holding-note cannot exceed two bars *moderato*. So, care must be taken, when this instrument is placed in the foreground, to write in such a manner as to allow it the requisite intervals of rest.

THE SARRUSOPHONE.

1.— The Sarrusophone is a rival of the Double-Bassoon, over which it possesses distinct advantages as regards both facility of emission and intensity in the low register. The column of air contained in its very wide tube is set in motion by means of a double-reed like that of the Bassoon, which instrument the Sarrusophone also closely resembles in its mechanism.

The Sarrusophone is sometimes accused of having a rather nasal and reedy quality of tone, so that the vibrations sound like a succession of little shocks. Each separate vibration, say its detractors, can be perceived as distinctly as those of a 32-ft. organ-pipe, when the ear is in the immediate proximity of the striking reed. This is most unjust criticism. When the instrument is in the hands of a player accustomed to the bassoon-reed, these defects in a great measure disappear. It then produces a full rich tone, forming an excellent bass of the Wood-wind group, since it can descend without hesitation to the extreme depths of the orchestra, an octave below the Bassoon:

2.— The Sarrusophone is written in C, and corresponds to a 16-ft. organ-pipe, just as the Bassoon corresponds to an 8-ft. pipe.

When used in conjunction with the Celli and Double-Basses, the Sarrusophone produces the effect of a Gamba-bass or very sweet Bombarde; it gives them a very characteristically penetrating tone.

3.— The Sarrusophone family is complete:

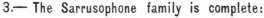

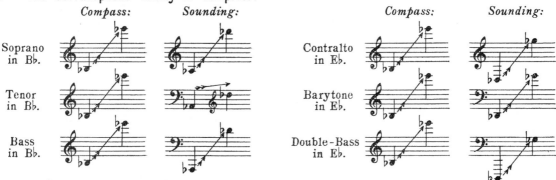

None of these interesting varieties have yet been used in the orchestra, Saxophones being preferred. As, however, the deepest-toned instrument of the Saxophone group cannot descend lower than the ordinary Bassoon — the size of the Double-Bass Saxophone making it practically inconvenient — the Sarrusophone in C stands without a serious rival in the extreme depth of the orchestra.

4.— This instrument possesses two really full-toned and remarkably powerful octaves (XY):

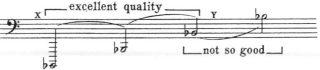

From Y upwards the tone of the Sarrusophone becomes dry, resembling the high register of the Bassoon; but this matters little, the lower octaves alone being really important.

All the notes of the Sarrusophone are as flexible and supple as those of the Oboe or the Cor Anglais; they can be attacked *forte* or *piano* — swelled or diminished — with equal ease.   All the notes can be produced with the same clearness and precision at the bottom of the scale as at the top.   Even in quick *tempo, staccato* passages, like the following, are practicable:

A Double-Bassoon in such a case would have no tone-power whatever, while the Sarrusophone overcomes the difficulty almost as easily as an ordinary Bassoon.

Articulation.

5.— The maximum speed attainable is about as follows:

The breath can be held about as long for sustained as for detached notes.   In moderate *tempo,* the lowest C can be sustained *forte* for two, or *piano,* for three bars:

The C an octave above can be held for 4 or 5 bars.

Shakes.

6.— All the shakes of the Bassoon are reproduced on the Sarrusophone, the fingering of the two instruments being the same.   Even in the lowest octave, shakes can be performed with speed and precision:

In short, the Sarrusophone stands in much the same relation to the Bassoon as the Double-bass to the Violoncello.   The two pairs of instruments may be treated in a parallel manner.

What the Bassoon can do, the Sarrusophone is likewise able to perform, within the limits assigned to low notes, which are, of course, heavy in proportion to their depth, and must be treated like people of consequence.

Saint-Saëns and Massenet have employed the Sarrusophone in several important works. It is an instrument which will come more and more into use, especially now that it has been perfected and its low register extended downwards; (a few years ago it could not descend lower than 16-ft. C). In Paris, it has been adopted by the Opéra, the Opéra-Comique, and the Colonne and Lamoureux Concerts.   It is now beginning to appear everywhere.

Chapter II.

—✛—

The Theory of the Tone-production of Brass Instruments.

1.— Let us take a tube; for instance, the long Trumpet that we see in ancient bas-reliefs. What are the sounds obtainable?

"Only those which correspond to the vibration of the whole column of air, or of half, or of a third, or of a quarter, etc., according to the amount of pressure exercised by the lips."

When the whole column of air is made to vibrate, the fundamental tone is sounded; when half the column of air vibrates, the second upper partial is obtained; when a third of the air-column is set in motion, the third upper partial is produced, and so on.

Let us assume the fundamental tone is 8-ft. C— the lowest note of the Violoncello;— the following series of harmonics can be successively obtained:

Just as the circular waves produced by a body falling into water draw mathematically closer and closer to each other in proportion as they get farther from the starting-point, so these sound-waves, first an octave apart (1-2), then a fifth (2-3), then a fourth (3-4), then thirds and seconds apart, finally almost merge into each other, separated only by thirds, fourths, and eighths of a tone. Just attempt writing down the 16 sounds of the 16-32 octave, the 32 of the following octave, the 64 of the next octave, the 128 of the still higher octave!

2.— The theoretical compass of all the brass instruments extends throughout the whole series of natural harmonics from 1 to 16, but, in practice, it is much more limited. Very wide tubes, like those of Tubas and Contrabass-Tubas, can alone sound the fundamental tone; the other brass instruments start from the second upper partial. Very narrow tubes, such as Horns and Trumpets, can alone reach and even go beyond the 12th, 13th, and 14th upper partials.

And yet these 13 or 14 notes, unequally scattered throughout two and a half octaves, have, for centuries, sufficed to give power and brilliancy to the orchestra. Neither Händel, nor Mozart, nor Beethoven, nor Weber ever suspected that a Trumpet would one day be able to play four chromatic semitones in succession, or a Horn come down the scale without jolting.

Owing to the breaks in the scale, the Trumpet could (up to the 7th partial at least) only proceed by skips, like a sparrow hopping from branch to branch.

Writing a Horn quartet was like solving a puzzle, each of the parts neglecting all kind of logical progression, in order to give chase to the sonorous note.

3.— The invention of valves removed the difficulty, setting the composer at liberty, and giving him very equal diatonic and chromatic scales throughout the whole of the harmonic series, also bringing exactly into tune the degrees which did not coincide with our tonal system, e. g. the 7th and 11th partials.

It then became possible to constitute, in the heart of the orchestra, two new groups of sound able to compete with the others in point of flexibility, viz. the Horn group and the Trumpet-Trombone-Tuba group. In short, the invention of valves loosened all fetters and flung wide the dungeon gates.

4.— The valve lowers the pitch of the instrument by lengthening it, as may be seen from the following table, which refers to the 4-piston Tuba in general use:

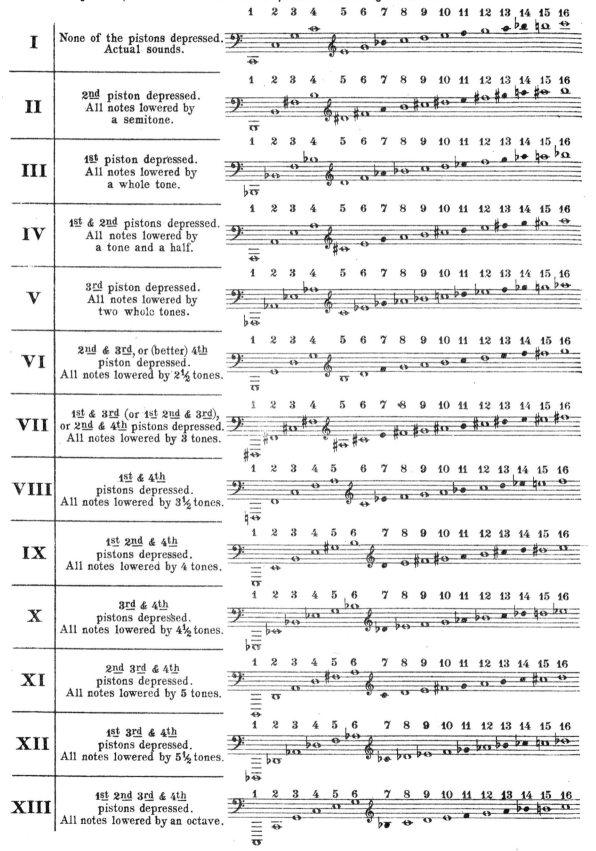

I	None of the pistons depressed. Actual sounds.
II	2nd piston depressed. All notes lowered by a semitone.
III	1st piston depressed. All notes lowered by a whole tone.
IV	1st & 2nd pistons depressed. All notes lowered by a tone and a half.
V	3rd piston depressed. All notes lowered by two whole tones.
VI	2nd & 3rd, or (better) 4th piston depressed. All notes lowered by 2½ tones.
VII	1st & 3rd (or 1st 2nd & 3rd), or 2nd & 4th pistons depressed. All notes lowered by 3 tones.
VIII	1st & 4th pistons depressed. All notes lowered by 3½ tones.
IX	1st 2nd & 4th pistons depressed. All notes lowered by 4 tones.
X	3rd & 4th pistons depressed. All notes lowered by 4½ tones.
XI	2nd 3rd & 4th pistons depressed. All notes lowered by 5 tones.
XII	1st 3rd & 4th pistons depressed. All notes lowered by 5½ tones.
XIII	1st 2nd 3rd & 4th pistons depressed. All notes lowered by an octave.

Such is the theoretical compass of five chromatic octaves, which might even be exceeded upwards. But we must add at once that no single performer is able to travel over such extensive ground; the most skilful cannot embrace more than three and a half octaves.

5.— Excepting the Tuba, Contrabass-Tuba, Valve-Trombone, and a few Barytone Saxhorns, all the other instruments have only three valves, so that the number of combinations tabulated above is reduced, in their case, to seven (I. II. III. IV. V. VI. VII.), corresponding to the seven positions of the Slide-Trombone. Such are the seven combinations possible on the Contrabass-Tubas in E♭ and B♭ of military bands. The others only concern instruments little used, and which, besides, cannot descend to the fundamental.

6.— Looking at the natural scale of harmonics, we see that the brass instruments fall into three groups:

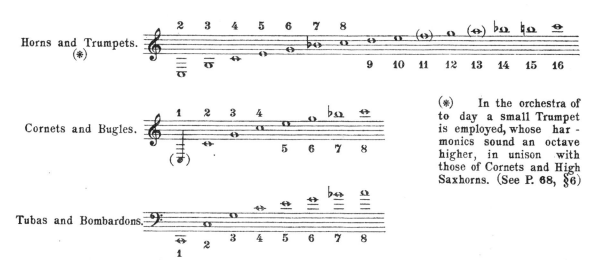

Horns and Trumpets. (*)

Cornets and Bugles.

Tubas and Bombardons.

(*) In the orchestra of to day a small Trumpet is employed, whose harmonics sound an octave higher, in unison with those of Cornets and High Saxhorns. (See P. 68, §6)

If we now compare the length of the tubes, we get the following figures, taking as a standard the key of B♭, common to all of them —

Cornet in B♭ . . . . length of tube 4 ft. 5 in.

Trumpet * . . . . — 8 ft. 5¾ in.   * Trumpet in B♭ *basso* an octave below the modern Trumpet.

Horn (in B♭ *basso*) . . . . . . — 17 ft. 7 in.

C.–B Tuba . . . . — 17 ft. 8 in.

So that Cornets correspond to 4 ft., Trumpets to 8 ft., and Horns and Contrabass-Tubas to 16 ft. Organ stops. However, in practice, things are somewhat different.

In reality, Cornets and Trumpets, enclosed within the same limits, play at pretty much the same pitch, and in such a parallel fashion that, in many secondary orchestras, without regard for the composer's intentions or the difference of *timbre*, the Cornet replaces the Trumpet, the latter being much more risky and dangerous to play.

7.— The distance between the harmonics diminishing as they rise, the subdivisions of the tube become so minute that the least hesitation, the least mistake in the pressure of the lips may cause accidents.

Take this theme:

The old Trumpet will play it, making use of the harmonics 4 to 12:

The Cornet in B♭ will sound the same notes, making use of the harmonics between 2 and 6:

(The notes marked with crosses could not be obtained but for the pistons.)

The Cornet, whose best notes lie between the 2nd and 5th or 6th harmonics, will reproduce this theme with a lightness of articulation, an ease and rapidity altogether superior to the Trumpet.   In this medium register, "diatonic and chromatic scales, shakes and runs are child's play for the Cornet: it is capable of as much execution as a Flute or a Clarinet."

On the other hand, can it compare with the Trumpet in point of *timbre,* especially in the high register, where it becomes poor and colorless?   Has it the same power, nobleness, and dramatic intensity?

8.— We have just (§6) classed Trumpets and Horns in the category of instruments which cannot emit the fundamental tone.   This is comprehensible in the case of the Trumpet, but what about the Horn, whose length, equal to that of the Contrabass-Tuba, ought to allow of descending quite as low?   The answer is that the Horn cannot sound its fundamental tone, because its tube is too narrow. In contrast with the bellying tube of the Contra-bass Tuba, the Horn has a slim and elegant figure which prevents the lips from acting efficiently in the lowest register.   Besides, there is the question of the size and shape of the mouthpiece, which affects not merely the *timbre,* but also the more or less easy emission of the notes.   The fundamental tone can only be sounded when the diameter and length of the tube bear a suitable ratio to each other (Cavaillé-Coll's law), and a special mouthpiece is also required, varying according to the family of instruments.

THE NATURAL HORN.

(Ital., *Corno*. Ger., *Waldhorn*. Fr., *Cor simple*.)

1.— It is only from the historical point of view that I mention the Natural Horn, now-adays almost universally discarded.

Without artificial aid, the *Waldhorn* can hardly sound any notes but the harmonics between 2 and 16 inclusively.

Remark: Horn-players read the F clef an octave lower than they ought; is it not ridiculous to use two clefs to write these four notes of the harmonic series, which ought really to be written in the F clef alone ?

Thanks to supplementary tubes, called "crooks," the harmonic series may be transposed, the fundamentals available (about a dozen in number) being as follows:

Horn in	Bb *basso*,	length of tube	17 ft.	7	in.
—	B♮	—	—	16 ft.	10	in.
—	C	—	—	16 ft.	1	in.
—	Db	—	—	15 ft.	3½	in.
—	D♮	—	—	14 ft.	6¼	in.
—	Eb	—	—	13 ft.	7½	in.
—	E♮	—	—	12 ft.	9	in.
—	F	—	—	12 ft.		in.
—	G	—	—	10 ft.	9½	in.
—	Ab	—	—	10 ft.	1½	in.
—	A♮	—	—	9 ft.	7½	in.
—	Bb *alto*	—	—	9 ft.	2	in.
—	C	—	—	8 ft.	4¾	in.

The lowest note obtainable is the C (✳) of the Horn in Bb *basso*, i. e. Bb for the ear.

The highest is the G (✠) of the Horn in A, i. e. E for the ear.

2.— To get the intermediate intervals, the horn-player inserts his right hand in the bell, cutting off half the air, and flattening the open notes by a semitone:

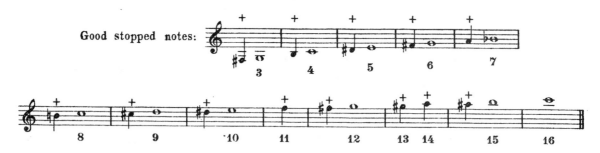

Remark: As the 7th, 11th, 13th, and 14th partials are out of tune in our scale, the player, in order to utilize them, has to flatten them by "stopping."

The semitones thus obtained below each of the open notes are excellent. *Muted* notes and *overblown* notes are also very valuable, on account of the variety of color they impart to the orchestra; we will speak of them at greater length in the following section dealing with the Valve-Horn.

The notes produced by cutting off more than half the column of air are dull, not quite true of intonation, and difficult of production:

Such is the instrument for which the classic masters wrote; breaks, deficiencies, and inequalities are to be met with at every step, and it is impossible below the 7th harmonic to come across two conjunct degrees of the same *timbre*. True, with the simplest means the most powerful effects are frequently obtained, and with such limited resources Weber has created masterpieces. Three notes suffice for Oberon's magic Horn:

THE VALVE-HORN.

(Ital., *Corno cromatico*.   Ger., *Ventilhorn*.   Fr., *Cor à pistons*.)

1.— Valve-Horns are made in several keys: E, E♭, D, etc., but nowadays only one kind is used: the Horn in F.

The indications to be met with at every page in modern compositions (Muta in D, in E, in F, in G) are for the convenience not so much of the performer as of the composer, who prefers (supposing there is a sudden change of key) to make use of the natural notes rather than of numerous accidentals.

He writes as simply as possible, and it is the player's part to understand him aright.

The chromatic scale of the Valve-Horn extends from:

(actual sounds)

Its 38 notes are perfectly homogeneous, and its compass, as will be observed, is much the same as that of the Bassoon, which, although it can descend a semitone lower, loses by comparison with the Horn in the upper register:

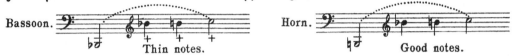

Bassoon. — Thin notes.   Horn. — Good notes.

2.— We may here notice an appreciable difference between the capabilities of the two instruments.

While the bassoon-player can perform all kinds of acrobatic feats throughout the entire compass of his instrument, and can pass from one register to the other as easily as a pianist on his keyboard, the horn-player has to choose between the high and the low register, as he cannot play satisfactorily at both extremities of the scale, because the lips assume a particular shape according to the register which the horn-player chiefly practises.   The 1st horn-player is to the 2nd what the Tenor Trombone is to the Bass Trombone.   The First Horns (of the two or three pairs in our orchestras) play the high notes, the Second Horns the low notes.

3.— To meet the requirements of both categories of horn-players, instrument-makers now construct two kinds of Horns: *ascending* Horns and *descending* Horns, a modification in the 3rd piston sufficing to enable one kind to rise easily and the other to descend easily.

N. B.   The 3rd piston raises the whole scale of the *ascending* Horns by one tone, and lowers the scale of the *descending* Horns to an equal extent.

The compass, in actual sounds, of our two chromatic Horns in F is as follows:

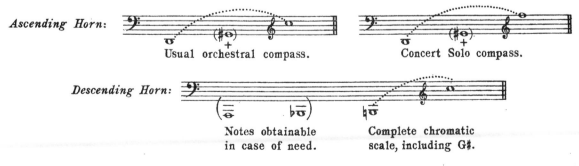

Ascending Horn: Usual orchestral compass.   Concert Solo compass.

Descending Horn: Notes obtainable in case of need.   Complete chromatic scale, including G♯.

N. B.   The G♯ marked with a cross is the only note wanting in the chromatic scale of the *ascending* Horn.

Notation.

4.—

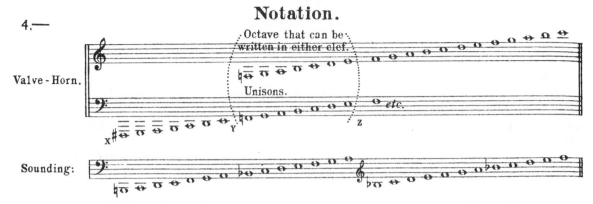

As we have already observed (P. 55), the notation of the Horn in the F clef is an octave too low.   Suppose, for instance, two Horns playing in the octave Y Z; if one be written in the G clef and the other in the F clef, what is in unison for the ear will be in the octave for the eye.   Triumph of absurdity!   Why not make the F clef the natural continuation of the G clef?

In this chromatic scale of 43 notes none are defective, and, with the exception of the G# (D#+) wanting on the *ascending* Horn, there are no breaks:

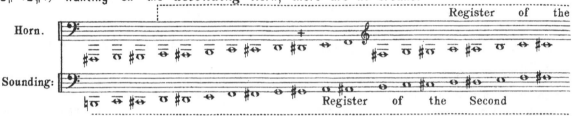

Three Varieties of Tone-Color.

5.— Besides the rich and poetic quality of the open notes, the Horn possesses two other kinds of very special and characteristic tone-color, viz. "stopped notes" and "overblown notes."

Stopped notes are obtained by means of a mute (*sordino*); *overblown* notes by the insertion of the hand in the bell.   The former are weak, the latter powerful.

Stopped notes, which should be indicated by the word   *sordini* (in German: *gedämpft*), are equivalent to the most absolute *pianissimo*— the echo, so to speak, of the open notes.

Nothing is more easily or more quickly accomplished than slipping the mute into the bell; the performer does not so much as interrupt his playing, for, while holding the Horn with his left hand, he slips in the mute with his right.

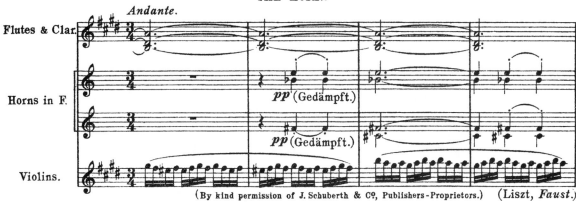

(By kind permission of J. Schuberth & C?, Publishers-Proprietors.)   (Liszt, *Faust.*)

Though barely audible beneath the undulating figure of the Violins, the velvety tone of the Horns is, in this case, extremely gratifying to the ear.

Overblown notes, whose production involves considerable effort, are obtained by closing half the tube with the right hand: the lips attack the semitone above the note required, and the insertion of the hand lowers the note to an equal extent. If, for instance, the player wishes to sound D as an overblown note, he attacks E♭, his hand at the same time lowering the column of air by a semitone.

The composer has several ways of indicating these overblown notes:

(1) simply by a cross placed above the note to be overblown:

(2) or by the word *cuivré* (in German scores *gestopft* *f*):

(3) or by a cross and the word *cuivré* (*gestopft f*):

It sometimes happens that the word *cuivré* is accompanied by the indication *piano*. In that case, the note can be overblown at the moment of attack only; immediately after the attack, the tone becomes very subdued, like that of the muted Horn.

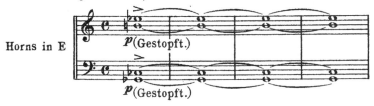

The Horn can be played *con sordino* throughout its entire compass. Stopped notes produced with the aid of the hand can hardly be obtained below the 3rd upper partial:

---

* *Gestopft* means simply "stopped," but accompanied by an accent >, or by the indication *f* or *sf*, it is understood in the sense of *overblown*.

In his *Requiem*, Berlioz has written an overblown F♯ (a semitone lower) for two Horns in unison , the effect still being tolerably good, but this is the extreme limit.

When Valve-Horns were beginning to come into vogue, they were assigned to the second pair of horn-players, being subordinated to the first pair, who still retained Natural Horns.

When the first pair was assigned a note not belonging to the natural scale, accompanied by the indication *forte* or *sforzando*, as no mistake was possible, the composer had no need to give any special directions; these stopped notes *forte* were necessarily overblown, as, for instance, in *Faust:*

Sometimes, as in the *Damnation de Faust*, the composer thought fit to specify the effect he desired in parentheses, although this was needless:

To sum up, in order to avoid all chance of misunderstanding, we must in future confine ourselves to the two following formulæ:

> *Con Sordini* for all *pianissimo* effects.
>
> *Cuivré* (with a +) for stopped effects *forte*.

It is sometimes necessary, after these special effects, to indicate the precise moment when the Horn is to come back to natural sounds. The word "open" (in French "ouvert," in German "offen") is used for this purpose. (See *Rheingold*, Page 181).

Speed of Articulation.

6.—Despite the great length of its tube, the Horn can articulate rapidly, making exclusive use of *single-articulation* in the lower register, but towards the higher part of its compass, from the 3rd partial upwards, *double* and even *triple articulation* may be employed, so that the Horn can bear comparison with the Flute in point of execution.

The opening of the 2nd act of *Tannhäuser*, for instance, would be impossible with *single-articulation,* considering the quick rate of movement.

The maximum speed attainable in the low register is:

in the medium register (*single - articulation*):

Register of *double* and *triple articulation*, where the speed that can be attained is almost unlimited:

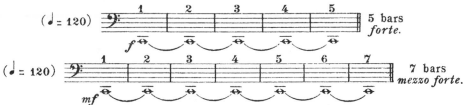

Remark: However, the strain on the lips involved in the production of high notes is hardly compatible with great speed of emission. It is prudent not to go beyond the 9th or 10th harmonic, when making use of *double* and *triple articulation*.

Length of Breath.

7.— The following are the results of experiments made with the kind assistance of Mr Pénable, Concert Colonne soloist:

In the medium register, from the 4th to the 8th partial , keeping the same metronomic rate of movement (♩ = 120), the human lungs allow of sustaining eleven bars *forte*, 14 *mezzo-forte,* and 25 *piano*.

We must add that this can only be accomplished with the utmost effort, and would be a dangerous experiment in the orchestra.

The production of the high notes, inasmuch as it involves great air-pressure, severely tasks the lungs, so that such long holding-notes can hardly be expected above the 8th and 9th harmonics.

Shakes.

8.— The pistons are never used for shakes; in this tube, so very narrow considering its great length, the air cannot travel fast enough to attain the object in view.

Consequently, horn-players make use of their lips only.

Major shakes come out well; (they are only possible from the 5th to the 12th, 13th, 14th, and 15th harmonics).

Register in which shakes are practicable: , and

the best part of this register is: Shakes between the 12th and 15th

upper partials are better avoided in orchestral writing; they are suitable for *virtuosi*, but dangerous for the majority of players.

Minor shakes do not come out so well; they are only possible with the hand in the bell, and are really of very doubtful quality.

Crooks.

9.— The Valve-Horn can change key as easily as the Natural Horn, when needful.

Each key has a special crook, a hollow ring interposed between the mouthpiece and the body of the Horn. The shorter the tube, the higher the scale rises and the nearer the sound seems to come to the lips; in the end, the player feels as if he held it tight between his teeth, so that it cannot escape. He is as sure of it as the draughtsman of his pencil, which he holds near the point for very minute work.

So, if the performer has to play very high, he makes use of the F♯, G, A♭, A♮, and B♭ crooks:

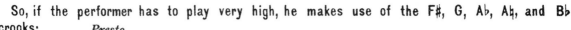

The crook corresponding to the key of F has two coils 8 inches in diameter, the A♭ crook a single coil of slightly inferior diameter, and the A♮ crook a coil only 5½ inches in diameter.

How could Schumann venture to write up to such giddy heights, between the 8th and 20th harmonics, for the first of the 4 Horns in his very interesting *Concerto?*

Virtuosi are so much afraid of this Concerto that, although they are willing enough to rehearse it in the orchestra, they will never venture to play it in public: the danger is really too great!

Siegfried's horn, which reaches the 16th upper partial, goes straight ahead, without any kind of hesitation or fear, because it moves forward by regular degrees, and because it feels that it is getting gradually nearer to the goal, where it expends its full force:

But Schumann's *Concerto* is far more dangerous; there is not a page without a stumbling-block.

10.— In paragraph 1 we spoke of the indications to be found in modern scores (Muta in D, E, F, G, etc.), rather for the convenience of the composer than in the interest of the performer, who usually transposes into the key of F.

Indeed, he plays everything in F, save in the exceptional cases which we have just noticed (§9).

If then, in the course of a piece, the composer thinks it necessary, for the sake of avoiding too many flats or sharps, to change the key of the Horns, he may do so without troubling himself about the means by which the change can be effected. Take, for instance, this passage beginning in F and finishing in E.

Here are two modern ways of writing it:

The result is the same; it is only a matter of determining the most favorable place for the change of key; it is a mere question of neat appearance for the eye. Performers are accustomed to this sort of exercise, and are never taken by surprise. The composer may implicitly trust to them.

THE HORN IN THE ORCHESTRA.

11.— Four Horns make an admirable quartet.

When the Horn-quartet is added to the Woodwind, the volume of sound is more than doubled.

A Solo Horn moving softly through the Strings blends with them most harmoniously. It is one of Wagner's favorite devices.

When blended with the Celli and Double-basses, the Horn acquires a singularly penetrating quality of tone, which one might fancy to be that of a soft Trombone:

(Liszt.)

The four Horns playing *piano* or *forte* can be heard through the whole mass of the orchestra:

(Widor, *3rd Symphony.*)

(J. Hamelle, Editeur-Propriétaire.)

The Horn and Clarinet in unison are exquisite:

(C. Franck, *Symphonie.*)

(J. Hamelle, Editeur-Propriétaire.)

In the following choral given to the Brass, the Solo Horn doubles the first **Trombone** very efficiently:

(Ganaye, *Ouverture dramatique.*)

The following combination of two Clarinets and two Horns, little known before Mozart, but so often used since, is very even in quality, the two kinds of tone-color blending admirably:

(Flauto Magico.)

The next example shows some light, bounding chords from the *Roi de Lahore*, that leave behind them a vibration as pleasing to the ear as the white mist of a summer's morn to the eye:

(By kind permission of Heugel et Cie, Editeurs - Propriétaires)   (Massenet, *Le Roi de Lahore.*)

Note also this charming effect of the Horn and Flutes, accompanied by the holding-notes of the Strings and the rhythmically recurring figure of the Harp:

(By kind permission of A. Durand et Fils, Editeurs-Propriétaires.)   (Saint-Saëns, *Danse Macabre.*)

In a chord played by all the wind instruments together, nothing can equal the stopped Horns at the extreme end of a *diminuendo*, to give the impression of a dying echo:

(Wagner, *Siegfried*.)

(By kind permission of Schott & Cº, Publishers-Proprietors.)

1st Remark: When the Horns are written in four parts, the bass is naturally obliged to expend more wind than the other parts, and to take breath oftener, being at the same time less sonorous. It is better, when sustained notes are needed, to make use of the Bassoon, which is less fatiguing for the player and forms a more solid basis to the harmonic group:

(By kind permission of Schott & Cº, Publishers-Proprietors.)   (Humperdinck, *Hänsel und Gretel*.)

2nd Remark: As we have usually four Horns in the orchestra, it must be remembered that the first Horn of each pair is an *ascending* Horn, and the second a *descending* Horn; consequently, the high register must be confined to the 1st and 3rd Horns, and the low register to the 2nd and 4th.

12.— AUTHORS AND WORKS TO BE STUDIED: Mozart (*Quintet*); Beethoven (*Sonata, Quintet, Sextet* and *Septet*); Schubert (*Octet*); Schumann (*Concerto*); Brahms (*Trio*); Saint-Saëns (*Romance*); Dauprat, Gallay, Mohr (Schools); Friedr. Gumbert (*Solobuch für Horn*), etc.

Read Händel, Bach, Mozart, Beethoven (who writes down to double Bb in the 9th Symphony), all Weber, all Wagner, and all the modern authors.

THE NATURAL TRUMPET.

(Ital., *Tromba.*   Ger., *Trompete.*   Fr., *Trompette.*)

1.— We have already seen (P. 51, §2) that the narrow diameter of its tube would not allow the Trumpet to sound its fundamental tone, its scale in practice only beginning with low E (actual pitch):

This E has nearly always been regarded as the inferior limit of the instrument.   In *Manfred,* Schumann ventured to write E♭, a semitone lower,   but prudent conductors usually transfer this note from the intimidated Trumpet to the 1st Trombone:

2.— Like the Horn, the Natural Trumpet has crooks, which lengthen the tube more or less, and transpose the harmonic series into nearly all keys:

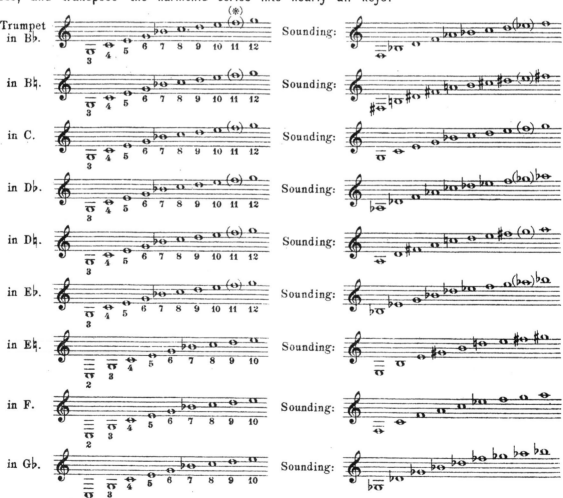

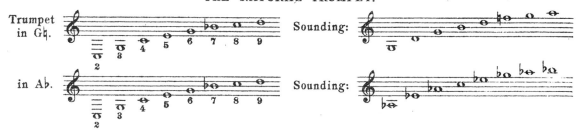

(✳) N. B. The 11th partial is always given in parentheses; we have already seen that it does not exactly coincide with the 4th degree of our scale.

This list of the keys of the Trumpet ought really to begin with A, but it is a key of very indifferent quality on the Trumpet, and consequently very little used.   In the *7th Symphony,* Beethoven writes his Trumpets in D;   likewise Mendelssohn in the *Italian Symphony,* but he changes to E for the last two movements.   Neither Beethoven nor Mendelssohn uses them in A.

The Trumpet in A would be in unison with the Horn in A; the Trumpet in B♭ is in unison with the Horn in B♭ *alto;* the Trumpet in B♮ is in unison with the Horn in B♮ *alto,* and so on.

3.— The Horn in C *alto* and the Trumpet in C are two *non-transposing* instruments producing the same actual sounds.

Their quality, however, is quite different. We have already observed that the shape of the mouthpiece greatly influences the quality of tone, and that the mouthpiece of the Horn is twice as deep as that of the Trumpet—sometimes even deeper; the little cup which serves as a mouthpiece for the Trumpet is not ½ inch deep, whereas the long, conical mouthpiece of the Horn measures about an inch.

The conical mouthpiece is necessary for instruments with a soft velvety tone, like the Horn, whose *timbre* blends so well with the Woodwind;   on the other hand, the hemispherical mouthpiece of the Trumpet produces power and brilliancy.

"It is easy to understand the influence exercised by the shape of the mouthpiece on the formation of the sound, when it is remembered that in this cup the sound-waves are generated.   We cannot therefore too strongly advise performers to employ exclusively such mouthpieces as long experience has shown instrument-makers to be the only ones suited to the *timbre* of the instrument for which the said mouthpieces are constructed."
(Mahillon, *Eléments d' Acoustique.*)

4.— It is hardly necessary to point out, as we did in the case of the Horn, how limited are the resources of the Natural Trumpet, for which the composers of former times could write nothing but the natural harmonics, conjunct degrees being available only from the 7th partial upwards.

They had not even stopped notes at their disposal, for their quality was so execrable that the two or three instances of their employment resulted in miserable failures.

THE VALVE-TRUMPET.

5.— As in the case of the Horns, the invention of valves remedied all the defects of the Trumpet, allowing of a regular chromatic succession, and bringing *into* tune the harmonics *out* of tune in our scale.   From low E to high B♭, the chromatic scale is complete; all the degrees are very even and true; all the notes are excellent *forte,* nearly all *piano:*

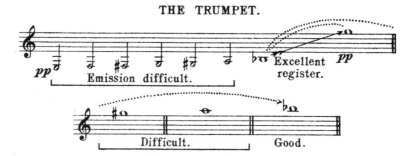

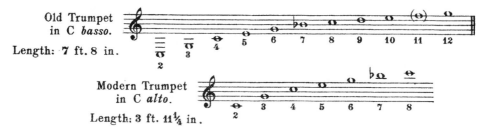

6.— Like the Horn, the Trumpet can change key when necessary. For a long time the keys of D, E♭, E♮, and F were in use, the two last having a quality of tone incomparable for its beauty and energy; but, within the last ten years, not only have the old keys been discarded, but the harmonic series has at a single bound skipped an octave higher; for this composers are responsible, as they have kept on writing higher and higher, obliging performers to seek for more practical means of playing in the high register.—

It is no longer an 8 ft. but a 4 ft. Trumpet that is used at present; it is a companion to the Cornet and has the same dimensions:

Old Trumpet in C *basso*.
Length: **7** ft. 8 in.

Modern Trumpet in C *alto*.
Length: **3** ft. 11¼ in.

7.— The modern Trumpet is played in the keys of A, B♭, B♮, C, D♭, and D♮.

The following figures show the length of tube of the various Trumpets.

Trumpet in D♮ = 3 ft. 5¼ in.
        „   D♭ = 3 ft. 8¼ in.
        „   C = 3 ft. 11¼ in.
        „   B♮ = 4 ft. 2 in.
        „   B♭ = 4 ft. 5 in.
        „   A = 4 ft. 8 in.

Their chromatic scale starts from F♯ and reaches C *in alt*.

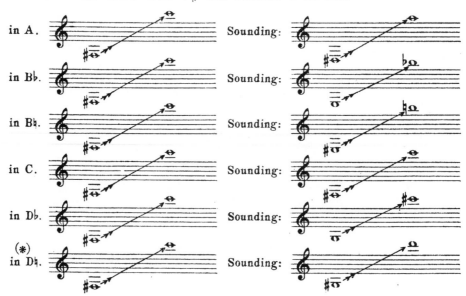

Remark: The Trumpet in D (✳) is required for Bach's works; it is not used otherwise, for, generally speaking, notes above Bb (actual pitch) lose the *timbre* of the Trumpet, and produce the sensation of a large Flute rather than of a brass instrument. Besides, G♯ and A cannot be attacked *piano,* and still less B and C, so what need is there for so high a key?

The true compass of the Trumpet is two octaves, from G to G (actual sounds.) and within these limits nothing is so fine and so powerful as the old Trumpet in F— (in F or in E, according to tonal necessities).

Compared with this manly and imperious instrument, the tone of the little modern Trumpet sounds almost like that of the Cornet à Pistons.

Wagner scrupulously avoids making too free use of the high notes; it is quite exceptionally, and to produce a special effect, that he writes up to C *in alt* (actual pitch) in *Parsifal.*

It is likewise quite exceptionally and in a *ff* that he sends the F Trumpet up to B♮ (actual pitch):

Trumpet in F

ff

(*March for the Centenary of American Independence.*)
(By kind permission of Schott & Cº, Publishers-Proprietors.)

However, the performers of to-day have all adopted the Trumpet in C, easy to play in the high register. Nearly all have a tuning-slide which allows of falling one tone below F♯ *basso;* when it is necessary for the Second Trumpet to descend still lower — to the E♭ of *Manfred,* for instance — it takes the B♭ crook, and its tuning-slide not only allows it to play E♭ but even D (actual pitch), so that the 2 Trumpets of a pair, the 1st in C, the 2nd in B♭, have the following enormous compass:

Trumpets: { in C. { in B♭.

Tuning-Slide. Natural Scale. (Actual Sounds.)

Remark: The tuning-slide is not used for keys lower than B♭.

Articulation.

8.— Like the Flute, the Trumpet makes use of three kinds of tonguing: *single, double,* and *triple articulation,* so that it is capable of great rapidity of emission:

Trumpet in E. *Allegro.*

(By kind permission of Heugel et Cie, Editeurs-Propriétaires.) (Delibes, *Sylvia.*)

Trumpets in D.

Flutes.
Oboes.
Clarinets.

Bassoons.

(Berlioz, *Menuet des Follets.*)
p. 259.

(By kind permission of Heugel et Cie, Editeurs-Propriétaires.) (Lalo, *Le Roi d'Ys.*)

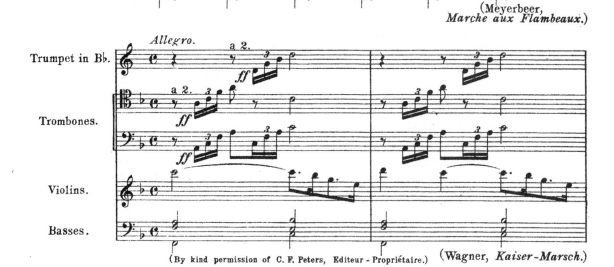

(Meyerbeer,
Marche aux Flambeaux.)

(By kind permission of C. F. Peters, Editeur-Propriétaire.) (Wagner, *Kaiser-Marsch.*)

The following are about the maximum speeds attainable in the low and medium registers:

However, the passage must not be very long, on account of the fatigue of emission and consequent heaviness of articulation.

Length of Breath.

9.— *Piano,* the Trumpet can, in moderate *tempo,* sound a holding-note of 8 or 9 bars in the low register:

and with the same rate of movement, it can hold a note in the medium register for 12 or 14 bars:

It is needless to observe that these numbers are halved in *forte* passages, because then the expenditure of breath is doubled.

Shakes.

10.— We have seen that the Horn does not make use of the pistons for shakes. With the Trumpet, it is just the reverse: it can *only* use its pistons.

The following are those which may be used: (the cross means *bad*; the double cross *impossible*).

Muted Trumpets.

11.— Neither Beethoven nor Weber made use of muted Trumpets. Wagner has brought them into fashion by employing them in *Siegfried* and in *Meistersinger*. Since then, they are constantly to be met with in modern scores:

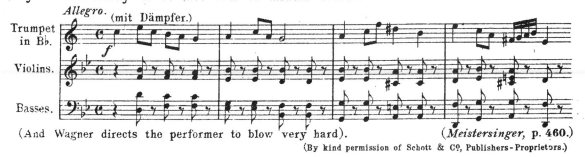

(And Wagner directs the performer to blow very hard). (*Meistersinger*, p. 460.)

There is no modern composer who does not use the Trumpet *con sordino:* Richard Strauss, Vincent d' Indy, Bruneau, Debussy. Examples abound: I will only quote the following exquisite use of muted Trumpets:

(By kind permission of Heugel et Cie, Editeurs-Propriétaires.) (Charpentier, *Louise.*)

The articulations of the Trumpets loom through the surrounding veil of orchestral haze; an experienced ear can only just detect them under the tremolo of the Violins and the silvery notes of the Harps.

THE BASS TRUMPET.

12.—The quality of tone of the Bass Trumpet is admirably full, rich, and even, from:

Its tube is 7 ft. 8½ in. long.
Wagner writes it in E♭, D, & C:

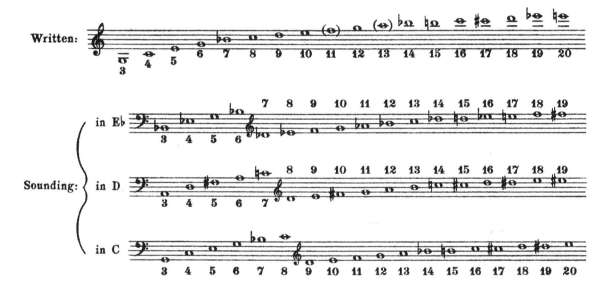

but, whatever the key indicated by the composer, it is always played in C (transposing when necessary), Bass Trumpets in E♭ and D not being made.

Avoid falling as low as the 3rd partial, or rising higher than E, the 20th partial, though F, a semitone above, is possible and tolerably sonorous.

13.—AUTHORS AND WORKS TO BE CONSULTED: Everything published since Bach and Händel. These two illustrious masters should be read more out of curiosity (as far as the Trumpet is concerned) than with the idea of imitating them, their manner differing altogether from our modern style.

Technically, we have little information about their almost prehistoric Trumpet. Was it an instrument analogous to our little Trumpet in C? So one would think from a passage in Deldevez's *Curiosités musicales:*

"Lately, an important discovery has been made at Heidelberg, which solves the problem; a tube 4 ft. long, in B♭, has been found, which, by means of a tuning - slide, can be raised to the key of D. At a meeting held in Berlin, Rosleck played it before an assembly that unanimously admired the easy and agreeable emission of notes sounding an octave higher than those produced by ordinary Trumpets."

Where is this Trumpet? Is it the instrument formerly in current use?

How is it that only this single specimen should have been discovered, although we have preserved numerous specimens of all kinds of Trumpets and Trombones from the time of Charles V onwards?

Was it merely a question of the mouthpiece employed, as is supposed by Eichborn (*Die Trompete in alter und neuer Zeit*, Breitkopf & Härtel) and the majority of the specialists I have been able to consult?—

"The radical mistake made by scientific men consists in thinking that the high tone of Soprano Trumpets was due to their tube..... No, it was due exclusively to the employment of various mouthpieces, whose very narrow bore obliged the player to contract his lips, the Soprano Trumpet having a much smaller mouthpiece than the ordinary Trumpet."

The truth is that the employment of a very narrow mouthpiece enables lips specially practised for playing in a limited part of the scale to reach heights generally deemed inaccessible. Besides, we must note that Bach's Soprano hardly ever plays outside of its own special octave.

The real Trumpet begins with Haydn and Mozart, the imperious and manly Trumpet of Beethoven, Weber, Wagner, and Berlioz, neither too high nor too low: two octaves from G to G:

This is the ancient Trumpet, the oldest instrument in the world, unchangeable like the Perfect Consonances, the Fifth and the Octave. It is for this kind of Trumpet that we ought to write.

THE CORNET À PISTONS.

(Ital., *Cornetto*. Ger., *Kornett*. Fr., *Cornet à pistons.*)

1.— For nearly half a century, in French, Belgian, and Italian orchestras, the Cornet à Pistons took the place of the Trumpet, gradually ousting it. This was due to the fact that the Cornet was easier to play, requiring less talent and artistic intelligence. Trumpet *virtuosi* became rarer and rarer, while cornet-players were to be met with everywhere.

Although the *timbre* of the two instruments could not for one moment be compared, the one being thick and vulgar, the other noble and brilliant, as they had the same compass, the difference in quality of tone was ignored; so much the worse for sensitive ears!

However, since the invention of the little modern Trumpet, which can rise as easily as the Cornet, makes use of the same harmonic series, and is not much more risky in its emission, the Cornet has gradually retreated before the reinstated Trumpet.

2.— Cornets are tuned in B♭ and A: the length of their tube is the same as that of little Trumpets in B♭ and A, and their scale, which starts from the same F♯, rises to the same C *in alt:*

Cornet in B♭ length of tube 4 ft. 5 in.

— A — 4 ft. 8 in.

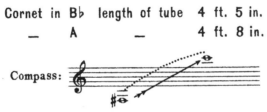

Compass:

Need we again call attention to the danger incurred by too frequently using either the highest or the lowest notes of brass instruments? We must ever bear in mind the doubtful quality of the first 5 or 6 degrees in the low register, from F♯ to C, and the increasing weakness and thinness of the *timbre* from the sixth partial (G) upwards.

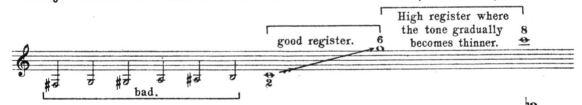

The highest notes can only be produced with some difficulty, except B♭ which is relatively easy.

It is dangerous to attack these extreme degrees without preparation, but when easier and surer notes precede them the danger is obviated. Nothing is more frequent than a cadence like the following, for instance:

Cornet in B♭

and the B♭ thus prepared is excellent.

So we see that the best notes of the instrument lie between C (2nd upper partial) and G (6th upper partial).

3.— Cornets and Valve-Trumpets have the same mechanism, the same capabilities, the same possible and impossible shakes.— Like the Trumpet, the Cornet makes use of single, double, and triple tonguing. Still more easily than the Trumpet, thanks to the shape of its mouthpiece, it can perform the wildest acrobatic feats: runs, iterated notes, chromatic scales, etc.

"But its technical resources," says Gevaert, "show to the best advantage in the secondary forms of art — military and brass bands — where it is treated as a *bravura* instrument." See Alex. Luigini's interesting *Caprice*.

However, we must not forget services rendered; Berlioz, Meyerbeer, Gounod, Bizet, and their contemporaries used Cornets instead of Trumpets in the orchestra.

Till within the last few years, composers in the West of Europe wrote for 2 Trumpets and 2 Cornets, and it is only quite recently that 4 Trumpets have again come into vogue.

(Berlioz, *L'Enfance du Christ.*)

(Meyerbeer, *Le Prophète.*)

(Gounod, *Faust.*)

(Choudens, Editeur - Propriétaire.)

(Bizet, *l'Arlésienne*.)

Trombones.
(By kind permission of Heugel et Cie, Editeurs - Propriétaires.)

(Widor, *Ouverture Espagnole*.)

At present, Cornets are gradually disappearing from the orchestra, and Trumpets are taking their place, thus resuming their legitimate position.

THE TROMBONES.

(Ital., *Tromboni.* Ger., *Posaunen.* Fr., *Trombones.*)

1.— Bach, Gluck, Mozart, and Beethoven (in his youth) always wrote for 3 Trombones —— Alto, Tenor, and Bass.

Despite its admirable *timbre,* akin to that of the Trumpet in F, the Alto Trombone has now become more or less obsolete, because its compass being much the same, it is almost a duplicate of that magnificent instrument.

Alto Trombone:

Trumpet and Trombone complete each other, the former being, as it were, the higher section, the latter the lower section of a single keyboard. If the Alto Trombone was necessary in the orchestras of yore, which never had more than two Trumpets, it is not so indispensable now that we have three or four Trumpets.

2.— In the last chapter (P. 74, §13) I mentioned the theories started in connection with Bach's Trumpet. Its inability to produce any notes but the natural harmonics prevented it from taking part in conjunct polyphony. It was never the *Trumpet* that played the soprano part in the quartet of brass instruments, but the *Cornetto,* or else a kind of high Trombone nowadays almost unknown. *"It was a characteristic German custom, on Sundays and Church holidays, to have the Choral for the day played by a band of Cornet and Trombone players, standing in the tower of the principal church. Bach introduced this effect into his Cantatas, the brass instrument group playing alone or doubling in unison each of the vocal parts."* (*Cantata No 25*).

So, the *Cornetto* and the Trombones were grouped together, and the Alto became an indispensable voice in this robust quartet.

The old formula *Alto, Tenor, Bass* remained in force till the *Symphony in C minor.* Afterwards, Beethoven adopted the system of writing the two first Trombones on one staff, never exceeding the limits of the Tenor Trombones, and Weber and his successors followed his example.

Then, when 4 Trumpets came to be used in the orchestra, the Trombones being ever more confined to the lower parts of the harmony, the Alto became more and more obsolete.

THE TENOR TROMBONE.

(Ital., *Trombone tenore.* Ger., *Tenorposaune.* Fr., *Trombone ténor.*)

3.— Compass: 35 notes, from   to

Its mechanism is simple; the slide, which can be drawn out to seven different lengths, displaces the harmonic series each time by a semitone.

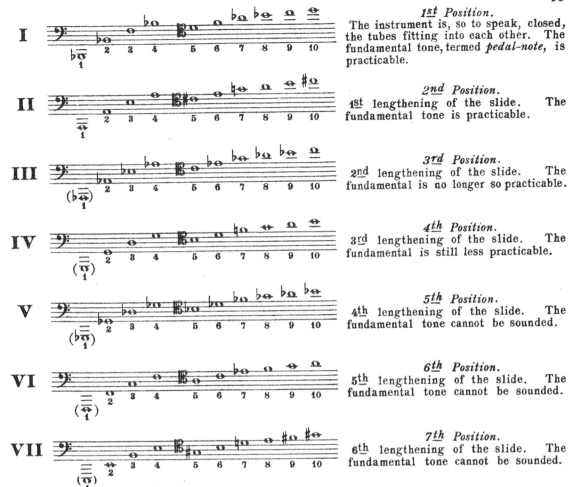

I — *1st Position.*
The instrument is, so to speak, closed, the tubes fitting into each other. The fundamental tone, termed *pedal-note*, is practicable.

II — *2nd Position.*
1st lengthening of the slide. The fundamental tone is practicable.

III — *3rd Position.*
2nd lengthening of the slide. The fundamental is no longer so practicable.

IV — *4th Position.*
3rd lengthening of the slide. The fundamental is still less practicable.

V — *5th Position.*
4th lengthening of the slide. The fundamental tone cannot be sounded.

VI — *6th Position.*
5th lengthening of the slide. The fundamental tone cannot be sounded.

VII — *7th Position.*
6th lengthening of the slide. The fundamental tone cannot be sounded.

Here is the complete scale, with indications above each note showing the position which allows of sounding the said note. As will be seen, some degrees are common to two or even to three positions:

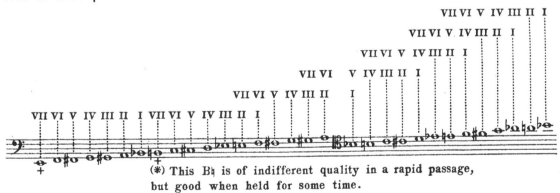

(✱) This B♮ is of indifferent quality in a rapid passage, but good when held for some time.

When possible, avoid the 7th position, which requires the maximum extension of the slide, and is therefore the most difficult of all, the two notes Double E + and B + a fifth above, which can only be produced in this position, are the worst on the instrument.

4.— The remark made on P. 57 (§2), concerning the Horn, applies equally to the Trombone: in the case of both instruments, performers have to choose between the high and the low register, as the lips cannot play in both registers with equal ease.

It is evident that, after having sounded the 8th, 9th, and 10th upper partials, the performer will find it difficult to descend without mistake or hesitation to the low notes: G, F, E:

As a matter of fact, the really sonorous register is comprised between Gamut G and B♭ in the G Clef:

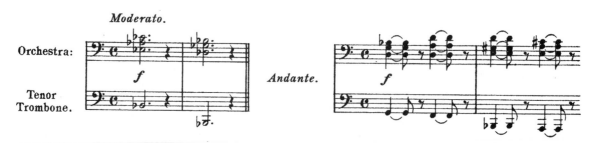

All degrees in this register are good, save two  which are somewhat difficult to attack; but this slight imperfection, which the player's talent should correct, need not be taken into account by the composer.

The low notes must not be too much relied upon, for they are lacking in strength, and the performer who has to play them is soon out of breath:

5.— Pedal-notes: This is the name given to the fundamental tone of each position. Theoretically, all seven should be practicable, including Double E; in reality, the only practicable ones are the first two: B♭ and A, A♭ being risky, and G very dangerous.

However, the manner in which B♭ or A is attacked is not indifferent. "The best way," says Berlioz, "is to proceed by skip of a fifth or an octave:"

A very correct remark: emitted thus, these pedal-notes do not seem to differ from the other notes, being neither slower of speech nor weaker in tone:

Length of Breath.

6.— The amount of wind required to play the Trombone is so great that in a *forte* the performer is obliged to take breath at almost every note:

Wagner, in this case, does not take the trouble to mark the breathing-places, for he knows that the performers will take breath everywhere; on the other hand, he carefully marks the *legato* passages, and, to preclude the shortening of the last note of each *legato* group, he places an accent over every note.

"Give me change for my money," Gounod used to say, "if I give you a shilling, I want twelve pence back; if I write a crotchet, don't play a quaver!"

In the theme of the 'Pilgrims' Chorus', the notes marked *legato* in bar Y do not indicate a punctuation, but a *sostenuto* of the phrase; "don't cut down my time-values," says Wagner, "let me have them complete." On the other hand, the slurs in bars X and Z show that breath is to be taken after the second beat, while— such is the meaning of the accent over the note —, at the same time, the length of the second crotchet is curtailed as little as possible.

This system of articulating and taking breath simultaneously (a method peculiar to the Trombone) corresponds to detached bowing on the Violin.

When the composer for the Violin wishes to have the full tone-power of the instrument, he asks for one bow per note; he marks no slurs, but to prevent any mistake, he writes above the passage: *sostenuto*, which means: "let there be no intermittence in the linking of the notes; let the *legato* be uninterrupted."

The Trombone proceeds in the same way; when able to economize breath (in *piano* passages), it can play *legato* as well as any other instrument; just as the violinist gives a bow to each note, so the trombone-player gives an articulation to each motion of the slide, and that, too, *sostenuto assai.*

Have we not always heard the following transition, placed by Schumann at the end of his *Larghetto,* "hermetically" slurred by the performers?

(*Symphony in B♭.*)

Remark: Schumann sometimes uses the Alto Clef for his two first Trombones, which he writes like Alto Trombones, as in the following extract from the 3rd Symphony and in the preceding illustration from the Symphony in B♭.

Note the extreme lip-tension required to sound the high E♭ + of the Horn and Trombone.

This is certainly a striking example of very dangerous composition. Yet, in our modern orchestras, we have players skilful enough to sound this E♭ harmoniously on their Tenor Trombone, the public not even so much as suspecting the difficulty, but professionals, aware of the danger, feel a thrill of suspense at the beginning of the piece, and only breathe freely when the difficulty has been overcome.

Let us be careful not to write so high.

7.— In the preceding paragraph, I referred only to slurs between notes belonging to different positions; it is hardly necessary to add that, like the Horn, the Trumpet, the Cornet, etc., the Trombone can emit a succession of harmonics having a common fundamental with one single articulation.

8.—This instrument, which is so short-winded in *forte* passages, and obliged to take breath at every note, is remarkable, in *piano* passages, for its astonishing sustaining-power:

(By kind permission of Schott & Cº, Publishers-Proprietors.)

Through eight long bars, the Trombones hold their respective notes quietly, and without giving any sign of fatigue; then the sound vanishes like mist, without our so much as noticing its slow tip-toe exit.

Articulation.

9.—It goes without saying that the lower the Trombone descends, the heavier the emission becomes. It is evidently difficult to sound the fundamental tone of a tube 8 ft. 10 in. long, like that of the Tenor Trombone (B♭), or 12 ft. ¼ in. long, like that of the Bass Trombone (F).

Not only did the classic masters dispense with these low notes, but they carefully avoided anything that looked like a *bravura* effect. Nowadays, thanks to the skill of instrument-makers, many things formerly forbidden have become possible. While Beethoven and Weber always wrote in semibreves, minims, and crotchets, Berlioz and the modern school are not afraid of much livelier rates of movement, or even of prolonged florid passages, which come out very well, on condition they are written in the sonorous medium register:

(Marche Hongroise.)

No one would formerly have thought of using the following articulations, from *Götterdämmerung*:

(By kind permission of Schott & Cº, Publishers-Proprietors.)

Or these, from *Parsifal*:

(The low G + is difficult to repeat.)

(By kind permission of Schott & Cº, Publishers-Proprietors.)

(By kind permission of Heugel et Cⁱᵉ, Editeurs-Proprietaires.)   (Saint-Saëns, *3rd Symph.*)

(By kind permission of Heugel et Cⁱᵉ, Editeurs-Proprietaires.)   (Widor, *La Korrigane.*)

The performers of to-day look upon these passages as mere child's play.

But set them to play the Scene of the Commander — ask them for Mozart's long sustained tones; you will see them shake their heads and beg for time to collect their strength, and indeed they have need of it all:

(Don Giovanni.)

The whole scene should be studied, note by note. Can there be anything more dramatic than the Trombones rising in octaves under the chromatic harmony of the orchestra, or anything more impressive than the *crescendo* of these sounds of brass?

Remark: The low Eb (＊) is possible on the Bass Trombone, for which instrument Mozart wrote the part.

Shakes.

10.—Shakes are impossible with the slide; they can only be produced by the lips: the only practicable ones are between degrees of the scale which stand one tone apart in the harmonic series, i. e. when the 7th, 8th, and 9th partials can be employed.

In reality, the only possible shakes are as follows (the positions being indicated):

Lately, as I was passing near a public ball-room, I heard such strange bellowings escaping from the Trombones that I went in and asked the performers, as soon as the dance was over, to show me their music. This was what they had been playing:

and to wind up:

Astounding effect! One would have thought it was the Beast in Revelations, with a cracker tied to its tail, roaring "Fire!" through a speaking-trumpet.

It is not likely that this effect will ever be used in a symphony, any more than the shake, and I only mention it here on account of its rarity.

This fantastic howl is produced by the combined action of the slide and the lips, as a *glissando* is performed by the finger on a stringed instrument. It is very easy to execute, and suitable for a nigger danee.

11.— AUTHORS AND WORKS TO BE CONSULTED: I must repeat the advice given in connection with the Trumpet; read all the scores published since the time of Bach and Händel; the special literature of the Trombone is as poor as that of the Trumpet, but all the masters have written for both instruments, each one treating them in his own personal manner, and it is these various manners which must be studied.

The brass instruments of Bach and Händel are written very high; those of Mozart, Beethoven, Weber, in their true register; Schumann's sometimes too high, sometimes too low; Wagner's usually in the rich medium register, but not without a secret predilection for the low register (Bass Trumpets, *Tuben*, Bass Trombones, Contrabass Trombones); those of the young contemporaneous school with just the contrary tendency, especially as regards Trumpets, a tendency to be regretted, for it is anti-instrumental.

We must read, compare, and take advantage of the experience acquired by our predecessors.

THE BASS TROMBONE.

(Ital., *Trombone basso*. Ger., *Bassposaune*. Fr., *Trombone basse*.)

12. It is the Tenor Trombone transposed a fourth lower.

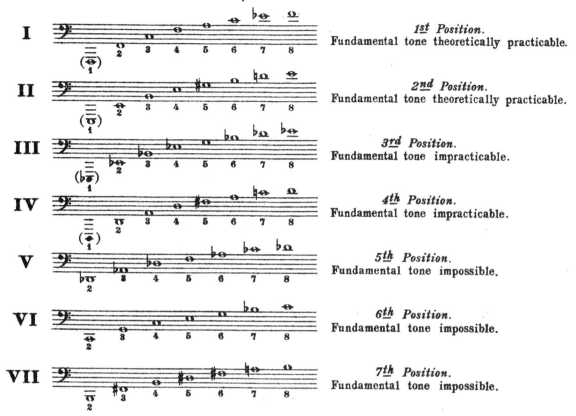

I — *1st Position.*
Fundamental tone theoretically practicable.

II — *2nd Position.*
Fundamental tone theoretically practicable.

III — *3rd Position.*
Fundamental tone impracticable.

IV — *4th Position.*
Fundamental tone impracticable.

V — *5th Position.*
Fundamental tone impossible.

VI — *6th Position.*
Fundamental tone impossible.

VII — *7th Position.*
Fundamental tone impossible.

The Bass Trombone is admirable as to tone, but difficult to play, requiring robust lungs and special lips.

Its compass is as follows:

All that has been said about the Tenor Trombone applies equally to the Bass Trombone, with two restrictions, the first concerning the slowness of speech of a tube 12 ft. long, the other referring to the difficulty experienced in producing the pedal-notes (fundamental tones).

If the Tenor Trombone can barely sound as pedal-notes anything but Double Bb and Double A ♯, the lower notes not coming out, still less can the pedal-notes of the Bass Trombone be obtained:

Not only have the great masters never employed them, but they are very careful not to indulge in too free a use of the lowest notes of the real scale. They rarely write lower than Eb ♯

Take, for instance, the score of *Tristan;* do you know how many times Wagner in-
dulges in a B♮?

Once only + (P. 76), and just see whether he tires the performer by the length of the
note:

He does not make the Bass Trombone descend to E♭ more than 8 or 9 times; the following exquisite holding-note + *pianissimo* (P. 250) is one of the cases in question:

(By kind permission of Breitkopf & Härtel, Editeurs-Propriétaires.)

Twice he writes D:

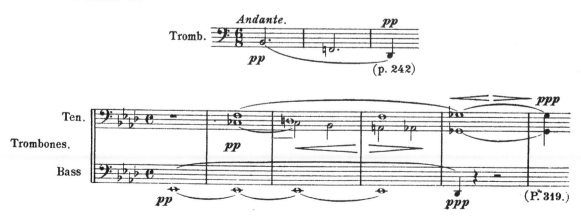

So that the whole of this score contains at the most one Double B♮, two D's, and a few E♭'s. And when it is a question of holding-notes, Wagner never employs anything lower than E♭, and always *piano*.

One of the rare examples of a holding-note *forte* is to be seen at the end of the 2nd act of *Parsifal*; but admire the prudence of the musician who has his Bass Trombone doubled by a Tuba, and only asks the Trombone to play *fortissimo* for 4 bars, while the Tuba continues for 8 more:

(By kind permission of Schott & Cº, Publishers-Proprietors.)

THE CONTRABASS TROMBONE.

13.—The Contrabass Trombone is an octave below the Tenor Trombone, like the Double-bass compared with the Cello, or, more precisely, like the Sarrusophone compared with the Bassoon. In its first position, its harmonic series is as follows:

Wagner makes use of this instrument in the *Tetralogy*.

It is hardly necessary to add that it is even more difficult to play, and requires a mouthpiece still more special than the Bass Trombone, and that all the remarks made about the latter instrument apply with still more force in this case.

(By kind permission of Schott & Cº, Publishers-Proprietors.)   (*Rheingold.*)

As Gevaert very judiciously remarks, it would be more practical to write the Contrabass Trombone an octave above the actual sounds, as is done in the case of the stringed Double-bass, the number of leger lines becoming troublesome to both performer and score-reader.

N. B. Instrument-makers are beginning to construct Soprano Trombones, as in the time of Bach. These instruments have the same compass as Cornets.

It need hardly be added that they are not capable of as much execution, the slide mechanism being unable to compete with the valve mechanism.

THE SAXHORNS.

1.— This is a separate group of absolutely different *timbre* from the other brass instruments, the tube of the Saxhorns being conical, instead of cylindrical like that of Trumpets and Trombones.

If we enquire into the origin of the Saxhorns, we can trace it back to the almost forgotten family of Keyed Horns and Ophicleides.

The group consists of seven instruments:

Sopranino.......Saxhorn, or Small Bugle in E♭

Soprano.......... — or Bugle in B♭

Alto................. — or Alto in E♭

Barytone......... — or Barytone in B♭

Bass (✶)......... — or Tuba in B♭ (or in C)

Deep Bass..... — or Bombardon in E♭ (or in F)

Double Bass — or Contrabass-Tuba in B♭

(✶) This is the instrument used in the orchestra as a bass to the Trombones. (V. §8, P. 94.)

Except the Tuba, which has four or even five pistons, all the members of this family are analogous to the Cornet, having the same number of pistons, making use of the same mechanism and of the same fingering.

2.— It is unnecessary to enlarge upon the differences in the dimensions of the tubes, upon the facility of emission of a Bugle 4 ft. 3½ in. long, compared with the increasing heaviness of the lowest notes of the Contrabass-Tuba in B♭, which is 17 ft. 8 in. long, or to repeat that, at such depths, speech becomes slow and *bravura* effects are not to be expected.

3.— It would be well to admit the Saxhorn group into our orchestra. This perfectly homogeneous mass, with a total compass of five octaves, would serve as a firm and mellow background for the brilliant flourishes of the Trumpets and Trombones.

It would serve as a foil rather than as an element of combination with them. This is what Wagner intended when he conceived his *Tenor-Tuben* and *Bass-Tuben* (respectively in E♭ and B♭), which are nothing but modified Alto and Bass Saxhorns.

The total compass of the group is as follows:

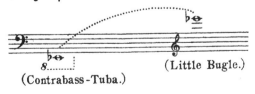

(Contrabass-Tuba.)   (Little Bugle.)

The Saxhorns are made of brass; their length is invariable, i. e. their key never changes, for they make use of neither tuning-slides nor crooks.

SOPRANINO SAXHORN.

(LITTLE BUGLE IN E♭)

4.—In German: *Flügelhorn piccolo in Es:*

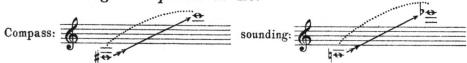

This is a very high, shrill instrument, capable of great execution; it is not very use-ful in the orchestra, unless for some special effect, but suitable for military bands, where it plays the *Sopranino* part; the following are the limits of its various regis-ters:

The notes of the high register, especially the three last semitones , are very dangerous and difficult. Even high A cannot be attacked without pre-paration; it has to be led up to by a scale or some kind of figure:

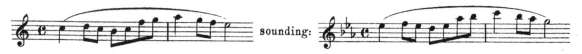

It is played like a Cornet à Pistons; it has the same mechanism, the same easy e-mission, and the same *single, double,* and *triple articulation.* It is a Cornet, but a Cornet higher by a fourth.

Its most characteristic name is the German one: *Flügelhorn Piccolo,* which clear-ly points to the fact that it is the Piccolo of the family; it is not a melodic but a *bravura* instrument.

SOPRANO SAXHORN.

(BUGLE IN B♭)

5.—In German: *Flügelhorn in B:*

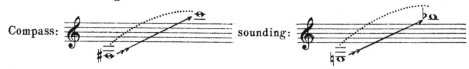

This is an instrument with a soft, mellow, poetic *timbre,* and is less vulgar than the Cornet, to which it corresponds in compass. It has hardly been employed more than once in the orchestra, and even then its part is usually played by the Cornet (*Robert le Diable,* last act); it is true, Meyerbeer, being dead, is unable to protest.

As its compass and mechanism exactly correspond to those of the Cornet, there is nothing special to note about the Bugle, the capabilities of both instruments being i-dentical.

F♯ is dangerous, but the two following octaves are excellent, and the high register is not inferior to that of the Cornet, which latter instrument frequently rises to C.

Remark: Except F♯, the low notes are of much better quality and purer of intonation than on the Cornet.

Although capable of great execution, the Bugle is more especially an expressive instrument, and ought to be used chiefly for melodic purposes.

ALTO SAXHORN.
(ALTO IN E♭)

6.— In German: *Althorn in Es:*

This is a rather inferior instrument, which does not play as a soloist, but usually forms part of the background to the polyphonic instruments.

It is the connecting link between the Soprano and Barytone Saxhorns. However, it articulates with considerable ease and can hold a note for some time.

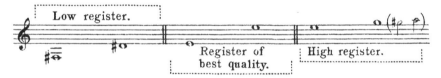

It is imprudent to descend lower than C , unless other instruments in unison or in the octave are at hand to make up for its defective quality.

It is a background instrument, a kind of orchestral padding.

BARYTONE SAXHORN.
(BARYTONE IN B♭)

7.— In German: *Tenorhorn in B,* or *Bass-Flügelhorn:*

This is a much more pleasing and attractive instrument than the Alto, and possesses the great advantage of being able to descend with relative ease, at the same time emitting without difficulty some pretty high notes. In reality it corresponds to a 16 ft. stop, while the Bugle corresponds to an 8 ft. stop.

It is written like the Cornet, but sounds an octave lower.

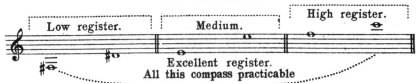

Apart from the highest notes, which, of course, gradually become thinner in quality, the whole of its compass, and in particular the medium, has a full, soft, rich tone, recalling that of the Horn. It is, besides, capable of very satisfactory execution. Like the Bugle, the Barytone is an expressive instrument, better adapted for melodic than for florid passages.

It is the most perfect instrument of the whole family.

BASS SAXHORN.
(TUBA)

8.— In German: *Basstuba:*

This is the only instrument of the Saxhorn family that has been introduced into the orchestra so far.

Thanks to the addition of supplementary valves, it can descend as low as the Contrabass-Tuba. However, as its tube is relatively narrow, the low notes which are common to the two instruments are nothing like as rich and full as on the Contrabass-Tuba.

Bass-Tubas are constructed in C and in Bb, this latter key possessing two extra semitones in the low register:

But, whichever instrument is used, the general practice is to write for the Tuba in C, the performer transposing when necessary.

If we consider this extensive scale, we find that the most interesting register (the very low one) is unfortunately the weakest:

Some exceptional performers can, with the 5-piston Bass-Tuba, descend as low as D , but it is imprudent, when scoring for the orchestra, to write lower than

, and even this note should be sparingly used, as well as all the degrees comprised in the third X Y.

On the other hand, the two octaves between Y and Z are remarkably intense and rich in quality.

The Tuba, which has with great advantage replaced the Ophicleide, is not so satisfactory a substitute for the Bass Trombone, for the two kinds of tone-color do not blend well; the soft thick tone of the Tuba jars with the metallic *timbre* of the Trombones, and the comparison is altogether to the disadvantage of the Tuba.

But let us try to be content with what we have got, and remember that neither Beethoven nor Weber had these deep bass notes at their disposal. We give some examples showing the use that can be made of them:

3rd Trombone.

Tuba.

(By kind permission of A. Durand et Fils, Editeurs-Propriétaires.)　(Saint-Saëns, *Suite Algérienne.*)

3rd Trombone.

Tuba.

(By kind permission of Heugel et Cie, Editeurs-Propriétaires.)　(Massenet, *Scènes Alsaciennes.*)

Bass Trombone.

Tuba.

(Glazounow, *6th Symphony.*)

9.— Despite its extreme depth, the Tuba is not incapable of some execution. Here is a scale, for instance, which comes out very well:

and some octave-skips which come out equally well:

Results of experiments made with the kind assistance of Captain Soyer, Bandmaster of the 24th Infantry Regiment, Paris.

10.— Of all the Saxhorn group, the Tuba is the only member having special mechanism and fingering. While the other Saxhorns are modelled on the Cornet with 3 pistons, the Tuba, having five pistons, is necessarily played in a different manner.

Such is, till some better instrument has been invented, the usual bass of the brass instruments; so far it is the most currently employed and most practical.

Doubtless, the future has something better in store for us.

THE DEEP BASS SAXHORN.
(BOMBARDON)

11.—In German: *Tuba in F, in Es.*
It is tuned either in F or in Eb.

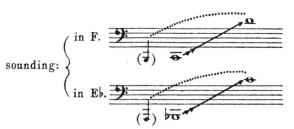

This instrument is not used in the orchestra, but only in military bands, as a connecting link between the Tuba and the Double-bass Saxhorn in Bb, which latter it usually doubles.

THE DOUBLE-BASS SAXHORN.
(CONTRABASS-TUBA)

12. In German: *Kontrabass-Tuba.*
It is tuned in Bb.

It is written like a 16 ft. stop, e. g.

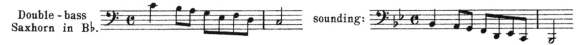

As will be seen, this is, of the whole family, the member that has the most limited compass, but, on the other hand, it is perhaps the most sonorous. All the notes of the scale come out well, down to G, and the execution is satisfactory, despite the great depth of the notes.

Wagner had a Contrabass-Tuba in C constructed for *Rheingold,* which could descend to 16 ft. Eb. These extremely low notes are not as satisfactory as could be wished, when played *forte* (V. P. 186). Their effect is better *mezzo-forte:*

(By kind permission of Schott & Co, Publishers-Proprietors.)

It is *mf* also that he gives this low F to the Contrabass-Tuba:

Bass Trumpet in C.

Tenor-Tuben E♭.

Bass-Tuben B♭.

Contrabass-Tuba.

(By kind permission of Schott & Cⁿ, Publishers-Proprietors.) *(Götterdämmerung.)*

Contrabass-Tuba.

(By kind permission of Schott & Cⁿ, Publishers-Proprietors.) *(Götterdämmerung.)*

The following is the compass of this Contrabass-Tuba in C:

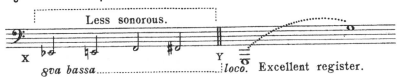

Remark: Instruments of French construction, whether tuned in B♭ or in C, cannot produce the 4 lowest notes (X Y.)

13.—To sum up, we have two kinds of deep basses among the brass instruments: the Bass Trombone and the Tuba.

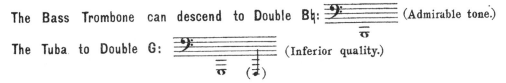

The Bass Trombone can descend to Double B♮: (Admirable tone.)

The Tuba to Double G: (Inferior quality.)

It is rather unwise to write F for the Tuba, for this note practically cannot be produced on the Tuba in C, and a considerable number of performers employ this C Tuba exclusively. (Low F can be produced by a Tuba in B♭).

Exceptionally, for special effects, Wagner's Contrabass-Tuba (which descends to E♭) may be required in the orchestra, but then we must remember what was said above about the 4 lowest notes of its compass.

Chapter III.

—⊹—

Percussion Instruments.

THE KETTLE-DRUMS.

(Ital., *Timpani.*   Ger., *Pauken.*   Fr., *Timbales.*)

1.—"The Kettle-drum consists of a hemispherical shell, over which is stretched a skin. The shell should be of good brass, free from any kind of flaw or dint; the "head" is usually made of ass's skin, but some instrument-makers employ goat-skin, dog-skin, sheep-skin, or calf-skin. The skin must be well curried, homogeneous, without cracks, and of uniform thickness. It is attached to the shell by means of screws; an iron ring, contracting and expanding in obedience to the action of these screws, serves to tighten or loosen the membrane. No precise dimensions can be given for Kettle-drums, but on large Kettle-drums the deep notes are of better quality." (Kastner)
This last proposition is self-evident.

2.— Nowadays, all Kettle-drum heads are made of well curried calf-skin, usually selected from the animal's back, that being considered the most serviceable part of the hide.
As the skin is not of absolutely uniform thickness, the drummer's experience comes to the rescue, sparing the thin parts, and beating out the thick ones. Before a rehearsal, a conscientious drummer may sometimes be seen hammering out parts of the head, very much like a gold-beater.
It sometimes takes 4 or 5 years to "mellow" a Kettle-drum. The instrument-maker constructs it, but the performer gives it the finishing touches, which take more time, as we have just seen, than the making of the Drum.
A well made Kettle-drum lasts a long time. "On the average, and if no untimely accident happen to it, about as long as the drummer," says Mʳ Henri Vizentini, the performer on this instrument in the Colonne Orchestra; and accidents are rare in the orchestra.

3.— Kettle-drums are made in three sizes.
The largest can at will be made to sound any one of the chromatic degrees comprised in the fifth:

The smallest size gives the following notes:

and the medium-sized ones play either in the fifth  or in the fifth 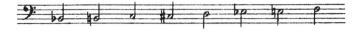, according to the custom of the various countries.

For the sake of completeness, we will also mention a little Kettle-drum with this compass , to be found in museums, but hardly ever used in practice, the two highest degrees, F♯ and G, being of poor quality. Even F♮ is not sonorous, and although Beethoven uses it he never fails to contrast it with the F an octave lower, its weakness being atoned for by the full and rich quality of the low F:

(8th Symphony.)

(9th Symphony.)

4.— So, it is not advisable to go beyond either high F or low F. E is sometimes required for a special effect, but has no tonal value except in a *pianissimo;* its tone suggests the idea of a cracked Bass Drum.

I am fully aware that Berlioz wrote the high F♯, and Wagner the low E, but only exceptionally, and if you feel inclined to borrow anything from them, it is better to ask them for something else.

Besides, there is another means of producing a roll deeper than that of the Kettle-drum: it consists in using a Bass Drum played with Kettle-drum sticks.

5.— In France, the oid system has been retained; the membrane is tightened and loosened by means of screws, varying in number from 9 to 11 for a large Kettle-drum, and from 7 to 9 for a small one. Taking into account the inequalities of the skin with which he is familiar, the drummer adjusts the several screws accordingly; otherwise there is some risk of the head cracking. Besides, quality and correct intonation depend on well-balanced tension.

The length of time required to change the tuning of the Drums depends on the interval, on the number of turns to be given to the screws. The head is sufficiently strong to bear tightening to the extent of a fifth, but it would be very unskilful on the part of the composer to require such skips.

The performer requires a relatively long time to change the pitch of a Drum by more than a major third, and if the great masters' works be examined, it will be seen that they carefully avoid exceeding this limit.

I take five scores at random:

Liszt: *Festklänge...* 4 Kettle-drums tuned in: G, A, B♭, C.
Changing to: F♯, A, B♭, B♮.
(*Maximum skip: a semitone.*)

— *Hungaria....* 3 Kettle-drums tuned in: A, B♭, D.
Changing to: F♯, B♮, D♯.
Then to: B♭, B♮, D♯.
And finally to: A, C, D♮.
(*Maximum skip: a major third.*)

— *Mazeppa......* 2 Kettle-drums tuned in: A, D.
Changing to: A, C♯.
Then to: A, B♮.
And finally to: A, D.
(*Maximum skip: a minor third.*)

Berlioz: *Marche Nocturne*................ 2 Kettle-drums tuned in: G, C.
      (L'Enfance du Christ.)   Changing to: G, B♭.
                                   (*Skip of a second.*)

—   *Fantaisie sur la "Tempête"*...2 Kettle-drums tuned in: A♭, C.
       (Lelio.)   Changing to: A♭, D.
                                    Then to: A♭, E.
                               And finally to: C, F.
                      (*Maximum skip: a fourth, but
a gradual one, by seconds.*)

About one bar of quadruple time, in moderate *tempo*, is required to raise or lower the pitch of a Drum by one tone. Naturally, more time is required for a third, a fourth, a fifth, if indeed such a skip be risked.

When only small intervals are in question, drummers manage to tune without consulting the ear; they know when to give a quarter, a half, three-quarters, or a whole turn to the screws. In fact, it is only thus that they can tune in a *forte*, amid the din of a *tutti*.

However, when wide skips are called for, they no longer trust to their manual experience; they may be seen gently touching the skin with a drum-stick, endeavoring to judge whether the instrument is in tune.

6.— In Germany, Russia and Great Britain this system has been discarded, and mechanically-tuned Kettle-drums exclusively adopted.

Two kinds are made: (1) Drums mounted on pivots, the head being tightened or loosened according as the instrument is turned to the right or to the left: (2) Drums with levers acting upon a number of notches corresponding to the series of semitones. This latter kind is in more general use.

The great advantage of mechanical tuning lies in its instantaneousness. In moderate *tempo*, figures such as the following can be executed on a single Drum.

All⁰ moderato.

(The sudden motion of the lever coincides with the stroke
of the stick, so as to avoid blurring.)

Curious *glissando* effects can be obtained by handling the lever slowly, very much like the violinist's finger on a string:

Andante.

The Paris Opéra had adopted these Kettle-drums, but has just discarded them again, alleging that their intonation is inaccurate. The skins contract or distend according to the temperature and the dampness or dryness of the air, so they say, and they complain that they have not sufficiently direct control over the tuning of the Drum.

Sub judice lis est!

7.—As for composers, they need not take sides' in the quarrel, but write as they think fit, without any other preoccupation than that of confining the instrument to its true office.

What do we require of the Kettle-drum?

A vibration, a sound dying away like a harp-string's. To abruptly cut short or suddenly damp this sound is antagonistic to the nature of the instrument. Is it really the Drum's function to run up and down rapid scales?

With three Drums all combinations are possible. As each Drum can be easily tuned in 4 successive semitones, all the degrees of the chromatic scale can be obtained, without involving a skip greater than a minor third.

It frequently happens that, at a first rehearsal, the performer is embarrassed by the composer having neglected to indicate the changes of key beforehand; it will be the drummer's business to study and arrange the proper changes for the next rehearsal. In such a case I think the composer is somewhat to blame.

It happens sometimes, in the course of a piece, that a single performer is absolutely unable to make the necessary change in the tuning. Suppose his Drums are tuned as follows:

and then that he needs to finish off on B♭, as follows.

If he is naïve, he will tell his troubles to the conductor, who will direct him to ask his neighbors for assistance. If, on the contrary, he is a bright man, he will, of his own accord, request one of his companions in the orchestra, while he himself is playing the C, to give two of his screws the half-turn necessary to raise the A Drum by a semitone.

Nowadays, anything can be written, technical difficulties constantly diminishing, but nothing ought to be written which is not in keeping with the nature of the instrument.

The Sticks.

8.— There are two kinds:

Sticks with skin knobs, for ordinary use *forte* or *piano,* and sticks with sponge knobs, for particularly soft effects.

Formerly, wooden-headed sticks were sometimes used, but the quality of tone produced is very hard and has very little *timbre,* recalling that of the Side Drum.

The drummer avoids playing on the extreme edge of the head, as this only produces a nasal, dry tone, without vibrating power. He also carefully avoids the centre of the head, and prefers playing mid-way between edge and centre.

Mode of writing.

9.— If any definite duration of sound is required, the Drum part must be as carefully written as that of any other instrument.

Beethoven, fearing the vibration of the E would last beyond the attack of the B♮, in the beginning of the overture to *Fidelio*, separates the two notes by a rest +:

whereas, for the remainder of the orchestra, the E is dotted:

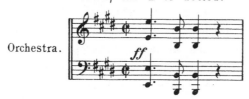

In the course of the work, it will be observed, Beethoven frequently marks the accented beat of a bar by means of a crotchet, when, not having any special intention, he might just as well have written minims; it is a mere question of habit:

In such cases, Mozart usually writes:

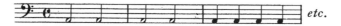

10.— When a roll is required, the great masters make use of two kinds of notation.

Some write the roll like a shake ![X shake notation],

others like the tremolo of the Strings ![Y tremolo notation],

and the same master frequently uses both systems in succession.

Remark: It is hardly necessary to add that with the Y system it becomes indispensable to specify time-values sufficiently rapid to produce a roll.

The X system seems preferable, precisely on account of its uniformity.

11.— When a roll lasts through two or more bars, the notes must be tied; otherwise, the performer may think the composer intends the first beat of each bar to be marked:

(Correct mode of writing.)   (Inaccurate mode of writing.)

It is precisely in such cases that the X system seems preferable, for is it not absurd to tie notes which are written as articulated notes?

Likewise, at the end of a roll, it is necessary to specify whether the last note is to be articulated, or whether it is simply intended as the unnoticed dying-away of the tremolo.

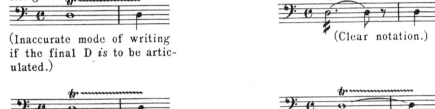

(Inaccurate mode of writing if the final D *is* to be articulated.)   (Clear notation.)

(Inaccurate mode of writing if the final D is *not* to be articulated.)   (Clear notation.)

12.— It is hardly necessary to recall the effect of swelling and diminishing the tone in a roll:

or to enlarge upon the propriety of giving accurate directions to the drummer if this effect is to be emphasized:

pp —————— *ff* —————— *pp*

Need we add that it is quite correct to end a roll without having reached an accented beat, as may be seen from the last example?

However, it is perhaps not superfluous to mention that a *crescendo* roll reaches its *fortissimo* terminus with the same energy and dash, whether executed on a single Drum throughout, or whether the Drum changes.

For instance, the *crescendo* D ————— E will reach its culminating point with the same continuity of swell as the *crescendo* D ————— D; the change from one Drum to the other being so rapid that not even the most practised ear could detect it:

Here is a curious *crescendo* coming to a climax + before the accented beat, singularly dramatic in its energy:

(Gernsheim, *3rd Symphony*.)

We must also mention the possibility of continuing a roll on the Drums by a tremolo on the Double-basses; the two qualities of tone follow each other without the least jarring:

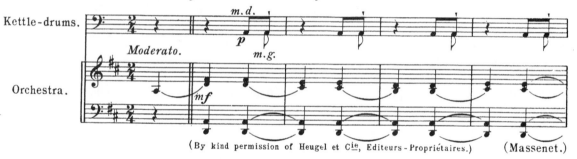

Here is a characteristic rhythm from *Les Erynnies:*

(Massenet.)

Here are some other formulæ in current use:

13.— From the harmonic point of view, the Kettle-drum cannot be counted on.

What can be expected of an instrument that never affords more than 2 or 3 notes to choose from? Can good "part-writing" be expected in the case of the Drum?

Let us be content with the best obtainable coincidences of the Drum notes with the notes of the harmony, introducing them freely into the polyphonic weft, without ever losing sight of the practical means of execution.

The Drum by itself can only serve as a true bass in cases where no tonal doubt is possible; see the following example, in which the true bass is sounded in the first bar by the orchestra, its effect still lingering in the ear when the Kettle-drum enters:

Here the tonal impression is quite pure and clear. But if in the first bar, the E♭ chord were replaced by the chord of B♭ (say), the case would be wholly different; confusion and uncertainty would arise.

14.— The Kettle-drum has so little harmonic significance that it may sometimes be treated as a neutral element in the orchestra, notes not coinciding with the harmony being given to it, as is done in the case of the Triangle, the Side Drum, or the Cymbals. Verdi and Massenet have sometimes treated it thus, wishing to avoid a sudden change in the tuning of the Drums, especially when the new note would be of use for a couple of bars only.

However, this licence is only excusable in a *forte,* when the Drum, drowned by the din of the whole orchestra, retains its rhythmic value only. It is never done in a *piano,* where it would be quite inadmissible.

15.— There is no reason why two Drums should not be struck together:

A roll for two notes attacked simultaneously requires two **drummers,** of course.

16.— It will hardly be necessary to point out that the deepest notes are always the heaviest, their length of vibration being in proportion to their depth.

With a light rhythm, it would not be advisable to write F, F♯, G, as these notes have a tendency to "boom":

The notes of the medium, on the other hand, have a very pleasing tone, resembling the *pizzicato* of the Cello. (D is exquisite).

Finally, we will point out that C is an equally good note on either the small or the large Kettle-drum.

THE SIDE DRUM.

(Ital., *Tamburo piccolo*.   Ger., *Kleine Trommel*.   Fr., *Tambour*.)

1.— We have seen that the head of Kettle-drums is made of calf-skin; in the case of the Side Drum sheepskin is used.

The sticks are of wood.

As no definite pitch can be assigned to the tone of the Side Drum, it would be more correct to call it *noise*. Whether the piece be in B♭, in A♮, or in F♯ is quite immaterial, the Side Drum being suited to all keys, because it has no key of its own and its effects depend solely on rhythm.

Remark: The **2** or **3** examples that could be quoted of the tuning of the Side Drum need not detain us, as they are not sufficiently conclusive.

Various Strokes.

2.—The single stroke of one stick is rarely used:

but, in its stead, the double-stroke, produced by the almost simultaneous attack of the two sticks on the membrane, is usually employed:

as is also the "coup de charge," differing from the above by the accentuation of the first short note:

Rolls.

3.—Rolls are called: *ra*.

They consist of 3, 4, 5, 6, 7, 8, 10 strokes, and so on:

There is also the continuous roll, similar to the Kettle-drum roll; it is written like a shake, or like the tremolo of the Strings:

care being taken, as in the case of the Kettle-drum (P.102, §10), to write time-values sufficiently rapid to produce a true roll:

Rhythmic Combinations.

4.— Some of the rolls in use in the French army are given below: they pretty well summarize all the capabilities of the instrument:

Notation.

5.— The Side Drum is usually written in the G clef, its clear acute *timbre* evoking the idea of high notes. However, in the majority of scores published nowadays, a single line without any clef is given to the Side Drum, as this arrangement economizes space.

The same practice prevails as regards Cymbals, Bass Drum, Triangle, Castanets, all of them being instruments without definite pitch.

Use of the Side Drum in the orchestra.

6.— I do not think it has ever been employed in a symphony. On the other hand, it is frequently used for dramatic purposes. "Meyerbeer," says Gevaert, "has known how to derive a peculiar and terrible effect from the association of the Side Drum with the Kettle-drums, for the famous *crescendo* roll of the *Bénédiction des Poignards* (in the *Huguenots*)."

These are, in fact, Berlioz's own words, expressing his admiration for Meyerbeer's device, then quite novel. Since his time, it has been so often used that it seems superfluous to quote examples. Everyone can call them to mind.

At random, I quote this theme of the "Marche de Turenne," which Bizet has turned to account in *L'Arlésienne*:

(Choudens, Editeur-Propriétaire.)

And this other delicate yet incisive effect, from the *Scènes Pittoresques:*

(Joseph Williams, Limited. Publishers-Proprietors.)   (Massenet, *Fête Bohême.*)

Muffled Drums.

7.— They may be heard at military funerals. If the head of the Drum be covered with a cloth, a very striking and mournful quality of tone is obtained, the vibrations of the parchment being more or less damped and, so to speak, driven back into the interior of the Drum. Nothing can be more dismal than a long roll, gradually swelling and diminishing, on a muffled Drum:

Sometimes the indication: *sans timbre* is met with; the effect required is obtained either by loosening the *snares,* or by muffling as described above; the choice of the means of execution is usually left to the performer.

The following passage illustrates the use of the muffled Side Drum:

(Mackenzie, *Solemn March from the "Story of Sayid".*)
(By kind permission of Novello & Cº, Lᵈ., Publishers-Proprietors.)

THE TENOR DRUM.
(WIRBELTROMMEL, ROLLTROMMEL, RÜHRTROMMEL.)

8.— The Tenor Drum is longer than the Side Drum, and is made of wood, instead of brass. Its sound is duller, and might be that of a small-sized Bass Drum.

It serves the same purposes and has the same mechanism as the Side Drum. Gluck, in *Iphigénie en Tauride* (Chorus of the Scythians), and Wagner, in *Die Walküre* and in *Parsifal,* have made use of the Tenor Drum.

THE TAMBOURINE.

(Ital., *Tamburino.* Ger., *Schellentrommel.* Fr., *Tambour de Basque.*)

1.— There are three ways of using it:
(1) **By striking the parchment with the back of the hand:**

(Choudens, Editeur - Propriétaire.)   (Bizet, *Carmen*, p. 182.)

(2) **By shaking the instrument, in order to call into play the "jingles", i. e. the small metal plates which are, so to speak, embedded in its hoop; a metallic rustle rather than a roll is thus obtained:**

(Choudens, Editeur - Propriétaire.)   (*Carmen*, p. 183.)

As in the case of the Kettle-drum and Military Drum, this rustle is written either like a shake, or like a tremolo for the Strings:

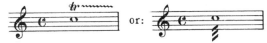

Note, as before, that when the latter mode of writing is employed, time-values sufficiently rapid to ensure continuity of sound must be indicated (P. 106, §3).
(3) By gliding the thumb over the parchment, a temporary roll can be produced, in which the sound of the jingles predominates. This, however, requires some skill.

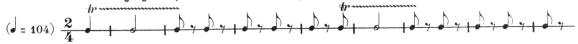

2.— The clef has no more value in the notation of the Tambourine than in that of the Military Drum, the Triangle, etc. A single line is usually employed, as in the above example.

THE TABOR.

(Fr., *Tambourin.*)

1.— This is a very long drum, without *timbre,* used in Provence. The tabor-player blows into a three-hole pipe, or *Galoubet,* which he holds in his right hand, while with his left he beats time with a single stick:

(Choudens, Editeur - Propriétaire.)   (Bizet, *L'Arlésienne.*)

THE TRIANGLE.

(Ital., *Triangolo*.   Ger., *Triangel*.   Fr., *Triangle*.)

1.— The Triangle may be written either on a single line, or in the G clef.   It is suitable for all kinds of rhythmic combinations, single, double, triple strokes, etc.

The *tremolo* is written as for the Drums:

2.— The single stroke sometimes seems too simple, and is replaced by a group of 2, 3, 4, or 5 notes, the last alone have any appreciable time value.

I. The short note preceding the true note gives it more sprightliness.

II. This group of 3 notes is excellent, the first and third being struck in the same direction, from right to left.

III. This group of 4 notes is not so natural, the first and last being struck in contrary directions.

IV. Groups of 5 notes, as well all odd-numbered groups (7, 9, etc.), are very good, for reason given above (See II).

3.— If a *pianissimo* is wanted, it is the top of the Triangle that must be touched, where the rod has only an inch or so of space to move backwards and forwards in. As the performer is likely to know his business, it is needless to note this in the score.

Remark: I think it may be as well to call attention to the fact that some Triangles produce a double sound; they may be said to be *out of tune;* the stroke of the rod ought always to produce a single sound.

4.— Always effective, the Triangle is absolutely indispensable in the orchestra, for to it alone is sometimes entrusted the duty of marking the rhythm of the piece. It can be heard through the whole of the polyphonic mass, even when struck *pianissimo*.

(Berlioz, *Damnation de Faust*.)

THE TRIANGLE.

(By kind permission of A. Durand et Fils, Editeurs-Propriétaires.) (Saint-Saëns, *La Jeunesse d'Hercule*.)

(Schumann, *1st Symphony*.)

(Joseph Williams, Limited, Publishers-Proprietors.) (Paladilhe, *Ouverture de Suzanne*.)

Here is a very delicate effect of the Triangle tremolo, with *pianissimo* holding-notes for the Strings.

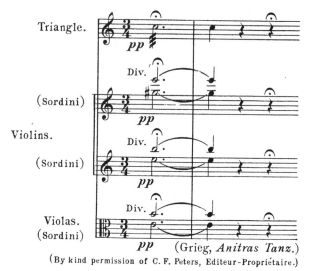

(Grieg, *Anitras Tanz.*)
(By kind permission of C. F. Peters, Editeur-Propriétaire.)

The Bacchanal of *Tannhäuser,* the Introduction and March of the Corporations in *Meistersinger* (from P. 453 onwards), the *Tetralogy,* etc. should be studied from this point of view.

In these scores, it will be observed that a stroke or tremolo on the Triangle stands out, even upon the most noisy orchestral background.

At the climax of a *crescendo,* when the orchestra would seem to have reached its maximum intensity, it suffices to add the Triangle, in order to convert red-heat into white-heat.

THE CASTANETS.

(Ital., *Castagnette.* Fr., *Castagnettes.* Ger., *Kastagnetten.* Span., *Castañuelas.*)

1.— They are made of wood or of iron, and are used in pairs, one pair being held in each hand. Like the Triangle and Drum, they can execute any rhythmic combinations imaginable.

For instance, they can mark the accented beat like a Triangle — a charming and little used effect:

(By kind permission of A. Durand et Fils, Editeurs-Propriétaires.) (Saint-Saëns, *La Lyre et la Harpe.*)

Usually, this instrument, so characteristic of popular Spanish music, is confined to certain formulæ current *tras los montes*, which are not very varied, as may be seen:

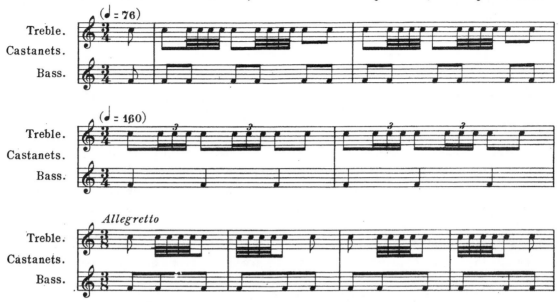

2.— The Castanets are usually written on a single line, without any clef.

The 2nd Scene of the 3rd Act of *Samson et Dalila* should be consulted. Note, beneath the veil of this persisting rhythm for the Castanets (both wooden and iron ones)

the skilful use of the percussion instruments alternating with and replacing each other, then drawing closer, and finally uniting to produce the maximum outburst of strength.

THE CYMBALS.

(Ital., *Piatti*.   Ger., *Becken*.)

1.— They may be played either together or separately.

They may be violently clashed one against the other, or one of them may be lightly struck with a drum-stick.

The sound may either be damped, or it may be allowed to vibrate.

In the former case, the Cymbals are written as follows:

in the latter case, thus:

Even if the bind only leads to a rest, it nevertheless retains its value as a bind, i.e. the vibrations must not be stopped. To make surer, the two preceding examples may also be written:

2.— There are two ways of producing a roll, or tremolo, with the Cymbals: (1) In a *forte* passage, they may be clashed against each other, the performer's wrist serving as an axis for the right to left motion; these shocks, as rapid as possible, of the two brass discs produce an uneven, but very violent and sonorous metallic jingle;

(2) in *piano* passages, or for a *crescendo*, one of the two Cymbals may be suspended by its strap, and a perfectly even and continuous roll performed on it by means of drumsticks; from *piano* to *forte,* the sound swells with great regularity — and vice versa.

As an example of the first kind of roll, the *tutti* passage which announces the peroration of the *Tannhäuser* Overture may be mentioned: eight bars *fortissimo* for the Cymbals:

and as a specimen of the other kind:

(By kind permission of A. Durand et Fils, Editeurs-Propriétaires.)   (Saint-Saëns.)

Curious *forte* effects, *crescendo* rolls, etc. are to be found in *Les Perses* (Xavier Leroux). See also *L'Apprenti Sorcier* (P. Dukas).

3.— When the Cymbals and Bass Drum are used together, this latter instrument must be thrown somewhat into the background, and the Cymbals alone must stand out conspicuously in the foreground, because it is to them that brilliancy is due.

Remark: If, perchance, the composer wished to produce the contrary effect, he would need to expressly indicate it. In the *Sanctus* of his *Requiem,* Berlioz writes the Cymbals and Bass Drum on two separate lines, and the traditional manner of performance, considering the character of the piece, is to bring the Bass Drum rather more to the front than the Cymbals. "The Bass Drum and Cymbals strokes" (says Berlioz in a note) "should be as weak as possible, the Cymbals being gently clashed against each other in the usual manner, and the instrument being allowed to vibrate."

See in the Overture, Entr'actes, and Stage music to *Phèdre,* the curious effects that Massenet obtains from the Bass Drum in the first piece, then from the Cymbals in the *Sacrifice* scene, and finally from the two combined in the last piece.

In the *Overture,* in the *Imploration to Neptune,* the Bass Drum always stands alone.

4.— Every one has noticed the charming effect of a Cymbal gently struck with a sponge-tipped drumstick, so as to equal or even surpass the *pianissimo* of the Triangle. Nothing could color a rhythm more delightfully; with each stroke a cloud of gold-dust seems to rise up out of the orchestra:

(J. Hamelle, Editeur-Propriétaire.) (Lalo.)

The two Cymbal strokes which are indicated in the above example are not to be found in the *Suite* from *Namouna* (P. 74); it was Vaucorbeil who very ingeniously added them during the rehearsals of Lalo's posthumous work at the Paris Opera-house. So characteristic, so unexpectedly picturesque was this metallic quiver, upon the reappearance of the theme, that it still rings in my ear, despite the many years which have since elapsed.

We now give another example of the skilful use of a Cymbal struck *piano* in the midst of the Strings:

(Th. Dubois, *Suite miniature.*)

ANCIENT CYMBALS.

5.— They are made after the model of those discovered at Pompeii, and preserved in the Museum of Naples, along with instruments of all kinds employed in the time of the Cæsars: Flutes, Organs, Pandean Pipes, Citharæ, etc.

They are much smaller than our Cymbals, varying from 6 to 8 inches in diameter, and have a more silvery and acute *timbre*.

Since their adoption by Berlioz in *Roméo* and in *Les Troyens,* Gounod, S! Saëns, and many others have employed them.

The composer writes for them as for ordinary Cymbals, avoiding rolls and tremolos, which would be difficult of production on such a small surface. However, such rolls are not impossible, and perhaps some special effect will some day be produced by their means.

On the stage, dancers and *figurantes* frequently keep step with the assistance of Ancient Cymbals held in the hand.

THE BASS DRUM.
(Ital., *Gran Cassa.* Ger., *Grosse Trommel.* Fr., *Grosse Caisse.*)

This is another instrument without precise intonation, like the Military Drum, Triangle, Castanets, etc. (Tuning the Bass Drum has sometimes been attempted, but the result obtained is not worth the trouble that it involves).

What is required of the Bass Drum is a full and rather heavy quality of tone.

"The Bass Drum ought to be large: the rods or braces which stretch the parchment ought to act equally upon the whole circumference", (Parès, *Treatise on Instrumentation for Military Bands*).

The Bass Drum is played by means of a large drumstick provided either with a single felt or cork knob (*mailloche simple*), or with a double knob, one at each end of the stick (*mailloche double*). With the *mailloche* held by the middle of its handle, a roll resembling distant thunder may be produced. The Bass Drum can likewise imitate cannon (Berlioz, *Marche Hongroise*).

We have already said (P. 99, §4) that, in order to obtain a roll deeper than that of the Kettle-drums, the Bass Drum might be employed, the player making use of Kettle-drum sticks for this purpose. The roll thus produced is very effective, but has rarely been used. We give one example:

(Busser, *Hercule au Jardin des Hespérides.*)
(By kind permission of Henry Lemoine et Cie, Editeurs-Propriétaires.)

Who has not been moved by the *pianissimo* attack of the united Bass Drum and Cymbals, accentuating a phrase, to which it lends mysterious solemnity and impressive grandeur?

(Gounod, *Faust.*)

The following bars illustrate a very skilful arrangement of the percussion instruments, with a view to produce an overpowering *fortissimo:*

THE BASS-DRUM.

(Balakirew, *Thamar.*)

THE GONG.

(Ital., *Tam-tam*. Ger., *Tam-tam*. Fr., *Tam-tam*.)

The Gong is terrifying when struck *forte,* and threatening even when struck *piano.*

The composer must beware of its long-sustained vibrations. Although the Gong is not able to give a tone of definite pitch, and is consequently adapted for use in any key, yet it seems to *borrow* the tonality of the chord in which it is struck, so that any change of harmony or any modulation must be avoided as long as the Gong continues to vibrate.

The Gong seems to be quite *in tune* in the first bar (X) of the above example, but appears to suddenly lose its *truth of intonation* when the harmony changes in the second bar (Y Z). In such a case, it is necessary to damp its vibrations at the end of the first bar; otherwise, it will seem, during the second bar, to hold the preceding chord, like a Pianoforte without dampers.

Different Altitudes of Percussion Instruments of Indeterminate Pitch and Long Vibration.

Let us suppose we are required to depict the Titans being hurled down from Heaven, and that we need to give the impression of violent shocks in quick succession.

If three such shocks at different sonorous altitudes might suffice to indicate the cataclysm, I think the percussion instruments would need to be disposed as follows:

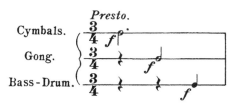

and we should get the very distinct impression of two successive skips of a fifteenth each:

So we have, in the   high   register: the Cymbals,
in the medium register: the Gong,
and in the lowest register: the Bass Drum.

Exceptional Percussion Instruments.

1.   The Glockenspiel.

2.   The Celesta.

3.   The Xylophone.

4.   Bells.

THE GLOCKENSPIEL.

1.— This instrument consists of a number of small steel bars, which are struck by means of little hammers; the pitch of these bars is in direct proportion to their thickness, and in inverse ratio to the square of their length.

If, for instance, it were desired to obtain the chromatic scale by means of bars all of equal length, "it would only be necessary to increase the thickness of each successive bar to an extent equivalent to the difference between each of the semitones." (Mahillon).

The compass of the Glockenspiel keyboard is two octaves and a tone:

(The actual sounds are *two* octaves above the written notes.)

The little keyboard of the Glockenspiel is similar to that of the Pianoforte, and the instrument may be treated in much the same manner as the Piano, provided time is allowed for the somewhat long vibrations to travel.

Wagner, in the finale of *Die Walküre*, Meyerbeer, in *L'Africaine*, Delibes, in *Lakmé*, Massenet, in *La Vierge*, etc. have employed the Glockenspiel.

The best notes of the instrument are, of course, those of the medium register, the lowest notes having a tendency to sound the fifth above, instead of the fundamental tone, which loses power the lower the note in the scale.

I believe Händel was the first composer to make use of the Glockenspiel, in *Saul*. After him Mozart employed it in *Zauberflöte:*

THE CELESTA.

2.— This is an instrument with a keyboard, like the Glockenspiel, the bars being re-placed by tuning-forks. Their tone is much weaker than that of the steel bars, but, on the other hand, infinitely more ethereal and poetical. Mustel, the inventor of the in-strument, was fully justified in giving it the name of *Celesta*.

Its compass is four octaves:

The Celesta may be treated like the Piano, or rather like 4 ft. and 2 ft. organ-stops, which it somewhat resembles. Its vibrations can be sustained almost like those of a wind instrument, and, at the same time, the crystalline percussion of the attack throws a delightful veil of mystery over the tone of the Celesta.

On P. 72 I gave an illustration from *Louise,* in which the Celesta is employed. I had already made use of it, at the Opéra, in the *Korrigane.*

THE XYLOPHONE.

(Ger., *Holzharmonika.*)

3.— This is an instrument consisting of a series of wooden bars, or rollers, of varying length, disposed like organ-pipes, which are struck by means of two little wooden mal-lets.

Compass: three octaves:

Saint-Saëns has used it in the *Danse Macabre,* and Gevaert remarks that the em-inent composer writes the notes an octave below their true pitch:

BELLS.

4.— Bells are made in all keys. The metal of which they are composed is an alloy of tin and copper. As for their dimensions, their height should be to their greatest diameter as 12 to 15.

To give an idea of the practical difficulty of employing them in the orchestra, it will suffice to say that the weight of a bell sounding Tenor C 𝄢 is over 22 tons, that the great bell of Notre-Dame (Paris) weighs 18 tons, and the Kremlin bell more than 195 tons.

So, bells may be classed with church Organs in the category of musical instruments difficult to manipulate.

When writing for bells, care must be taken to indicate whether deep or acute sounds are required.

Gevaert remarks that in theatres the actual pitch is rarely lower than G *in alt* 𝄞 He goes on to say that the two large bells used at the Paris Opera-house, for the tocsin of S.t Bartholomew's Day, in the 4th act of *Les Huguenots,* have always been considered as rarities: yet they only sound the upper octave of the notes written by the composer 𝄢

Large bells not being very practical, "attempts have been made to replace them by hemispherical alarum-bells cast in bronze; their relatively thin sides allow of attaining much deeper notes with a far smaller weight of metal."

These are the bells to be heard, arranged as follows, at the end of the 1st act of *Parsifal:*

Bells
(on the Stage)

Do they satisfy all desiderata? Hardly; something better will surely be found.

Besides, I once heard at Moscow a much more successful "bell-effect," much deeper and truer. It was obtained simply by means of a deep piano-string stretched in a deal case, a system which has long been in use for some kinds of clocks.

Bells are usually written in the F clef.

Chapter IV.

— ✢ —

THE SAXOPHONES.

1.— This family of instruments, more used in French military bands than in orchestras, was invented by Sax.

The tone is produced by means of a reed fitted into a mouthpiece similar to that of the Clarinet; the air-column is conical, and the tube is made of metal.

Of all wind instruments the Saxophones are perhaps the most expressive; like the Oboe they can swell and diminish their tone without ever losing their *timbre,* which always remains rich and full (bearing some analogy to the tone of the Cello, the Cor Anglais, and the Clarinet). The mechanism and fingering are much the same as for the Oboe.

The following are the four members of which the family is officially composed:

Soprano Saxophone	in	Bb
Alto	„	in Eb
Tenor	„	in Bb
Barytone	„	in Eb

They all have about the same compass as the Oboe, including the low Bb; however, the Soprano and Barytone stop at Eb in the highest register, whereas the Alto and Tenor can rise to F.

Compass of Soprano & Barytone.

Compass of Alto & Tenor.

2.— The Soprano and Tenor cannot descend very easily, so it is better to avoid writing the very low notes for them; the Alto and Barytone, on the contrary, are excellent in their lowest register.

As for the Bass Saxophone, it is not used in practice, on account of its great weight; it is usually replaced by the Sarrusophone, which can skip down with the most graceful ease to the extreme depths of the orchestra.

Proceeding by analogy of tone-color and of pitch, the following comparison may be established:

Soprano Saxophone	— 8 ft. stop	=	Oboe, Clarinet.
Alto	„	_ 12 ft. „ =	Cor Anglais.
Tenor	„	_ 16 ft. „ =	Cello.
Barytone	„	_ 24 ft. „ =	Bass Clarinet.

The Saxophones are written in the G clef, whatever their actual pitch may be. ✳

✳ Avoid attacking *pianissimo* the notes comprised in the lowest sixth: ; this restriction applies equally to all the members of the Saxophone family.

SOPRANO SAXOPHONE in B♭.

Its office in military bands is to reinforce the Clarinets, or to replace them in case of need. It is a rather shrill-toned instrument, and is not used in the orchestra.

ALTO SAXOPHONE in E♭.

It is the best of the family, the instrument to be heard in *Hamlet, L'Arlésienne, Hérodiade, Werther,* etc.

Its tone is even, and it can rise easily, at the same time possessing good bass notes. It is powerful enough to be a match for 4 or 5 Clarinets.

Remark: By saying that it can rise easily, I do not mean that the highest notes are as practicable as the notes of the medium register. The 5 or 6 highest notes can only be written for *virtuosi.* They naturally become thinner and thinner.

(Choudens, Editeur - Propriétaire.)   (G. Bizet, *Arlésienne.*)

"It is to the Alto Saxophone that florid figures, quick scale passages, shakes and arpeggios are given in military bands." (Parès).

Avoid, however, the following shakes:

TENOR SAXOPHONE in B♭.

5.— It is an octave below the Soprano, nearly in unison with the Alto Clarinet.

Its *timbre* is as full, as even, and in every respect as satisfactory as that of the Alto. Like the Alto, the Tenor Saxophone is capable of great execution, and well adapted for the execution of *bravura* passages, chromatic figures, etc.

It is better to avoid giving it the 4 or 5 highest notes to play.

BARYTONE SAXOPHONE in E♭.

6.—

Compass:  sounding:

This instrument is heavy to carry; in military bands it plays much the same part as the Bass Clarinet in the orchestra.

Its mechanism is not quite so simple as that of the Saxophones of higher pitch.

7.— Such, then, is the official family of Saxophones. There is another group, but it is neglected, and I only mention it for the sake of completeness.

It consists of the following varieties:

Sopranino	Saxophone	in F
Soprano	„	in C
Alto	„	in F
Tenor	„	in C
Barytone	„	in F

As for the **Bass Saxophone** in C, it is not used any more than the Bass Saxophone in B♭, which, as we have just seen (§2), on account of its great weight, is replaced by the Sarrusophone.

8.— All the shakes and tremolos possible on the Oboe can be performed on the Saxophone, for, as I have already said, the two instruments have the same mechanism. "All figures possible on the Oboe, Clarinet, and Bassoon are equally suitable for the Saxophones, but *legato* passages suit them best." (Gevaert).

The quartet of the Saxophones produces the illusion of the Organ.

However, breathing must not be lost sight of, and the composer, when writing holding-notes and long *legato* passages, must be careful not to exhaust the players.

A note in the medium register cannot be held for more than 10 bars, in moderate quadruple time.

Upon comparing the Clarinet with the Saxophones, it will be found that each instrument can sustain a note for about 40 seconds. However, this is a maximum which can only be expected in the case of a soloist playing *piano*.

9.— What may be the future destiny of the Saxophones in the orchestra? Will the whole family be some day admitted, or will only individual members be invited, as has been done so far? Time will show.

If I may venture to express an opinion, I confess the tone of the instrument seems to me rather loud and out of proportion with that of its neighbors, excepting, however, the example by Bizet, quoted above, which is perfectly pleasing. But since the Saxophone here seems to harmonize so well with the surrounding instruments, if elsewhere it seems out of place, it must be because it is then seen at a disadvantage, and is consequently not to be criticized.

All means are good, provided they are properly used, each in its own time and place.

THE HARP.

(Ital., *Arpa*. Ger., *Harfe*. Fr., *Harpe*.)

1.—The following figure shows the compass of the Harp, which comprises 47 diatonic degrees:

This diatonic scale becomes chromatic by means of seven pedals which act on *all* the octaves at once. According as a pedal is hitched into one or other of two notches, the pitch of the string is raised by a semitone or by two semitones. Example:

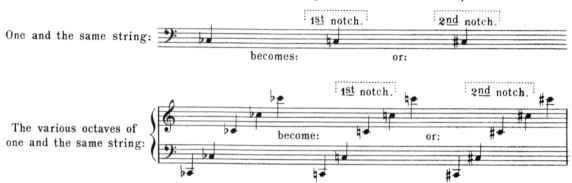

2.—When the pedals are not used, the scale naturally produced is that of C♭, as shown above. For the scale of C♮ the seven pedals are hitched into one set of notches, and for the scale of C♯ into the other set.

Natural Scale:	*Raised by a semitone:*	*Raised by 2 semitones:*
C♭	C♮	C♯
D♭	D♮	D♯
E♭	E♮	E♯
F♭	F♮	F♯
G♭	G♮	G♯
A♭	A♮	A♯
B♭	B♮	B♯

At first sight, it would seem as if this simultaneous action of the pedals throughout the various octaves were a serious defect, such passages as the following appearing to be impossible:

This passage, quoted by Berlioz as impossible, on account of the presence of both F♮ and F♯ (and so it was, formerly, for single-action Harps), is very easy, nowadays, for double-action Harps, F♮ being played as E♯ on the E string.

So this double-action system is very ingenious. It was invented by Sébastien Erard, and, as Gevaert remarks, for a whole century it has been adapting itself to the manifold conditions of modern music, allowing of executing chromatic passages and those *glissandos,* diatonic or otherwise, which seem to throw a kind of poetic haze over the whole orchestra.

3.— The following figure shows the various registers of the Harp:

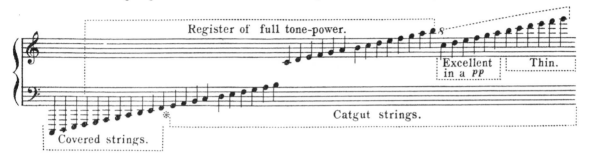

The first three low notes are rather hollow. From the lowest F to B♮ *in alt* the tone is rich and full, whether used *forte* or *piano*. The next octave, from B *in alt* to B *in altissimo,* is less sonorous, but still excellent in *pianissimo* passages. The highest notes alone are rather poor and thin in quality, the strings becoming shorter and shorter.

4.— The first eleven low notes are produced by covered strings; from Gamut G ❋ upwards the strings are of catgut. (Harmonics are only possible on catgut strings, as we shall see later).

5.— As has already been said (§2), each string of the Harp can be raised either a semitone or two semitones; consequently, twenty-one notes (nearly double the number of chromatic degrees) are available in each octave. How is it that we have not got 24, which would give us two strings for each semitone? It is because three notes: D +, G +, and A +, have no enharmonics, no synonymic or homophonic equivalents, as may be seen from the following diagram:

$$
\begin{array}{lll}
\text{C♭} & \text{C♮} & \longrightarrow\text{C♯} \\
\text{D♭} & \text{D♮} & \longrightarrow\text{D♯} \\
\text{E♭} & \text{E♮} & \text{E♯} \\
\text{F♭} & \text{F♮} & \longrightarrow\text{F♯} \\
\text{G♭} & \text{G♮} & \longrightarrow\text{G♯} \\
\text{A♭} & \text{A♮} & \text{A♯} \\
\text{B♭} & \text{B♮} & \text{B♯} \\
\text{C♭} & \text{C♮} &
\end{array}
$$

6.—What curious combinations we can get, by tuning the strings in all sorts of fanciful ways! What extraordinary scales we can imagine!

Many others can be found, or the scale may be transformed into a succession of minor or even major thirds:

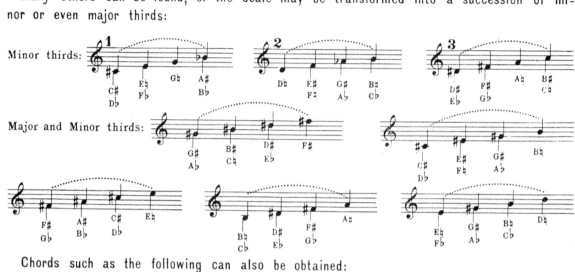

Chords such as the following can also be obtained:

(Gevaert, *Traité d'Instrumentation*, p. 86.)

All the combinations mentioned in this paragraph employ the complete series of strings comprised in the octave. When these strings are grouped so as to produce a chord with four notes, three of the notes are sounded each by two homophonic strings, whereas the fourth note is produced by a single string. Once the pedals are fixed, the harpist has only to slide his fingers over the strings, gently or violently, in order to produce the prepared harmonic effect.

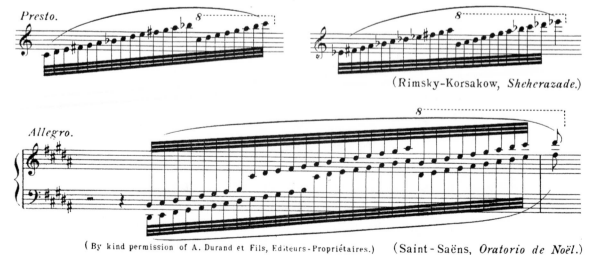

(Rimsky-Korsakow, *Sheherazade.*)

(By kind permission of A. Durand et Fils, Editeurs-Propriétaires.)　　(Saint-Saëns, *Oratorio de Noël.*)

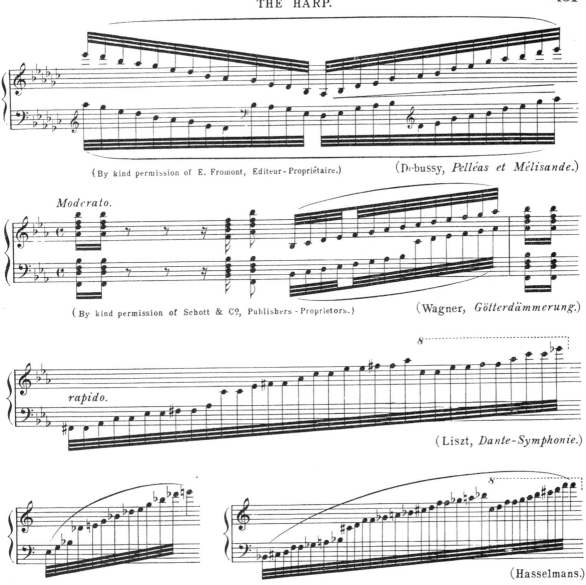

(By kind permission of E. Fromont, Editeur-Propriétaire.)　　　(Debussy, *Pelléas et Mélisande*.)

(By kind permission of Schott & Cº, Publishers-Proprietors.)　　　(Wagner, *Götterdämmerung*.)

(Liszt, *Dante-Symphonie*.)

(Hasselmans.)

Sometimes, for a particulary complicated figure, a prudent composer takes the precaution of indicating the tuning of the Harp himself. When this has once been done, it becomes needless to write the accidentals before each note:

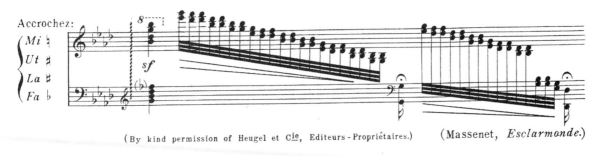

(By kind permission of Heugel et Cⁱᵉ, Editeurs-Propriétaires.)　　　(Massenet, *Esclarmonde*.)

7.— The harpist, having two strings at his disposal for each degree of the scale, can easily play iterated notes, even in the quickest *tempo*, each of the strings being alternately plucked, without the ear in the least detecting the ingenious subterfuge.

(Saint-Saëns, *Ascanio*.)
(By kind permission of A. Durand et Fils, Editeurs - Propriétaires.)

(Wagner, *Lohengrin*.)

(Oberthür.)

It would be impossible to perform the preceding passages (§§ 6 and 7) if we did not, thanks to Erard's invention, possess the means of tuning the Harp instantaneously according to our fancy, making all imaginable kinds of harmonic combinations, as we nearly always have two strings at our disposal for each note.

Harmonics.

8.— Harpists never use any other harmonic than the second, which is produced by the division of the string into two equal parts, and is consequently an octave above the fundamental of the open string.

We have already seen (§4) that the catgut strings alone produce satisfactory harmonics. When Verdi writes this descending *arpeggio*, the low E + is added only for symmetry's sake; it cannot be heard:

(*Falstaff*.)

9.— Harmonics can be produced within the following limits:

It is possible to go still higher, but at the expense of quality. In reality, it is better not to rise so high, as the tone becomes thinner and thinner; the register of good quality is limited to two octaves from Gamut G upwards:

10.— Double-action Harps allow of sounding 2, 3, sometimes even 4 simultaneous harmonics with the left hand, on condition the intervals are small, and require no extension of the fingers. The right hand can never play more than one harmonic at a time.

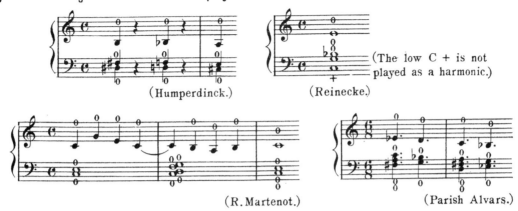

(Humperdinck.)   (Reinecke.)   (The low C + is not played as a harmonic.)

(R. Martenot.)   (Parish Alvars.)

Of course, harmonics cannot be made use of in *forte* passages: they are mysterious and poetic like dew-drops glistening in the moonlight.

They recall sounds echoing through a dream; they can only be heard when all is hushed in silence and sleep.

Nowadays, harmonics are always written an octave below the actual sound, with a zero placed over the written notes:

Written: sounding:

In the time of Berlioz, the note was sometimes written at its true pitch, accompanied by the indication: *harmonic.* Hence frequent mistakes were possible; e. g.

Does the composer wish these two bars to be sounded as written, or an octave higher? There remains a doubt. So composers have done well to give up this mode of writing.

11.— Besides harmonics, the Harp has yet another color of tone at its disposal,   viz. *étouffé* sounds: the vibrations of the string are stopped as soon as produced, giving the illusion of a brief *pizzicato,* very analogous to that of the Violas or Violins.

(By kind permission of Heugel et C<u>ie</u>, Editeurs-Propriétaires.)   (Widor, *Choral et Variations.*)

In the whole of this passage, which is played *staccato* with a single finger, the sound of the Harp closely resembles that of the Strings, forming an absolute contrast to the full rich arpeggio which concludes the phrase.

If, like a violinist playing *sul ponticello,* the harpist plucks the strings at their lower extremity, close to the sounding-board, the tone produced may easily be mistaken for the metallic *timbre* of the Guitar.

Mode of writing for the Harp.

12.—The Harp should be considered as a kind of magnificent Pianoforte without dampers: that is to say, the sound-waves must be allowed time to travel and disappear. Music written for the Harp must be in *tempo* slow enough to prevent all kind of confusion, all harmonic incoherence; in short, the instrument must be treated like an Organ in an empty cathedral, as far as possible in consonant harmony and diatonically.

As to its special technique, observe first that, as the strings are closer to each other than those of the Pianoforte, it is the tenth rather than the octave that corresponds to the natural span of the hand, which fact does not prevent the use of the octave and of all sorts of intervals; observe further that it is not only inadvisable to leave too great a distance between the hands, but that it is of the first importance to balance the intervals skilfully.

Example of very sonorous writing in slow *tempo:*

Note also that if the rate of movement is accelerated, it becomes necessary to simplify the bass parts, *giving octaves only to the left hand;* otherwise the music becomes heavy, thick, and incomprehensible, like the buzzing of chords played in the lowest octaves of the Pianoforte:

Note that immediately after the accented beat, Meyerbeer assigns to the bass nothing but octaves or single notes, because he needs clearness and rhythm. Few composers have treated the instrument as well as he. Oversights such as the following are quite the exception in his works:

Here he seems to forget that it is quite useless to write chords of five notes, harpists being unable to play more than four, since they never make use of the little finger. Take this other figure, which I have often heard criticized on account of its weak and confused character:

"It is written too low down," say *virtuosi*, "and besides it has the serious defect of not being built upon its true bass; a simple *arpeggio* would be infinitely more sonorous."

The most powerful effects are produced by the simplest means. True. But is that a reason why we should always follow the beaten track, and confine ourselves to one and the same *arpeggio?*

Shakes.

13.—The shake performed with the aid of a single hand is nearly as bad as the one a tipsy violinist might attempt to play *pizzicato* on the first string of the Violin.

With two hands, and *piano,* it is, on the contrary, excellent:

It is better to keep to this *piano,* and not attempt a *forte,* if the shake is to remain at all airy and delicate.

14.—All scales, all *arpeggios,* major or minor, can be executed with equal ease; thanks to the pedals, whatever the key, the fingering always remains the same, just as if the fingers had a keyboard of white keys to play upon.

However, it is always better, unless a great number of double flats are involved, to choose the keys of C♭, G♭, D♭, rather than those of B♮, F♯, C♯.

Avoid repetitions of the same chord in the same hand:

Avoid great spaces between the hands:

(Poor and thin quality.)

Let the distance between the hands be neither too great nor too small, and avoid having a string which has just been plucked by one hand immediately set in motion again by the other hand.   Give the sound-waves time to travel; let the vibrations die out of themselves.

What can be finer than the following bass-notes of the Harp, marking the beginning of each bar, and filling the orchestra with their long deep tones?

(Massenet, *La Navarraise.*)
(By kind permission of Heugel et Cie, Editeurs-Propriétaires.)

This deep register of the instrument is admirable; even the lowest notes, which we had called rather hollow, when considered by themselves (§3), are admirable in octaves:

15.—Here follow some figures practised by harpists, sonorous because they are easy:

(By kind permission of Heugel et Cie, Editeurs-Propriétaires.)   (Th. Dubois, *Fantaisie, Harpe et Orchestre.*)

(By kind permission of A. Leduc, Editeur-Propriétaire.) (Hasselmans, *Ballade*.)

(By kind permission of A. Durand et Fils, Editeurs-Propriétaires.) (Hasselmans, *Gitana*.)

(By kind permission of J. Geo. Morley, Publisher, Proprietor.) (Hasselmans, *Conte de Noël*.)

Andante.

(By kind permission of J. Geo. Morley, Publisher-Proprietor.) (Hasselmans, *Prelude.*)

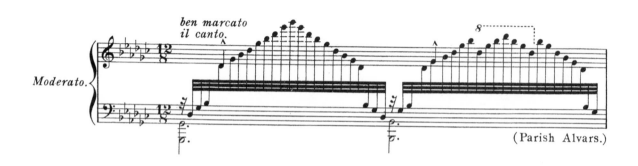

Moderato.

ben marcato
il canto.

(Parish Alvars.)

AUTHORS AND WORKS TO BE CONSULTED: Mozart, Boieldieu, Reinecke, Parish Alvars, Ober-thur, John Thomas, Zabel, H. Renié (*Concertos*): Th. Dubois (*Fantasia for Harp and Orchestra*); Pierné (*Concertstück*), Hasselmans, Widor, Posse, Zamara, Schuecker, Sas-soli (*Concert-pieces, Fantasias*); R. Martenot (*Harp School*). Read the scores of Liszt (admirably written for the Harp): *Dante, Orpheus, Tasso, Was man auf dem Berge hört*, the *Preludes, Mephisto-Walzer* (in which the *glissando* is used for the first time); also read the scores of Wagner, Berlioz, Meyerbeer, Saint-Saëns, Mas-senet, Richard Strauss, and of all the modern Russian school.

16.—In this section, I have spoken of the double-action Harp only, neglecting the so-called *chromatic* Harp, in which the pedals have been suppressed, but the strings in-creased in number.

Its inability to execute the greater part of the figures characteristic of the instrument, and the difficulties of fingering in certain keys, have prevented it so far, despite all its efforts, from obtaining a foot-hold in the orchestra.

It is needless to add that when the number of strings is multiplied on a sounding-board, the volume of sound diminishes in proportion.

Appendix to Chapter IV.

Frequently, two homophonic strings are employed, either with a view to increasing the intensity of the sound, or in order to obtain the waving effect of a *Voix céleste*   organstop; thus we write:

one and the same hand setting in vibration simultaneously two neighboring strings, of which one is tuned to B♭, and the other to A♯.

This device is only applicable to notes whose time-value is not too short; in the following example, for instance, homophones could only be employed in the case of the quavers, not of the semiquavers (++):

This passage the performer would play as follows:

It need hardly be added that it is impossible to make use of this device in the case of those degrees of the scale which have no homophones.

Here is another instance of two sounds for one note, the left hand producing the harmonic, while the right plucks the string that sounds as written:

This effect can, of course, only be utilized in soft passages, as harmonics are always very weak, and unable to make themselves heard unless the orchestra is playing *pianissimo*.

THE ORGAN.

Speaking of the Organ used in combination with the Orchestra, Berlioz in his *Treatise* says: "a secret antipathy seems to exist between these two powers. The Organ and the Orchestra are both kings, or rather, one is Emperor, the other Pope; their mission is not the same; their interests are too vast and too diverse to allow of amalgamation."

I.

Whom did Berlioz consult on this subject? On what organist did he unluckily stumble? I have never been able to ascertain, although, in order to jog the memory of Aristide Cavaillé-Coll, I sometimes went so far as to charge him with indifference to the Master's fame.

And indeed, what more reliable authority could Berlioz have found than Cavaillé-Coll, with whom he had frequent intercourse, and who would have been better qualified than any one else to give him correct information?

Although it is true that organ-stops are of three kinds: *Foundation-stops, Mixture-stops* and *Reed-stops,* it is nevertheless an indisputable fact that the *Foundation-stops* and *Mixture-stops* alone suffice to constitute the old, the true, the genuine Organ, dating from the time of Guido d'Arezzo, sanctioned by Bach, and whose traditions we should hand down to our successors.

If Berlioz failed to understand the function of these *Mixture-stops* it was the fault of his informant.

"Organ-builders and organists," he writes, "agree in praising the effect of this manifold resonance; however it decidedly causes several different keys to be heard simultaneously.— 'It would be insufferable', they say, 'if the two upper notes could be singled out, but *they are never heard,* the fundamental tone drowning them'. It then remains to be explained how a good effect can be produced on the ear by what is not heard!"

When Berlioz wrote these lines, the importance and function of the partial tones in the composition of the fundamental had not yet been demonstrated by Cavaillé-Coll with his *Enregistreur Harmonique.* This instrument, consisting of 32 pipes, can sound, in succession, or simultaneously, the first 32 upper partials of an 8 ft. A, our ear not being able to appreciate the value of sounds beyond the 32nd harmonic.

If, beginning with the most acute notes, the pipes of the instrument are made to speak one after another, the volume of this synthetic A increases proportionally, until it becomes 32 times as powerful as the A sounded by the deepest-toned pipe itself. If the 32 pipes are allowed to speak simultaneously, a single fundamental tone is heard, of incomparable power and absolute truth of intonation.

We are troubled by no manifold resonance, no divergency of key, no doubt or uncertainty for the ear. On the contrary, we get a sound so crystalline and clear, so full and powerful that the great masters of the 18th century made it their *Organo Pleno,* the richest means of expression of polyphony.

Besides, this is merely the repetition of what takes place in nature for any sound whatsoever, of the phenomenon that we might ask **Voltaire's** mechanician to explain:

L'Univers m'embarrasse et je ne puis songer
Que cette horloge existe et n'ait point d'horloger.

Just as a pebble falling into a pond inevitably produces circular waves, which, while receding in obedience to a well ascertained mathematical law from their common centre, are separated from one another by ever diminishing distances, until they finally seem to blend, so a sound originates other sounds, which the *ear does not hear,* but which nevertheless *produce a good effect.*

These secondary tones that are generated by the fundamental tone, these circular waves around the spot where the pebble disappeared, these harmonics which the orchestra has not yet succeeded in reproducing, are employed by the Organ either one at a time, or in groups, grading at will any one of them; according as the one or the other becomes more or less intense, the *timbre* of the instrument changes.

In his most recent Pianoforte *Concerto,* Saint-Saëns has made an ingenious application of this theory. The quality of the Pianoforte seems to be completely altered, having more affinity with the Xylophone than with the Erard.

It is the whole mass of 8 foot *Foundation-stops,* corresponding to the Strings in the orchestra, that are the backbone of Organ music; it is these stops that produce the feeling of infinite calm and sweetness. Quick rates of movement and powerful effects are to be obtained from the *Mixture-stops.* Bach's *Organo Pleno,* as I have already said, is composed of these two groups, without any *Reed-stops* on the manual. If Bach and his contemporaries neglect indicating the rates of movement and the registering, at the beginning of their compositions, it is because, only making use of two rates of movement always the same, *Andante* and *Allegro* (when perchance they want an *Adagio* they mark it), and nobody, consequently, being able to mistake the *tempo* of the piece, nobody should make a mistake as to the suitable orchestration, the *Foundation-stops* being always reserved for pieces of a serious character, the *Mixture-stops* for pieces in quick *tempo.*

If Berlioz speaks of "a medley and tangle of sounds, of disorder, of hideous pasquinades fit only for depicting an orgy of savages or a dance of demons," it is because the wretched organist who set him on the wrong track must have been in the habit of serving up Bach's music for Berlioz's consumption with a spicy dressing of Bombardes and Trumpets, an effect comparable to that of a String quartet with all parts doubled by Trumpets and Trombones.

This anonymous organist seems to have been totally ignorant of the most intense and most profound work of Bach, which is, at the same time, the one most characteristic of the instrument: his three books of Chorals. He gave his illustrious visitor insight into the mechanical side of the question only: Bach appeared to Berlioz only as a kind of road-surveyor, as a manufacturer of velocity exercises at the rate of so many notes per second. Of course, the illustrious visitor could not discover what his guide failed to show him.

Here a curious remark may be made. If, in the history of art, there are two techniques diametrically opposed to each other, certainly they are those of Bach and Berlioz.

Yet these two antipodic minds, these two inhabitants of planets far distant from each other, these two travellers setting out in opposite directions, have the same tendencies, are attracted towards the same horizon, are pursuing the same ideal. They are both landscape painters; both are fascinated by the picturesque; what appeals to them, although they are musicians, is above all a pictorial impression — a picture.

When there is a break in the series of *Little Chorals* for each Sunday, it is because the text of one of these chorals did not suggest anything picturesque to the musician's imagination. When the composer of the celebrated *Aria* destined to be sung out of doors at a spring festival, wishes to insert this air in one of his Church cantatas, as he needs a green background, as his music sings of May, he instinctively chooses Whitsuntide.

It is needless to point out the same tendency in Berlioz; all his works afford ample proof.

* * *

II.

In Bach's time, reed-stops were rare in the Organ. One or two only were to be found on the manuals, and they were exclusively destined to play the *Solo theme* of the Choral. In general they were not introduced into polyphony. In the Arnstadt Organ, the first to which Bach was appointed, out of 24 stops there was only one Trumpet. At Weimar the proportion was the same. At the church of Leipzig University there were three manuals, 38 stops, and one poor Chalumeau! At the church of S.t Thomas in Leipzig there were 31 stops, one Cremona, and one Trumpet. On the other hand, several reed-stops were always grouped on the pedal; usually a 16 ft. Trombone, an 8 ft. Trumpet, and often a 4 ft. Clarion, forming an excellent bass to the mass of the foundation-stops and mixture-stops on the manuals.

For the last century, organ-builders in France, England, and America have gradually been increasing the number of reed-stops at the expense of the mixture-stops, whose number they have proportionally reduced. Many Organs with 30 or 40 stops have only one or two mixture-stops, as compared with seven, eight or ten reed-stops. Hence results a modification in the quality and character of the instrument. The tone of the whole mass of stops becomes heavy; it is no longer possible, as with the old Organs, to follow the progression of the various parts, as the designs of white lace can be traced when thrown into relief by a dark background. The strata of air set in motion seem to be thick and viscous, and here we are in the medley and tangle of sounds, in the savage and fiendish disorder of which Berlioz speaks.

However, we must add that this modern Organ meets a new requirement: the necessity of adapting the masses of sound to the size of our cathedrals or concert-rooms.

Formerly, music was performed in churches of relatively small dimensions; the instruments were not very powerful, and the choir was composed of very few singers. Palestrina's choir consisted of 32 voices, Bach's of 16 only. Even when, by way of exception, an Organ with 100 stops was built, no one ever dreamt of using more than 30 (say) of these stops simultaneously, for it was impossible, on account of the material weight of the mechanism, to couple together more than two manuals at once. A hundred stops meant 100 varieties of *timbre,* but nowise the whole mass of such a number of stops.

So that our *Full Organ* has had to submit to playing a more decorative than polyphonic part. Nowadays, some care has to be taken with the enormous volume of sound produced by coupling together all the keyboards, and time allowed for the sound to travel to and fro under the roofs of our cathedrals. The composer no longer has the same liberty left him; his style can no longer be so close. Everything has to be punctuated, measured, minutely dosed. These masses of 16 ft., 8 ft., and 4 ft. reed-stops cannot possibly be written for in four parts in the medium, where they are stifled. It is indispensable to rise higher in search of breathable air, in order to avoid suffocation and absorption by the formidable bass-stops.

It is needless to try to conceal the fact that the ideal of this modern *Full Organ* is rather too nearly akin to that of Brass Bands. Forgetful of the traditions of the past, abandoning the sunny land of Counterpoint, it remains cooped up within the narrow limits of *struck* chords, and harmonies according to a few set formulæ.

Luckily, a reaction has set in: of late, works have been specially written with a view to protesting against this artistic decadence, and French organ-builders are now coming back to those mixture-stops which the Germans, with their native good sense, had always held in esteem. Besides, did not the genius of Aristide Cavaillé-Coll alway turn a deaf ear to unwise advice, inconsiderate criticism, and momentary impulses?

In the Organs of S.t Sulpice, Notre-Dame (*Paris*), S.t Ouen (*Rouen*), were not great masses of reed-stops always balanced by equally large masses of mixture-stops? One of Cavaillé-Coll's chief claims to celebrity is based upon his having given us these means of unveiling, of contemplating in all its brilliancy, and in its true light, the colossal work of the master of Eisenach, of hearing Bach as he wished to be heard. Cavaillé-Coll's instruments, with their admirable tones and their incomparable mechanism, have attracted and passionately interested a number of composers, who have found in them a genuine orchestra, varied, supple, and powerful, respectful of tradition, yet ready to welcome a new ideal.

*   *   *

III.

In the time of Berlioz, the Swell was known, but was still very imperfect. What is its origin?

It would be hard to say. England claims the invention of the Swell, attributing it to Jordan (1712), and we know that Händel was able to admire one of the first specimens of the new invention in London; we know also that about 1780 the Abbé Vogler recommended its use to German organ-builders, but this very ingenious means of creating the impression of a modification of intensity in an organ-pipe was still a mere curiosity without practical application. So that Berlioz denies the possibility of changing suddenly from *piano* to *forte,* or of creating sudden contrasts, of swelling and diminishing the volume of sound at will, and consequently of blending the Organ and the Orchestra into one harmonious whole, the cold tones of the former being incompatible with the nervous sensitiveness of the latter. "On almost all occasions," he says, "when this singular combination has been attempted, either the Organ very much "overcrows" the Orchestra, or else the Orchestra, having been raised to undue preeminence, well-nigh drowns its adversary."

How times have changed! Nowadays, no concert-room is built without its Organ. It is now possible to graduate the sound mass, to pass suddenly from an imposing *fortissimo* to an almost imperceptible *pianissimo,* and, when accompanying a singer, to follow all the lights and shades of vocal expression.

I am fully aware that this "expression" of the modern Organ can only be subjective; whereas the Strings and the Wind instruments of the orchestra, the Pianoforte and the human voice, are captivating only on account of their impulsiveness and spontaneity, the Organ, wrapped in its primitive majesty, speaks like a philosopher; it alone among the instruments can for ever furnish the same volume of sound, and generate the idea of Religion out of the conception of Infinity." No, the expression of the Organ is neither spontaneous nor impulsive; there is nothing that is neuropathic about the Organ. Of a thoughtful and deliberate nature, the Organ rises architecturally from *piano* to *forte,* following the straightest diagonal. The least inflexion would constitute a defect in its outlines, which should be as straight and precise as those of an engineer's plan.

The Philistine who "sentimentalizes" on the Organ forthwith turns the instrument of Majesty and Dignity into a big accordion. His outlines are like the wild zigzags of a weather-chart, or the marks left by a feather-brush carelessly passed along a dusty wall.

It is precisely because our present means enable us, with almost too ready facility, to embody any and every musical idea, that we must avoid all disrespect towards the majesty of the Organ, and that we must employ this "expression" with conscientious reserve and artistic feeling. Otherwise we shall ignore the essential characteristics of the instrument, and convert it into a pseudo-orchestra, witness those heavy, clumsy arrangements of symphonic pieces, overtures, marches, suites, etc.

Modern builders enclose a whole Organ in Swell-boxes, and so obtain, first by adding stop upon stop, and then by opening the Swells one after the other, the magnificent *crescendo* of the whole mass of sound. Then, immediately after this exhibition of colossal strength, they challenge with a simple 8 ft. Bourdon the *pianissimo* of any orchestral instrument.

Thanks to their skill, we can obtain, at will, sudden contrasts, instantaneous changes, *crescendos* and *diminuendos;* nothing is easier than to compete with the orchestra in point of suppleness, and to keep the Organ constantly well balanced with regard to the orchestra.

So, here we are far from the supposed antipathy between "Emperor and Pope" of which Berlioz speaks. No such thing exists nowadays, and a minute examination of the case leads us to doubt whether it ever really existed. Is not Berlioz's ignorant guide to blame in this case too? Does not the whole mass of Bach's vocal work point to the opposite conclusion? Is it not entirely based upon the suitable combination of the Organ with the Orchestra? And was not this combination satisfactory even at a time when the Organ was not expressive? Listen to the "arrangements" of Bach's *Cantatas* for concert-rooms that have no Organ, and compare the effect produced with Bach's original version. And what about Händel and his *Concertos?*

If Berlioz were still alive he would forswear his views of yore, or rather the views that were so unfairly instilled into his mind. Admirable new effects may yet be drawn from the union of the two former rivals, "the Emperor and the Pope," who, converted into fast allies, manifest ever growing mutual sympathy. A number of recent compositions I could quote furnish conclusive evidence on this point.

IV.

What was the Organ like in former times? When did the manuals become more numerous? When was the pedal invented? No one can say for certain. Two or three broad facts are known: Some 200 years before the Christian era, attempts were being made to improve the bellows; pressure was then obtained by means of water, and the *Hydraulic Organ* was to the Romans, in the time of the Cæsars, pretty much what the Pianoforte is to us.

Vitruvius gives us a description of the instrument, sufficiently clear and complete to furnish a fair idea of its construction. And after Vitruvius, the Emperor Julian says: "a skilful artist with swift fingers directs by means of his touch the valves adapted to the pipes, which, being made to vibrate softly by the action of the keys, breathe forth a sweet melody." The bas-reliefs, mosaics, and terra-cottas of those times show the organist standing with his head projecting above the pipes — an attitude which proves that the pedal was not yet known.

The Circus instruments must have been pretty large; had they several keyboards? It is not very likely.

The Organ emigrated with the Emperors to Byzantium, whence a few centuries later, it came back to the West, in the reign of Pepin or Charlemagne. The Christians, having had time to forget the instrument whose tones had accompanied the martyrdom of their ancestors, took it for a new instrument, and forthwith adopted it in their places of worship.

Is it not likely that Guido d'Arezzo's early polyphonic attempts, his harmonizations in fourths and fifths, first suggested the idea of mixture-stops, which simply reproduced the choir-parts without making any pretence of obeying the laws of sound, or of reinforcing the harmonics of the fundamental tone?

We hardly know anything of the history of the Organ during the Middle Ages. In any case it cannot have been of much use, music being at that time almost exclusively choral. It only begins to attract attention again with Frescobaldi and Scarlatti, under the fingers of the great Italian masters, the fore-runners of the great German organists.

The classical Organ sanctioned by Bach, who determined its compass, consisted of two or three manuals and one pedal-board, the former extending from CC to F *in alt* (54 notes), and the latter likewise beginning at CC and rising to F above middle C (30 notes).

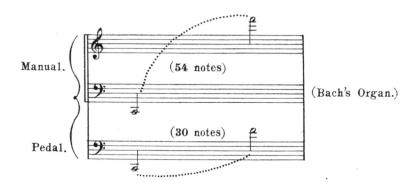

(Bach's Organ.)

On the manuals German, English, and American builders now go up to C *in altissimo,* while retaining the pedal-board of 30 notes:

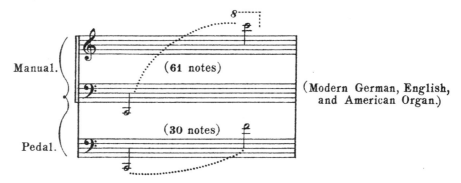

Manual.

(61 notes)

(Modern German, English, and American Organ.)

Pedal.

(30 notes)

Aristide Cavaillé-Coll had adopted for his large French instruments another somewhat illogical system: 30 notes on the pedal-board, from CC to F above Middle C, as usual, but 56 notes on the manuals, from CC to G in *altissimo.*

Fortunately, we have been able to induce his intelligent successor, M. Mutin, to apply the theory derived from Bach, which requires the adoption of the same limits for the feet as for the hands: from C to G. The following are the henceforth recognised divisions:

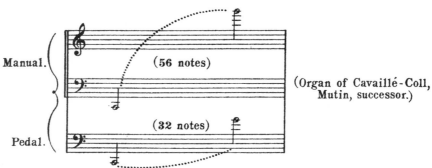

Manual.

(56 notes)

(Organ of Cavaillé-Coll, Mutin, successor.)

Pedal.

(32 notes)

It would be highly desirable that organ-builders should come to an agreement on this point. No harm comes of the precise upper limit of the manuals being undetermined; the danger lies in the compass of the pedal-board varying from one Organ to another, for an organist should never need to look down at his feet when playing: his guiding-marks should be invariable, otherwise he treads on the wrong key.

So, let us request the German, English, and American builders to adopt the French pedal-board of 32 notes, the maximum stretch possible for the organist's legs. As the Organ may be said to be in C, it will not strike them as being very illogical to take the dominant as the last note of the pedal-board, the hands continuing up to the tonic.

Concave pedal-boards are the most practical. Pedal-keys ought to be narrow, rounded and polished, in order to enable the performer to execute all the requisite *legatos* and *glissandos.*

I say *narrow,* because it is necessary to leave between the keys intervals about equal to the width of the keys, in order to allow of depressing them with the foot either perpendicularly or from the side, according to circumstances.

* *

V.

To form an idea of the amount of music modern Organs have given rise to, consult publishers' catalogues. The mere list of composers inspired by the Organ would fill a large volume.

In Paris, the production of Organ music was formerly nil, when, all of a sudden, the meeting of a great *virtuoso* and a skilful builder set the stone rolling.

Lemmens, a Belgian organist, was coming back from Breslau, where he had gone piously to collect from Hesse the traditions of Bach in all their purity. Cavaillé-Coll was preparing his plans for the Organs of Ste Clotilde, St Sulpice, Notre-Dame, etc.... The advice of the one came in the very nick of time to guide the tottering footsteps of the other, who had thus far been groping alone in the dark. To these circumstances we owe our magnificent instruments.

Thanks to them, a few years have given birth to more works than all the hoary past. And this movement has not been confined to one centre only; it has spread from country to country, making its influence felt pretty well everywhere.

Is there at the present time one single country that is not justifiably proud of a fine Organ played by an excellent musician? Is there any fine instrument which has not spurred on the imagination of its organist?

When, by the mere depression of a finger, the organist obtains a note of unlimited duration, and that too without the slightest strain on poor human lungs — when he feels that he is, so to speak, master of Time and Power — then he appreciates the true character of the instrument he plays, comprehends the language it behoves it to speak, and realizes the style that exactly befits it.

And if the essential qualities of good style are: *purity, clearness* and *precision,* Organ music certainly possesses them in the highest degree, not to mention other minor excellencies.

The great voice of the Organ should reflect the calm of the Absolute; it is made to be heard under stone roofs and is based on natural harmonies. While orchestral instruments strive after effects obtained by more or less diseased virtuosity, the Organ attains the maximum of strength by means of the common chord of C, by sustaining tones which seem to have neither beginning nor end.

This great voice requires to sing in time; it needs rhythm, punctuation, and a definite plan. Let us remark and admire in Bach's works those cadences which here and there come and interrupt the *continuo* of the text, in order to give us a minute's repose. Whatever the rate of movement, the great master thus avoids any impression of anxious hurry and precipitation. He never loses his self-possession, never troubles the serenity of his audience.

And this great voice of the Organ does not admit of the use of set formulæ, commonplaces, and fillings-up. Every note is meant to carry, and should, consequently, be in its proper place, like the Stringed Quartet, which eschews superfluous ornament.

When the organist has before him the 4 or 5 key-boards of St Sulpice, of Sheffield, or of Moscow, he fully realizes that the Organ is no drawing-room toy or fancy instrument.

It is a stupendous mass, a monument of granite, the most powerful means on earth of expressing what is great, unchangeable, eternal.

In its presence let us call to mind the monumental constructions of the past; let us bow down in reverence, and imagine that we are going to move to song Egyptian Pyramid or Roman Coliseum.

The Origin of the Swell, Pedal-board, Manuals, and Stops of the Organ.

The *Swell* was for the first time introduced in 1712 by Jordan the Elder, in the Organ of the Church of S! Magnus the Martyr (London). This primitive form of Swell was provided with movable shutters which were slid one over the other, a system soon superseded by the *Venetian Swell,* which at first was furnished with horizontal, and later with vertical *shades* or *louvres.*

The *Pedal-board.* Its invention is erroneously attributed to Bernhard the German, an organist and builder at Venice, who is said to have first introduced the pedal in 1471. The Organ at Halberstadt (1361) was provided with pedal-keys. A pedal was added to the Organ in the Church of S! Nicholas at Utrecht not later than 1450. And lastly, the Organ at Groningen, built in 1479 by R. Agricola, was already provided with a pedal-board of ten stops, but of a peculiar arrangement.

One of the first specimens of pedal-boards starting from C and possessed of a complete chromatic scale dates from 1673 (Nieuwe-Kerk, Amsterdam). From that time onwards, German and Dutch Organs have had pedals analogous to French ones, but with a compass of only 27 notes (from C to D). It was Bach who extended it to F.

Manuals. In the tenth century, the manual consisted of 15 keys embracing two octaves (A, B, C, D, E, F, G. A, B, C, D, E, F, G, A). About the middle of the 11th Century, semitones were beginning to come into use. In 1361, an Organ was built with three manuals, but what manuals! The keys were nearly three inches broad, and could only be depressed with a blow of the clenched fist. And while the first and second manuals had 22 keys, the third manual and the pedal-board had only 14.

Stops can be traced back to the end of the 15th century; at that time they were merely laths of wood (separating the rows of pipes from each other); the organist, suspending his playing, had to go to one side of the instrument and draw them out or push them back: at the end of each lath was a hole through which passed a piece of string; such was the mechanism in all its primitive simplicity!

Sliders, levers, and stop-handles did not come into use before the end of the 16th or the beginning of the 17th century.

Chapter V.

—— ✛ ——

The Strings.

——

THE VIOLIN.

(Ital., *Violino.* Ger., *Violine.* Fr., *Violon.*)

1.— It is needless to give a minute account of the mechanism of the instrument, which has not changed since the time of Beethoven.

Its maximum compass may be stated as 3 octaves and a fifth:

But, in the orchestra, it is dangerous to employ without preparation the notes contained in the highest third:

It is almost impossible to attack B♭ *in altissimo* ✳, unless it is led up to by conjunct degrees, or preceded by a fairly long rest (at least one bar of moderate quadruple time), for the player's finger must be allowed sufficient time to run up to the top of the scale and find its very narrow resting-place.

And if it is nearly impossible to play B♭ without preparation, still more is this the case with B♮, C, C♯, and D above.

N. B.   E *in altissimo,* however, is excellent when played as a harmonic (V. List, P. 160). Wagner and many others do not hesitate to write it.

B♭ *in altissimo* may be said to be the highest sonorous note on the Violin; the four semitones above becoming thinner and thinner.

However, if a number of Violins move upwards by conjunct degrees, these 4 notes are still tolerably sonorous; hence their occasional use by the great classic masters.

2.— Here follows the table of the seven positions of the Violin:

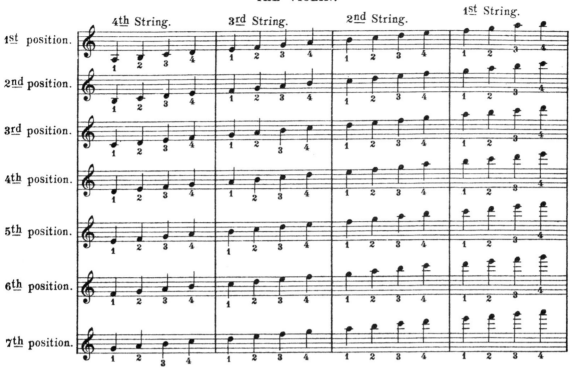

3.— Diatonic scales are excellent on stringed instruments; chromatic scales do not come out nearly so well, because they can only be obtained by sliding the finger from the true note to the altered note, and in rapid *tempo* this sliding is inevitably of but approximate accuracy.

However, the ascending chromatic scale is quite practicable; it is only in the descending scale that real difficulties of execution arise.

4.— The maximum stretch on one string cannot exceed an augmented fourth or a diminished fifth:

From the perfect fifth upwards, inclusively, two strings have to be employed, and then the execution becomes heavy, the bow having to oscillate from one string to the other.

Remark: The utmost stretch possible for the hand on two strings (in orchestral playing) is the minor ninth, and even this interval should not be used without care. (The minor ninth is opposite to the diminished fifth: it corresponds on two strings to the stretch required for a diminished fifth on a single string).

5.— Is it necessary to speak of the different qualities of tone on the Violin: of the admirable 4th string, of the rather subdued *timbre* of the 3rd and 2nd strings, of the brilliant 1st string?

If a theme be given to the fourth string, *sul G,* the notes of the lower octave will be the loudest, the power of the tone being in proportion to the length of the string. However, the quality will remain full and homogeneous up to Treble C (7th position), which limit it is unwise to exceed.

I am aware that in a solo higher notes can be reached:

(Widor, Concerto.)

but in writing for the orchestra it would be very imprudent to go beyond C.

Double Stops.

6.— It is, of course, easy to play all double stops that include an open string.

LIST OF DOUBLE STOPS IN THE ORDER OF INCREASING DIFFICULTY.

EASY: all *major and minor sixths:*

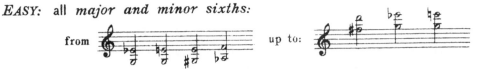

EASY: all *major, minor, and diminished sevenths:*

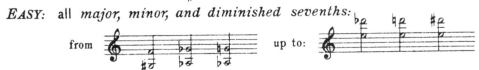

EASY: *major and minor thirds:*

POSSIBLE: all *perfect and augmented fourths:*

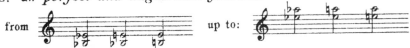

POSSIBLE: all *diminished and augmented fifths:*

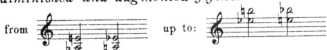

POSSIBLE: *octaves:*

From this *D* upwards they become more and more difficult.

POSSIBLE: *major seconds.*

RISKY: *minor seconds,* which should only be used with great care.

8.—As for the *perfect* fifth, it is hardly *perfect* on stringed instruments. It is better to consider it as very dangerous in orchestral work; if ever it becomes necessary to use it in a chord, carefully avoid going beyond F C on the first string:

It may be as well to repeat the remark already made at the end of §4:   the maximum stretch possible for the hand is the minor ninth:

It is impossible to reach the major ninth.

9.— We now give a list of sevenths in all keys, and of the various positions of the common chords on which they resolve. (For much assistance in this matter   I am indebted to M.ʳ Sechiari, Solo Violinist of the *Lamoureux Concerts*).

Chords of the Dominant Seventh.

The crosses + show the difficult or unsonorous chords; the asterisks * show the resolutions that are impossible in the minor mode.

Resolutions not specially marked are possible in either mode.

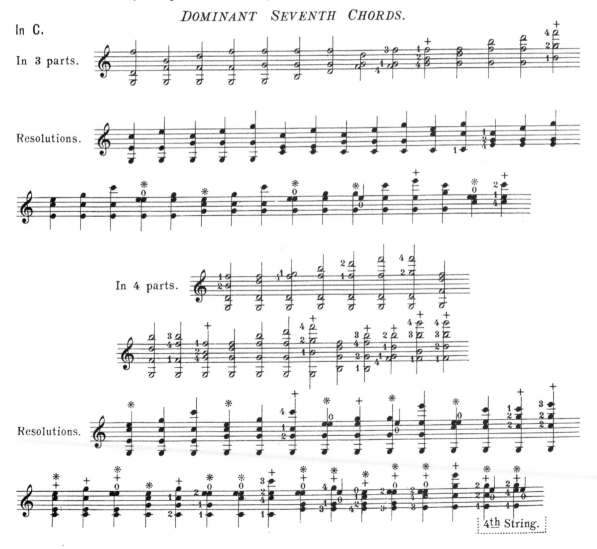

DOMINANT SEVENTH CHORDS.

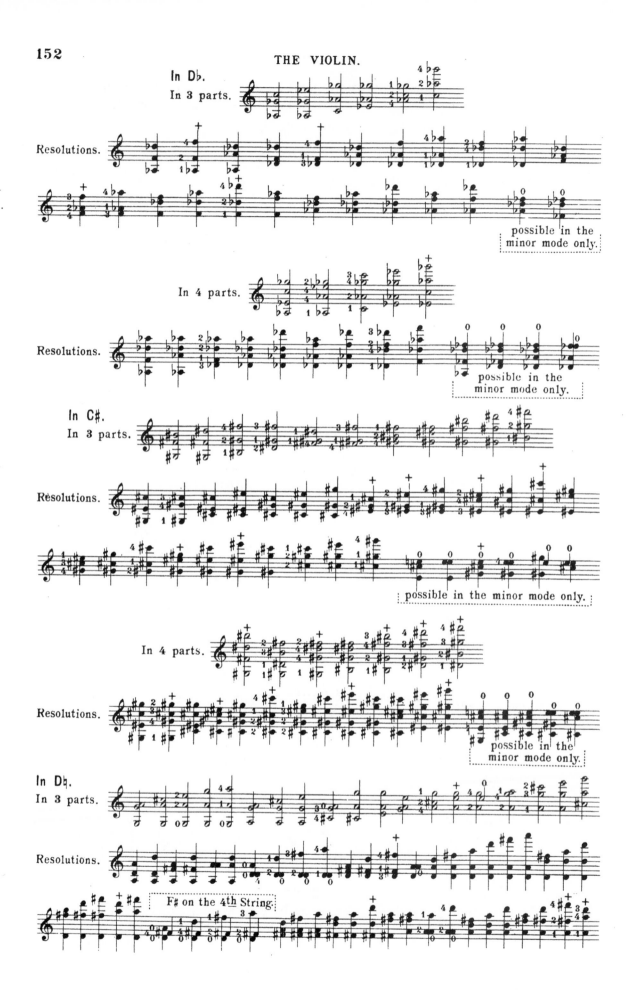

possible in the
minor mode only.

possible in the
minor mode only.

possible in the minor mode only.

possible in the
minor mode only.

F# on the 4th String.

possible in the minor mode only.

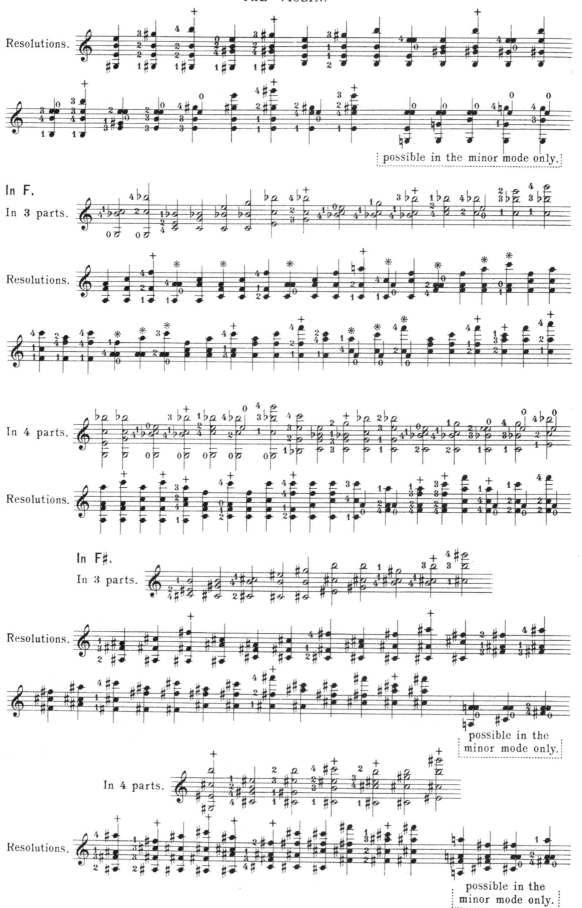

possible in the minor mode only.

In F.
In 3 parts.

Resolutions.

In 4 parts.

Resolutions.

In F♯.
In 3 parts.

Resolutions.

possible in the minor mode only.

In 4 parts.

Resolutions.

possible in the minor mode only.

In G.
In 3 parts.

Resolutions.

In 4 parts.

Resolutions.

In A♭.
In 3 parts.

Resolutions.

In 4 parts.

Resolutions.

In A♮.
In 3 parts.

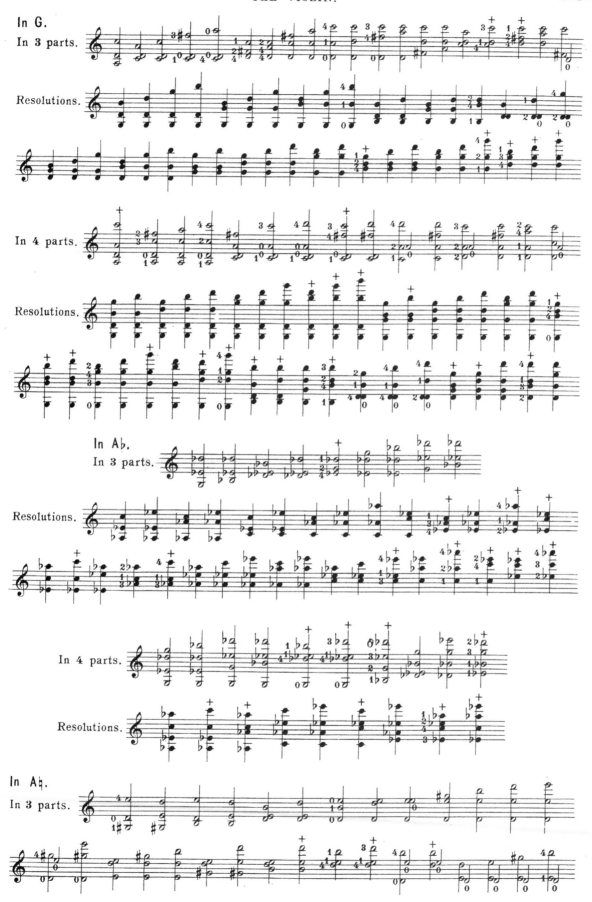

possible in the minor mode only.

In 4 parts

Resolutions.

possible in the
minor mode only.

Chords of the Diminished Seventh*

In 3 parts.
On the three
lower strings.

On the three
higher strings.

In 4 parts.

Chords of the Major and Minor Ninth.

In 3 parts.
On the three
lower strings.

On the three
higher strings.

In 4 parts.

Chords of the Augmented Fifth

are easy in four parts within the following limits.

Rising chromatically up to:

* All the Chords of the Diminished Seventh may be written enharmonically.

Harmonics.

10.— Taking as a fundamental tone the note produced by each of the open strings, the 2<u>nd</u>, 3<u>rd</u>, 4<u>th</u>, 5<u>th</u>, and 6<u>th</u> upper partials can be obtained with the help of a *single* finger lightly touching the string.

If we take Fiddle G as a fundamental tone, we get the following series of natural harmonics:

The 2<u>nd</u> partial is obtained by touching the string mid-way between the nut and bridge, i. e. at the point where the depressed finger would produce the same note.

The 3<u>rd</u> partial can be obtained in two different ways:
either (1) by touching the string at a distance from the nut equivalent to ⅓ of its length, i.e. at the point where the depressed finger would produce the perfect fifth:

or (2) by touching the string at a distance from the nut equivalent to ⅔ of its length, i. e. at the point where the depressed finger would produce the same note:

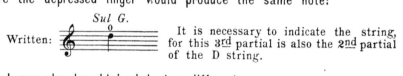

It is necessary to indicate the string, for this 3<u>rd</u> partial is also the 2<u>nd</u> partial of the D string.

The 4<u>th</u> partial can also be obtained in two different ways:
either (1) by touching the string at a distance from the nut equivalent to ¼ of its length, i.e. at the point where the depressed finger would produce the perfect fourth:

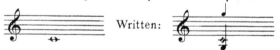

or (2) by touching the string at a distance from the nut equivalent to ¾ of its length, at the point where the depressed finger would produce the same note:

The 5<u>th</u> partial can be obtained in four different ways:
either (1) by touching the string at a distance from the nut equivalent to ⅕ of its length, at the point where the depressed finger would produce the major third:

or (2) by touching the string at a distance from the nut equivalent to ⅖ of its length, at the point where the depressed finger would sound the major sixth:

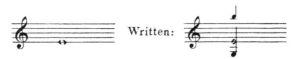

or (3) by touching the string at a distance from the nut equivalent to ⅗ of its length, at the point where the depressed finger would produce the major tenth:

or (4) by touching the string at a distance from the nut equivalent to ⅘ of its length, at the point where the depressed finger would produce the same note:

Remark: The first two ways of obtaining the 5th partial are the only ones used in the orchestra, the others being rather risky; with the 3rd way the harmonic is strangled and does not come out immediately; with the 4th way the tone is very pure, but it requires considerable stretching to reach this position, which would be still more difficult on the Viola, on account of its larger dimensions.

The 6th partial can be obtained in two ways:

either (1) by touching the string at a distance from the nut equivalent to ⅙ of its length, at the point where the depressed finger would produce the minor third:

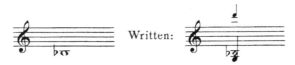

or (2) by touching the string at a distance from the nut equivalent to ⅚ of its length, at the point where the depressed finger would produce the same note:

this indication is vague, for this 6th upper partial of the fundamental G 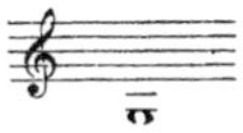   is also the fourth partial of D (open string)

It is therefore necessary to indicate whether the harmonic is to be played on the G or on the D string.

If the first way of producing it is employed, the harmonic comes out with difficulty, without beauty or charm; the second way involves a painful stretch, so it is advisable to abstain from using the 6th partial, the same note coming out better as the 4th partial of the neighboring string, a fifth above.

List of Natural Harmonics
practicable in the Orchestra.

Artificial Harmonics.

11.—This is the name given to sounds whose fundamental tone is not a note sounded by an open string. These artificial harmonics can only be produced by means of two fingers, the fore-finger serving as an artificial nut, the other finger lightly touching the string at a given point.

Of this class of harmonics the only one employed in the orchestra is the 4<u>th</u> partial, two octaves above the fundamental; the system explained on P. 158 (fourth partial (1)) is followed; the little finger touches the string at the distance of a fourth from the artificial fundamental, i. e. a quarter of the way between the depressed fore-finger and the bridge.

Written:

These artificial harmonics are all possible from the lowest Ab up to:

12.— Other artificial harmonics are made use of by *virtuosi,* e.g. the third partial, which can be obtained by touching with the little finger the fifth above the depressed fore-finger, i. e. a point a third of the way between the fore-finger and the bridge.

Written: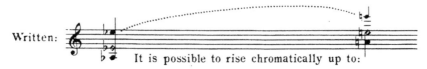

It is possible to rise chromatically up to:

13.—The 5$\underline{th}$ partial can be produced by touching with the ring-finger the major third a-bove the depressed fore-finger, i. e. a point a fifth of the way between the fore-finger and the bridge:

but this is not often done, for the quality of tone so obtained is poor.

Remark: A careless composer may write any note, putting a zero above it, so that the performer may know that this note is to be produced as a harmonic, leaving him to choose the best means of execution.

In this case, the composer must not forget that the complete chromatic scale at his command does not begin till G *in alt:*

Below this G, he has at his disposal none but natural harmonics, which are limited to the notes of the perfect major chord on each string (V. List P. **160**.)

Bowing.

14.—When the bow is drawn over the string from the heel to the point, the violinist is said to be playing a *down-bow,* when from the point to the heel an *up-bow,* and the following indications are used when needful:

Down-bow ⊔ Fr. *Tiré.*
Up-bow   V Fr. *Poussé.*

When a *down-bow,* and when an *up-bow,* is to be used, it is not easy to decide, cases varying widely, but it may be stated in a general fashion that a down-bow is used for an accented beat, and an up-bow for an unaccented beat or an unaccented part of a beat.

Varieties of Bowing.

15.—The *Grand Détaché* is produced by using the bow throughout the whole of its length, from the heel to the point, and *vice versâ,* the bow never quitting the string, and no slur being written over the notes.

A powerful tone is thus obtained.

If the effect is to be not only powerful, but even violent, the heel of the bow alone is made use of, but then there is some intermittence between each stroke of the bow, for each note requires the repetition of the same motion, and it becomes impossible to play as fast as with the *Grand Détaché.*

The *Détaché Moyen* is obtained by using a third of the bow; it is used in rapid *tempo*, and a still sufficiently intense tone can be produced by this means.

The *Petit Détaché,* which is produced with the point of the bow, is used in very rapid *tempo* and for soft effects.

The *Martelé* is played with the extreme tip of the bow, each note being attacked drily, as if with a hammer.

It may be used *piano,* as well as *forte.*

The *Sautillé* is obtained by making the middle of the bow rebound after each note; it is especially suited to passages requiring great lightness of execution, and the quicker the rate of movement, the better the effect.

Iterated notes suit it capitally, but it is absolutely devoid of strength.

Some composers very improperly indicate the *Sautillé* by the word *Staccato.* This is quite a mistake, the *Staccato* being obtained by an upbow from the point to the middle of the bow, and by detaching each note; written:

Frequently used in solos, the *Staccato* is rare in the orchestra, on account of the difficulty of executing it with regularity. As for the *Staccato* with the down-bow, it is never used in the orchestra.

Slurs and Legatos.

16.—Are all possible, whatever the number of articulations. The longer the stroke of the bow, the weaker the tone; even *ppp* it is well not to require more than *4 bars in moderate quadruple time* if holding notes are to be played, or *two bars in like tempo* if a figure has to be performed:

17.—Notes are said to be played *Louré* when each one is articulated, although a number are played with the same bow. This is indicated by little dashes over each note under the slur:

This is a very good means of expression, very much used in *cantabile* passages, and is one of the favorite devices of modern art.

The Pizzicato.

18.—It will suffice to quote the two following examples, which give a better notion of the way in which the *Pizzicato* is used than any description could:

Tempo of the Jota Aragonesa.

Piccolos. Oboes. Clarinets. 1st Violins. 2nd Violins. Violas. Violoncellos. Double-basses.

(Gevaert.)

Violins. Violas. Violoncellos. Double-basses.

Allegro. *animando sino al fine.*

(By kind permission of Heugel et Cie, Editeurs-Propriétaires.) (Delibes, *Sylvia.*)

It is impossible to change from *Pizzicato* to *Arco,* and vice versa, in quicker *tempo* than that of the two preceding examples.

Remark: More time is required to take the bow again after a *Pizzicato* than to pass from an *Arco* to a *Pizzicato* passage.

19.—The quality of the *Pizzicato* is fairly uniform from **Fiddle G** to **E** *in alt:*

but from this E upwards, in proportion as the string becomes shorter, so the tone becomes poorer.

However, here is a *Pizzicato* rising up to **C** *in altissimo,* of which the effect is equally good *forte* or *pianissimo:*

(By kind permission of Heugel et C͞i͞e, Editeurs-Propriétaires.)   (Philipp, *Sérénade,* orchestrated by Malherbe.)

Remark: This final C *in altissimo* ✱ would be impossible if it were not reinforced by the full tone of the chord given to the 2nd Violins. Thus placed, it comes out with a tone nearly as clear as on the Pianoforte.

The last high notes, used alone, become thinner and thinner, but when doubled or accompanied by an open string, they are admirable:

Excellent:

20.—The maximum speed possible for *Pizzicati* played in semiquavers is $\quart$ = 104, and even then the passage must not be long.

Remark: The speed of *Pizzicati* may be considered as unlimited when it is merely a question of plucking the notes of a chord which could be played as a struck chord, e. g.

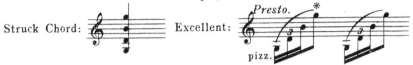

* The slur is necessary, this effect corresponding to the *glissando* on the Harp.

N. B. This descending arpeggio would be possible if the instrument were held the other end up, like a Violoncello.

21.—All the chords that we mentioned in §9 can be arpeggioed:

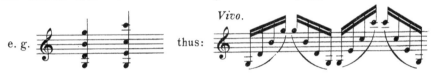

They may also be subdivided into two or more groups:

22.—The old tremolo of our ancestors is passing out of fashion and being replaced by crossed tremolos of the 1st and 2nd Violins, Violas, etc.

However, the former tremolo (X) is more sonorous than the latter (Y), and there are cases when nothing better could be used in order to reach a *fortissimo*.

A tremolo figure may finish off on an unaccented part of the bar, without reaching a culminating point:

(By kind permission of Schott & C⁰, Publishers-Proprietors.)

23.—When the back of the bow is to be employed for a special effect, the words *col legno* are written above the passage.

THE VIOLA.

(Ital., *Viola*. Ger., *Bratsche*. Fr., *Alto*.)

1.— All that has been said about the Violin applies to the Viola, which is in reality nothing but a Violin tuned a fifth lower, and consequently of rather larger dimensions.

Its compass may be said to comprise 3 octaves:

By transposing the positions of the Violin a fifth lower, those of the Viola are obtained; the mechanism and fingering are the same for both instruments.

The only difference lies in the slightly larger dimensions of the Viola, which diminish the *stretching* capabilities of the fingers.

2.— We noted that, on a single string, the hand of a violinist could reach the diminished fifth, and, on two strings, the minor ninth.

On the Viola, the perfect fourth and the octave are the respective limits.

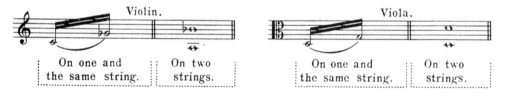

Here is an impossible passage written by an unskilful composer:

Conscientious performers will play the ninth marked with an asterisk ✳ as follows: 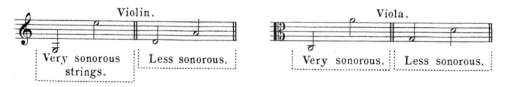, just touching the bass note, as a small hand would do on the Pianoforte; unscrupulous players will leave it out altogether, sounding the higher **E** only.

In either case, they will think very little of the said composer.

3.— As on the Violin, and all four-stringed instruments, the two best strings are the outer ones, the bow not venturing to bring much stress to bear on the two middle strings, for fear of touching one of the neighboring strings.

Double Stops.

4.— Are excellent or possible: all *minor and major sixths.*

All *diminished, minor, and major sevenths.*

All *minor and major thirds.*

All *perfect and augmented fourths.*

All *diminished and augmented fifths.*

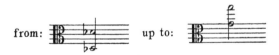

All *octaves.*

All *minor and major seconds.*

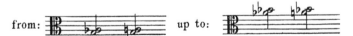

5.— We remarked on P. 151, §8, that the *perfect fifth* on stringed instruments was but approximately true, and we repeat the remark in this connection.   We observed that the extreme limit of *perfect fifths* on the Violin was F C ♪.

  In the case of the Viola, it is B F♯ ♪. It would be very dangerous to go higher in orchestral writing.

Dominant Sevenths and their resolutions.

6.— The crosses + mark the difficult or unsonorous chords. The asterisks * show the resolutions impossible in the minor mode.

Resolutions not specially marked are possible in either mode.

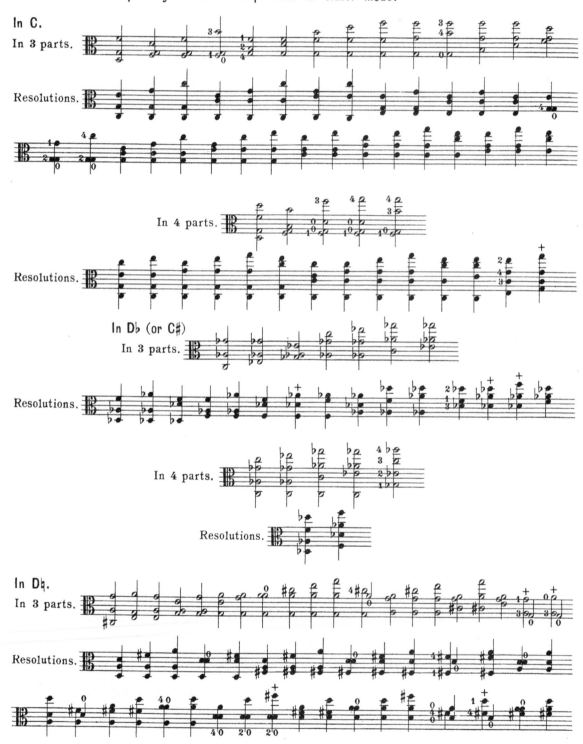

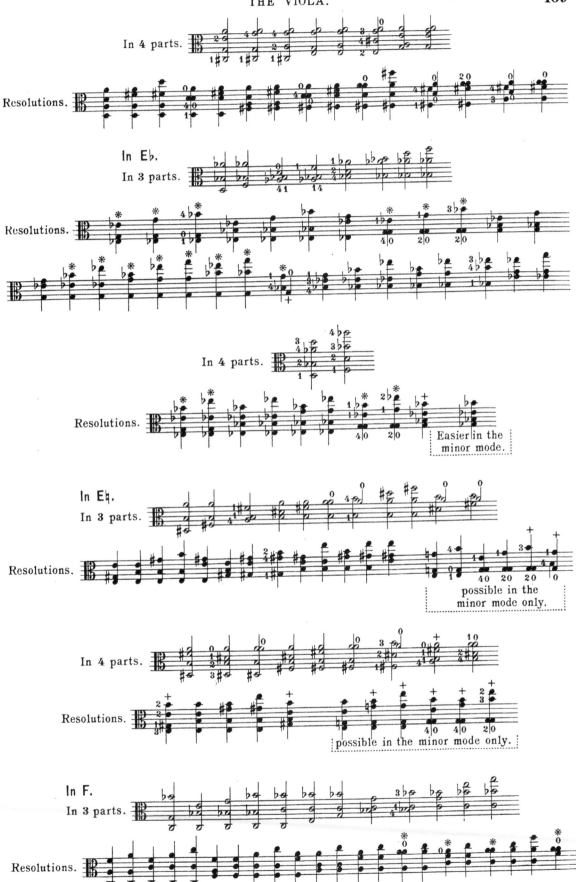

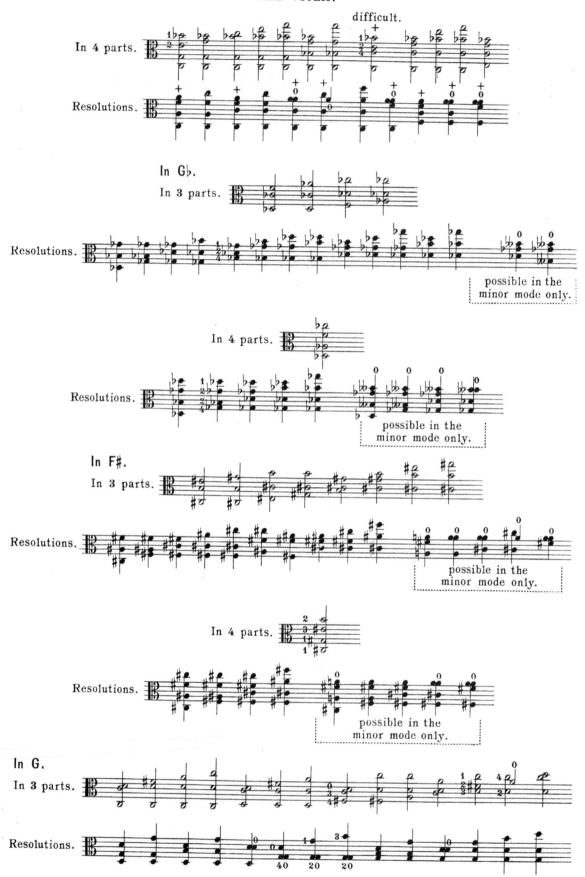

In 4 parts.

Resolutions.

In A♭.

In 3 parts.

Resolutions.

In 4 parts.

Resolutions.

In A♮.

In 3 parts.

Resolutions.

In 4 parts.

In 3 parts, resolutions possible in the minor mode.

possible in the minor mode only.

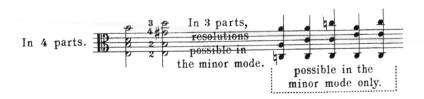

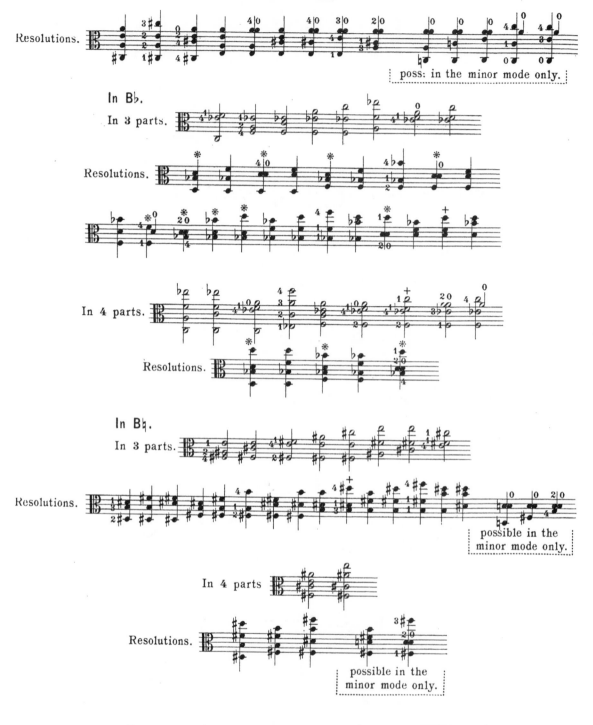

Chords of the Diminished Seventh.

On the three
higher strings.

In 4 parts.

Chords of the Major and Minor Ninth.

In 3 parts.
On the three
lower strings.

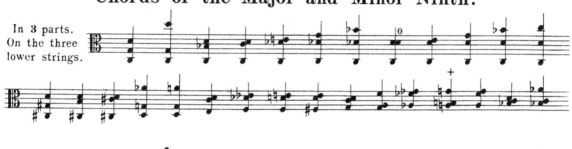

On the three
higher strings.

In 4 parts.

Chords of the Augmented Fifth.

In 3 parts.
On the three
lower strings.

In 3 parts.
On the three
higher strings.

In 4 parts.

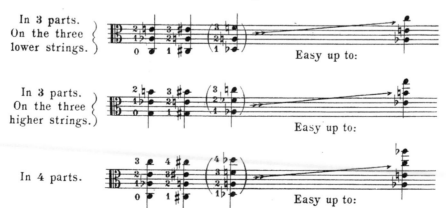

Easy up to:

Easy up to:

Easy up to:

7.— As on the Violin, all these chords can be arpeggioed and subdivided into any kind of groups.

List of Natural Harmonics practicable in the Orchestra.

N. B.   The three upper strings are written in the G clef, to facilitate reading.

In a word, all harmonics can be obtained on the Viola from:

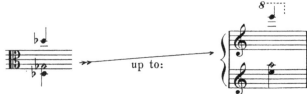

up to:

Remark: As in the case of the Violin (V. P. **161**, §13) a negligent composer may write any note, with a zero above it (from the 4th partial upwards), and leave the choice of the means of execution to the performers:

from: up to:

Below Treble C, he has at his disposal none but natural harmonics, which are limited to the notes of the common major chord on each string (V. List above).

Bowings.

8.— All that was said about Violin bowing applies to Viola bowing. All the varieties: *Grand Détaché, Détaché moyen, Petit Détaché, Martelé, Sautillé, Staccato,* etc., all *slurred, legato,* and *louré* passages are equally practicable on either instrument.

Likewise for the *Pizzicato:* as it seems prudent on the Violin not to go beyond the octave on the first string, let us also be content with the same octave on the first string of the Viola.

As on the Violin, all chords may be converted into arpeggios, or subdivided into 2 or 3 groups, etc. (See above §7).

THE VIOLONCELLO.

(Ital., *Violoncello.*   Ger., *Violoncell.*   Fr., *Violoncelle.*)

1.— Its compass is about three octaves and a third, from Double C to E above Treble C:

This E is here given as the extreme limit in orchestral writing, because it is at once the last sonorous note obtainable by *depressing* the string, and also one of the best *harmonics* on the instrument, so that performers can play it either as an ordinary note, by depressing the string, or as a harmonic, according to circumstances.

Above this E the notes become harsh and painful to the ear. Of course, I am now speaking of the orchestral instrument only, and not of the *Solo Violoncello,* which can go an octave, even an eleventh higher:

(J. Hamelle, Editeur-Propriétaire.)   (Widor, *Concerto.*)

2.— The fingering of the Cello differs from that of the Violin and Viola throughout all the essential part of its compass, i. e. in the lower register.   From Double C to A in the G clef, each semitone is produced by a different finger , but from this A upwards, the fingering is the same as on the Violin. The chromatic scale, so difficult of execution on all the stringed instruments we have so far considered, becomes quite easy and natural in the lower register of the Cello, but above A (in the G clef) it is better to avoid it, when writing for the orchestra.

Such is — owing to the six chromatic degrees which separate each open string from its neighbor — the fingering of the Violoncello; this fingering is the same for all the strings alike, and suits any key.

And this scale can be played very easily, despite the inevitable "shifting" of the hand after each series of four semitones.   In fact, *virtuosi* manage the "shifting" so skilfully that the ear never perceives the change of position.

Thumb Positions.

3.— The highest note obtainable with the ordinary method of fingering is this B♮ 𝄞 ○ .

Above this note, it becomes necessary to employ the thumb as a kind of artificial "nut," the fingering being the same as on the Violin.

"Thumb-positions" are sometimes used in the medium, or even in the low register. Some passages can only be executed in this manner — e. g. octaves, which are always played with one single kind of fingering, viz. *thumb and ring-finger.*

(The sign ϙ indicates the thumb.)

The very difficult figures to be found in *Rheingold* (P. 287 to P. 289) are quite as impracticable *without* the use of the thumb on the G, D, and A strings as they are *with* the employment of the thumb-positions, and whatever means of execution is adopted, it is difficult to secure truth of intonation.

4.— Thumb-positions should, in general, only be employed with considerable care. Skipping suddenly from a note produced by the usual fingering to a note that involves the use of the thumb is very risky, unless, indeed, this note happens to be the first harmonic of an open string, in which case the danger is minimized, because this first harmonic will come out, even if the position of the finger is not mathematically accurate.

Quality of the Strings.

5.— As in the case of the Violin and Viola, the first string of the Cello is the most brilliant, the one to which the melody is usually given, and which creates the most intense impression. The veiled quality of the second string is also very useful. The third string even, may be used in a *solo* with very good effect, but it more frequently has the bass of the harmony to play, like the fourth, whose full quiet tone is able to sustain the weight of a considerable orchestral mass.

On each string, the octave can be reached. However, the admirable effect obtainable on the fourth string of the Violin, where even the eleventh may be reached (P. 150, §5), must not be expected in the case of the Violoncello. It is usually in order to simplify the fingering that whole passages are played on a single string; sometimes, too, this is done for the sake of preserving a uniform tone-color.

6.— The following curious fact is not mentioned, as far as I am aware, in any Treatise on Instrumentation, or in any Violoncello School.

If the fifth be exceeded on the 3ʳᵈ string, four bad notes make their appearance: 𝄢 ♭○ ♭○ ○ ♯○ *; their tone is rough, harsh, incongruous, and uncertain; this is equally true of all Violoncellos used for orchestral purposes,   whoever may be the maker.*

What can this be due to? Why are not A♭, A♮, B♭, B♮ on the fourth string, and B♭, B♮, C, C♯ on the second, equally bad? Who can explain this mystery?

7.— As in the case of the Violin and Viola, the two outer strings, the 1ˢᵗ and 4ᵗʰ, are the most sonorous; the attack can be more vigorous, because the bow is not hampered as it is when playing on the middle strings, where it constantly runs the risk of *grazing* the neighboring strings.

8.— We have noticed that the maximum stretch possible for a violinist's hand, on a single string, is an augmented fourth:

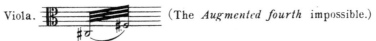

(The *Perfect fifth* impossible.)

and, in the case of the Viola, the player's hand cannot stretch beyond a perfect fourth:

(The *Augmented fourth* impossible.)

but, for the cello-player, the greatest stretch possible is a major third:

(The *Perfect fourth* impossible.)

Pizzicato.

9.— The shorter the string the drier the tone; what is the upper limit for *pizzicato* playing on the Cello? No definite answer can be given, as both performers and instruments vary somewhat; however, I think G♯, A, B♭ may be considered the highest notes which it is safe to write *pizzicato*. G♯ is still sonorous enough to leave behind it a vibration that recalls the bluish haze hovering over a distant landscape on a hot summer's day.

A is duller in tone, but when used as follows it is still satisfactory, thanks to the strengthening effect of the open string:

B♭ a semitone higher is somewhat dry; in case of need it may be written, but should certainly not be exceeded.

10.— As we are dealing with *pizzicati,* I wish to call attention to the fact that some conductors do not trouble much about the way in which the players execute *pizzicato* passages, and hardly seem to suspect of what an amount of variety and manifold shading this style of playing is capable. Truth to say, many teachers deserve equally severe criticism, for if you question their pupils, they will tell you that, their attention not having been directed to this point, they have never thought the matter over, and consequently play in a happy-go-lucky fashion, without any special intent. — This is a mistake.

11.— We have already seen (P. 165, §20) that the maximum speed attainable in a *pizzicato* passage in semi-quavers cannot exceed ♩ = 104. This speed is common to the Violin, the Viola, and the Violoncello. Likewise, the chords mentioned in the final remark of the same paragraph, which can be arpeggioed in any *tempo,* in a fashion analogous to that of Harp *glissandos.*

We also remarked that this *Pizzicato* was very good rising:

but impossible falling:

In the case of the Cello, this figure is equally practicable whether rising or falling. Either of the two following arpeggios may be written; both will sound equally well:

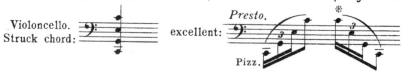

N. B. These descending arpeggios ✻ are very little used, but might sometimes prove very useful.

Double Stops.

12.— Seconds and octaves, which involve the use of the thumb, are to be avoided in orchestral writing, unless one or other of the notes is an open string:

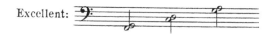

Thirds may be classified as follows:

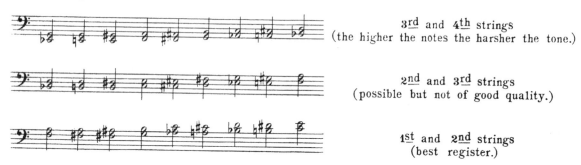

3rd and 4th strings
(the higher the notes the harsher the tone.)

2nd and 3rd strings
(possible but not of good quality.)

1st and 2nd strings
(best register.)

The following thirds are difficult for orchestral players, and could only be used in a *fortissimo:*

From this point onwards, they become more
and more difficult and much harsher in tone.

Perfect and *Augmented* Fourths:

(Avoid writing higher for the orchestra)

Perfect fifths are more satisfactory than on the Violin; they may be considered practicable:

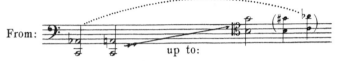

All *major and minor sixths* are excellent:

Minor sevenths are more difficult, and their truth of intonation more doubtful, when they are assigned to orchestral players:

Common Chords.

13.— All *major and minor chords* are easy, up to E♭:

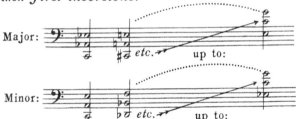

Quite easy too are their *first inversions:*

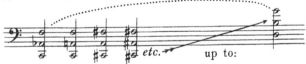

And likewise their *second inversions:*

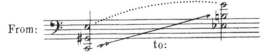

Chords of the augmented fifth:

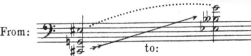

Major chords with diminished fifths:

From:

First inversions of chords of the augmented fifth:

Chords of the diminished fifth:

Their first inversions:

Chords of the dominant seventh:

Chords of the leading seventh: *And their second inversions:*

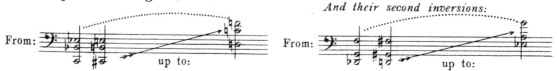

Chords of the diminished seventh:

Quadruple Stops.

14.— The following are practicable:

Common chords:

Their first inversions:

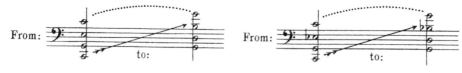

Their second inversions:

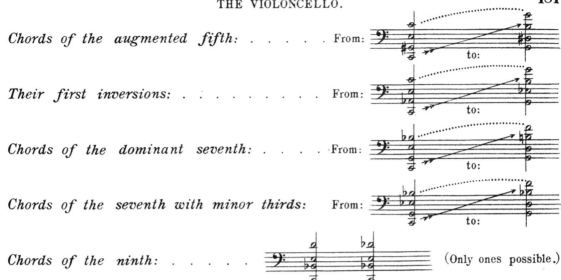

Chords of the augmented fifth: . . . . . From: . . to:

Their first inversions: . . . . From: . . to:

Chords of the dominant seventh: . . . . From: . . to:

Chords of the seventh with minor thirds: From: . . to:

Chords of the ninth: . . . . . (Only ones possible.)

Bowing.

15.— All remarks made concerning Violin bowing apply equally in the case of the Cello; the different varieties, such as *martelé, détaché, sautillé, staccato,* are practicable on all stringed instruments alike. The same holds good of slurs.

However, we must not omit to mention an effect peculiar to the Cello, due to the manner in which the instrument is held by the player, which is just the reverse of the way in which a violinist holds his fiddle. This special effect is obtained by using an up-bow when attacking a chord, in order to produce an impression of great energy; this practice is, of course, exceptional, for the maximum degree of strength on stringed instruments is usually obtained with a down-bow.

Harmonics.

16.— Here follows a list of natural Harmonics:

The limits within which artificial harmonics are practicable are as follows:

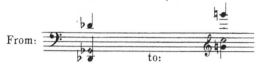

Remark: As in the case of the Violin and the Viola, a careless composer may write any note, placing a zero above it, (but only from the 4<u>th</u> partial upwards):

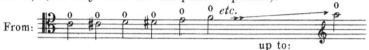

Below Middle C, he will only have natural harmonics at his disposal (See the List of natural harmonics given on P. 181).

Notation.

17.— As in the case of the Horn and the Bass Clarinet, the traditional mode of writing the Cello parts too often leaves room for doubt regarding the composer's intention, and it is high time that musicians should agree to adopt some definite system.

According to a long-established custom, the G clef, whether used from the outset, or only introduced incidentally later on, is regarded in the same light as a 16 ft. organ-stop, the notation being an octave above the actual sounds. When the composer wishes the G clef to retain its usual altitude in the scale of sounds, he is compelled to employ the C clef in the first place, making use of the G clef in the second place only.

However, of late years, there have been numerous protests against this absurd custom. I need only mention Grieg, Reinecke, Hans Huber, Luzatto, N. von Wilm, Ph. Wolfrum, who have always employed the G clef with its true signification, not to speak of Saint-Saëns's *Second Concerto,* in which he uses two staves (the lower one with an F clef, the upper one with a G clef), as if he were writing for the Pianoforte. His system is, of course, the safest.

We must nowadays combine to root out all old-fashioned methods, and agree to use the signs of musical notation with their true meaning only. Disregarding all devious practices, let us always use the F, C, and G clefs at their true altitude: *Ne varientur.*

The Violoncello in the Orchestra.

18.— I need not, in this place, enlarge upon the part it is called upon to play in modern polyphony. Formerly, the Violoncello played the thorough-bass, being so inseparably connected with the Double-bass that only one part was written for the two instruments; the Cello merely served to strengthen the first harmonic of the Double-bass. A melodic part was never given to the Cello alone.

Nowadays, things have changed. The two instruments are written on separate staves, the Violoncello has become a Tenor, the most intense means of expression of the String Quintet, not even excepting the fourth string of the Violin, and the Double-bass is usually left to bear unsupported the enormous weight of the harmonic mass.

All musicians have noticed the following curious musical phenomenon: the Cello alone constitutes a rather weak bass to the harmony (save in some special cases, when the music is calm and peaceful, as in the 2<u>nd</u> act of *Meistersinger,* for example); on the other hand, the Double-bass seems dull and devoid of tonal precision. Yet, when used in combination, the Violoncello and Double-bass constitute the most admirable fundamental tone that could be wished for; it is clear, bright, full, rich, and extremely flexible.

As an illustration of the use of Violoncellos without Double-basses, we give a few bars taken from the exquisite Hans Sachs scene; it will be observed that, in this case, the Celli, although *divisi,* amply suffice to sustain the harmony of the Violins, Violas, and Horns:

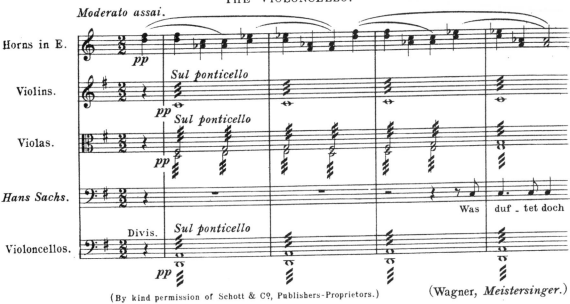

(Wagner, *Meistersinger*.)

Here is another example of Violoncellos by themselves constituting a very satisfactory bass, with nothing more than a high A sounded as a harmonic:

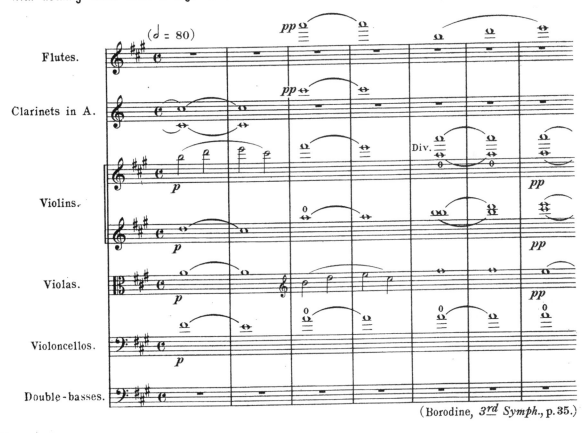

(Borodine, *3rd Symph.*, p. 35.)

N. B.   The composer in this case writes the real note, with a zero above, leaving it to the performer to choose the means of execution.

THE DOUBLE-BASS.

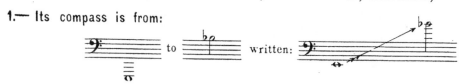

(Ital., *Contrabasso*. Ger., *Kontrabass*. Fr., *Contrebasse*.)

1.— Its compass is from:

Virtuosi can play some still higher notes. They are quite accustomed to C and D (the two notes above B♭), however it is better to avoid these extreme notes in orchestral writing, although Verdi, in *Falstaff,* did not scruple to use E♭ ✳:

(Actual sounds.)

M.ͬ Ed. Nanny, Double-bass soloist at the Opéra-Comique, considers that performers on this instrument should practice the high notes up to G, and he tells of the admirable effects which might be obtained by means of the Double-basses doubling the Celli in unison in *cantabile* passages:

Violoncellos.

Double-basses.

(Actual sounds.)

2.— The Double-bass, corresponding to a 16 ft. pipe, sounds an octave below the written notes. The part is written in the F clef. This instrument is tuned in fourths.

Written: Sounding:

Formerly, the Double-bass had three strings only, and its tone was perhaps better. Even at the present time, *virtuosi* prefer this classical type of instrument for solos, because the smaller number of strings increases the resonance of the sounding-board.

"Without entering into the question of the respective advantages and disadvantages of three-stringed and four-stringed Double-basses," says Bottesini; "without discussing their greater or less depth of tone, I will begin by treating of the true Double-bass, the kind which for the sake of the quality of tone, as well as of easy fingering, is furnished with three strings only."

This three-stringed Double-bass was the one used in the time of Beethoven, who never had the low E of our modern instruments at his disposal, and still less the 16 ft. C which is now obtainable on some Double-basses. He used to write one and the same part for Celli and Double-basses, the latter instruments playing as best they could, and simplifying their part whenever they came to a difficult passage. The low C's at the beginning of the Finale of the 5ᵗʰ Symphony were in his time played in the octave above, just as they are nowadays.

There has been no end of discussion on this subject. For a long time, this fourth string capable of sounding 16 ft. C was supposed to have existed. If it really ever had existed we should find in our museums ten, twenty, ay, thirty specimens of Double-basses with this fabulous C string, side by side with Bach's little Trumpet, whereas, in reality, neither of these will-o'-the-wisps is to be seen in any collection, but in their stead we come across numbers of three-stringed Double-basses. Were they, to use a chemical expression, all volatilized at one and the same time? Is it credible that, whereas instruments used in the time of Louis XIII and Louis XIV are to be seen on all hands, not a single Double-bass dating from 1815 or 1820 can be discovered anywhere? ✳

By their manner of writing, composers manifested for the Double-bass players of yore a contempt and disdain fully justified. "Those men", said a musicographer to me lately, "did not deserve the name of musicians — they were no better than *drawers of water.*"

3.— Nowadays, we have the E string, which might descend to C, provided the size of the instrument were slightly increased, as has been done in the case of the Double-basses used at the Brussels Conservatory, all of which are furnished with five strings, tuned as follows:

These five-string Double-basses are coming into vogue in Germany and England; they are likewise used in the Monte-Carlo orchestra (conducted by Jéhin), not to mention many other places.

Even with the ordinary instruments descending to E, it is possible to obtain one extra low note, without complicating the fingering to any great extent.

However, we must note that the degree of tension of the 4th string is proportionally diminished, so that the low D can be really satisfactory in *piano* passages only; in a *forte* passage it would not be very good.

Our orchestras ought really to possess, besides the ordinary Double-basses, two or three five-string instruments descending to C, like those of the Brussels Conservatory. Just as we have *ascending* Horns and *descending* Horns (P. 57, §3) so we should have *Solo* Double-basses and *Tutti* Double-basses.

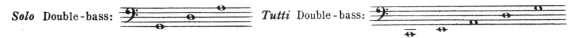

Solo Double-bass: *Tutti* Double-bass:

Fingering.

4.— In the case of the Double-bass, the strings are so long that the maximum stretch possible between the 2nd and 3rd and between the 3rd and 4th fingers is less than a semitone. It is only between the 1st and 2nd fingers that this interval can be reached.

The following figure shows the fingering of the diatonic scale:

(0 = Open String; 0 & 3 = Harmonic.)

(+ = Depressed String, or Harmonic.)

✳ Dr. Riemann calls my attention to the fact that N. W. Koch (Musikalisches Lexikon, 1802) not only speaks of the four-stringed Double-bass (E, A, D, G), as being already known at that time, but even mentions the possibility of descending a tone lower, to D.

5.— It is well not to lose sight of the fact that the bow with which the Double-bass is played is very short; in the case of *piano* holding-notes, the performer is at liberty to change from a down-bow to an up-bow, or *vice-versa,* without attracting undue notice, but in a *forte* each attack of the bow is distinctly audible.

The composer should therefore mark his intention clearly, and determine the exact points at which the change of bow is to take place.

Quality of the Strings.

6.— The Double-bass is not so much a melodic instrument as a prop on which the whole of the orchestra leans. Its four strings of catgut (of which the two lowest are covered with brass wire) may be considered as being all equally good, although the most sonorous register lies between:

The great *virtuosi* of the present day can succeed in rendering the 1st string as intensely expressive as a Cello string.

If Beethoven were still alive he would certainly write a *Concerto* to please Double-bass players, for they are no longer "drawers of water," but first-rate musicians.

Shakes and Tremolos.

7.— All major and minor shakes are currently used, and possible up to B♭:

(extreme limit.)

The minor third is only practicable from G♯ upwards on the 4th string, from C♯ upwards on the 3rd string, from F♯ upwards on the 2nd string, and from B♮ upwards on the 1st string, i. e. only the upper notes can be used, to the exclusion of the two first tones on each string, the reason being that it is only at this distance from the nut that the intervals become small enough to allow of a minor third "stretch" between the 1st and 4th fingers.

Tremolos practicable on one and the same string and that may be written without danger.

On the 4th String.

On the 3rd String.

On the 2nd String.

On the 1st String.

Staccato passages in octaves are very good, whatever the rate of movement:

Legato, these octave skips are impossible in quick *tempo.*

Pizzicato.

8.— The *Pizzicato* can be used in any part of the instrument's compass, but the most sonorous register lies between:

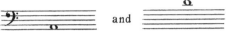

Pizzicati are frequently written up to A and even B♭:

but at such heights the tone becomes dry and unattractive, losing all charm.

Remark: *Pizzicato* playing should be avoided in very quick *tempo,* on account of the fatigue it causes the performer, who is soon exhausted, and therefore plays without vigor. When obliged to employ the *Pizzicato* in rapid *tempo,* the composer will do well to write for the Double-basses *divisi,* giving a few bars to each group alternately:

Double-basses.
(*Divisi*)

Double stops.

9.— The following double stops are practicable:

All, *minor and major thirds:*   from: up to:

All *perfect fourths:* . . . . . from: to:

All *perfect fifths:* . . . . . . from: to:

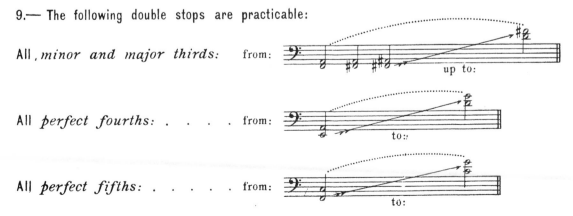

10.—Sixths are impossible, except in the high register, where they can be played by *virtuosi,* but are impracticable in the orchestra; the same remark applies to sevenths and octaves (unless the lower note happens to be an open string):

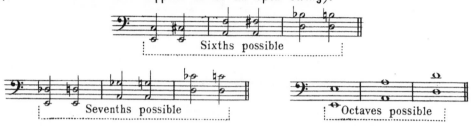

The following perfectly sonorous passage illustrates the use of double stops:

(E. Nanny.)

Harmonics.

11.— On the Double-bass, natural harmonics are alone practicable, because, as we already know, artificial harmonics are usually obtained by means of a *stretch* of a fourth, and Double-bass players cannot reach this interval on one and the same string. Even among the natural harmonics some are hardly practicable, viz. those of the very thick E string, on which only the 4th and 5th upper partials can be produced:

List of Harmonics.
(ACTUAL SOUNDS.)

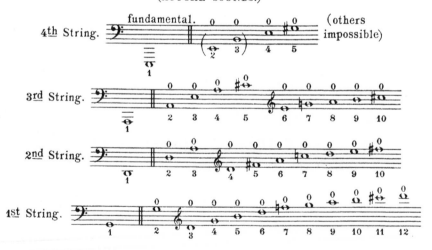

It would be dangerous, in orchestral writing, to make use of all the harmonics tabulated above; it is better to err on the side of over-caution and only employ the following:

By writing harmonics for the Double-basses *divisi,* chords of an admirable tone-colo. can be obtained:

Harmonics:

"Owing to the great length of its strings," says Berlioz, "the Double-bass is well adapted for the production of harmonics." Verdi has proved the correctness of Berlioz's remark by successfully employing the harmonics of the Double-bass in the 3rd act of *Aïda.*

Bowing.

12.—All remarks made in connection with the bowing of the Viola and Violoncello apply equally in the case of the Double-bass (save the restriction mentioned in §5 concerning the short bow of the Double-bass).

We repeat that strength, accent, and rhythm exclusively depend on the use of down-bows.

So much is this the case that when a composer neglects to mark the bowing, if the passage be *forte* the performer of his own accord makes use of down-bows:

Double-bass.

Runs.

13.—Rapid runs are very frequently written for the Double-bass, and are extremely effective and powerful:

(Mozart, *Symphony.*)

(Berlioz, *Invocation à la Nature.*)

(Gluck, *Armide.*)

(Widor, *Les Pêcheurs de St. Jean.*)
(By kind permission of Heugel et Cie, Editeurs-Propriétaires.)

In all the examples given above, the Celli play the same notes as the Double-basses, with which they blend as perfectly as does a fundamental tone with its first harmonic.

By themselves the Violoncellos seem weak, especially when playing on the two middle strings.

On the other hand, passages played by the Double-basses quite alone do not come out clearly, the deep notes becoming heavier and thicker the lower they are written. Yet when used together, these two instruments form the brightest, most supple, and most powerful bass in the orchestra.

It is the same phenomenon as that observable on the Organ: when to a dull, slow-speaking 16 ft. Bourdon any one of the 8 ft. stops — even the weakest — is added, an astonishingly robust and tonally precise quality is obtained.

The Mute.
(SORDINO)

So far, we have not, when treating of the stringed instruments, referred to the Mute, because it seemed needless to describe such a well known accessory.

The Mute is employed to damp the strength of the vibrations of the strings of Violins, Violas, and Violoncellos, while it at the same time renders their *timbre* more penetrating.

(It is better not to use it much in passages intended to be played on the 4<u>th</u> string of the Violin, because, in this case, it somewhat too effectually muffles the tone of the instrument.)

The Mute is not employed on the Double-bass.

When all the other stringed instruments are muted, the strength of the bass part may be suitably balanced by assigning it to *one* or two Double-basses only, the indication *Solo* or *Due Soli* being employed in that case. In this manner, the parts will be so well-balanced that no one will ever perceive that *all* the Strings are not muted.

It would seem that the Mute was still in use in the time of Berlioz, who says: "Mutes are employed on the Double-bass, just as on the other bowed instruments, but the effect obtained is not very characteristic; the Mute only somewhat diminishes the strength of the vibrations, rendering the quality darker and duller."

Tempora mutantur: nowadays the Mute is no longer employed by Double-bass players.

The Bridge.
(PONTICELLO)

"The tone of bowed instruments varies considerably according to the part of the string on which the bow is brought to bear. Whereas, close to the bridge the maximum brilliancy is obtained, above the finger-board the quality is weak and dull."

When the bow is used near the bridge the *timbre* of the instrument is metallic and, so to speak, *glittering:* while incomparably powerful in an impressive *ensemble,* the tone-color becomes *sparkling* and ethereal in *pianissimo* passages.

A similar change in the *timbre* of the Harp may be observed when the strings are plucked close to the sounding-board: it is near the bridge of the bowed instruments and near the sounding-board of the Harp that the strings can bear the greatest degree of tension.

Hence this peculiar effect, this characteristic quality.

The Back of the Bow.
(LEGNO)

Some composers, e. g. Meyerbeer in *L'Africaine,* Wagner in *Meistersinger,* Saint-Saëns in the *Danse Macabre,* have succeeded in making effective use of notes produced by striking the strings with the back of the bow.

The tone thus obtained is very curious, resembling a very dry and short *pizzicato,* which recalls the pattering of hail-stones on plate-glass. Although strange and characteristic enough, this effect should not be used without a very marked intention.

Here follows a list of French, Italian, and German expressions used in connection with the Strings.

French.	*Italian.*	*German.*
Pizzicato. . .	Pizzicato. . .	Pizzicato.
Archet. . . .	Arco.	Bogen.
avec Sourdines. . .	con Sordini. . .	mit Dämpfer.
sans Sourdines. . .	senza Sordini. . .	{ ohne Dämpfer. / die Dämpfer fort.
Divisés. . . .	Divisi. . . .	Geteilt.
Unis.	{ Tutti. . . . . / Insieme. . . .	Zusammen.
sur le Chevalet. . . .	sul Ponticello. . .	sul Ponticello.
sur la Touche. . . .	sul Tasto.	sul Tasto.
sur la 4e Corde. . .	sul G.	sul G.
Soutenu. . . .	Sostenuto. . .	{ Ausgehalten. / Getragen.
Staccato. . . .	Staccato. . .	Staccato.

TABLE
showing the compass of the various Instruments.
(also see p.213)

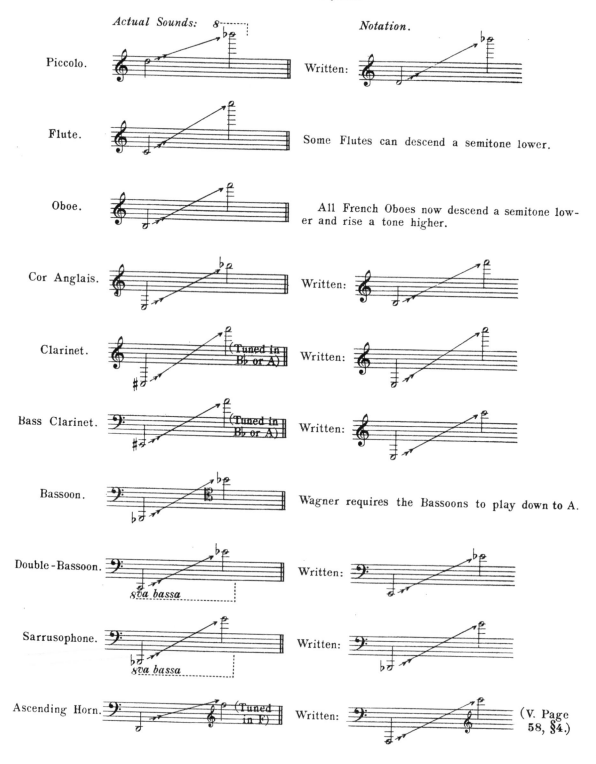

Piccolo. *Actual Sounds:* / *Notation.* Written:

Flute. Some Flutes can descend a semitone lower.

Oboe. All French Oboes now descend a semitone lower and rise a tone higher.

Cor Anglais. Written:

Clarinet. (Tuned in B♭ or A) Written:

Bass Clarinet. (Tuned in B♭ or A) Written:

Bassoon. Wagner requires the Bassoons to play down to A.

Double-Bassoon. *8va bassa* Written:

Sarrusophone. *8va bassa* Written:

Ascending Horn. (Tuned in F) Written: (V. Page 58, §4.)

193

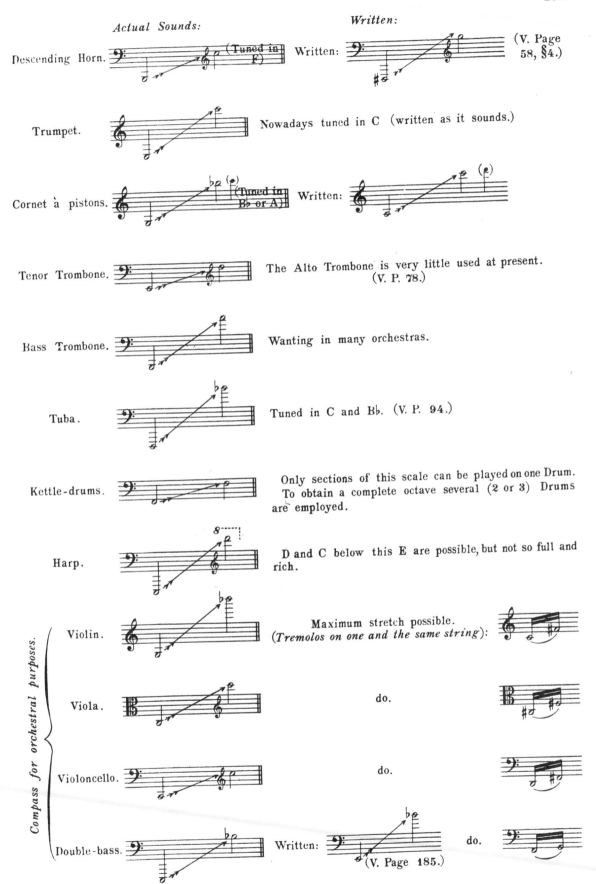

194

List of Shakes practicable on Woodwind Instruments.

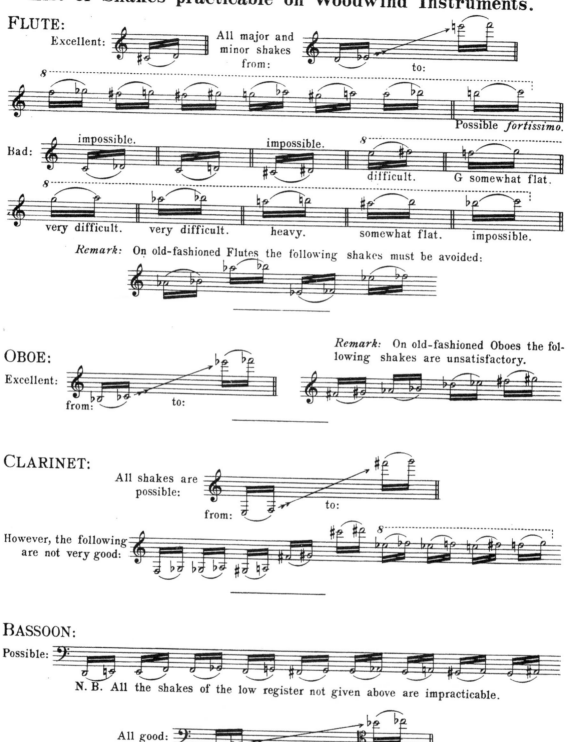

List of Harmonics.

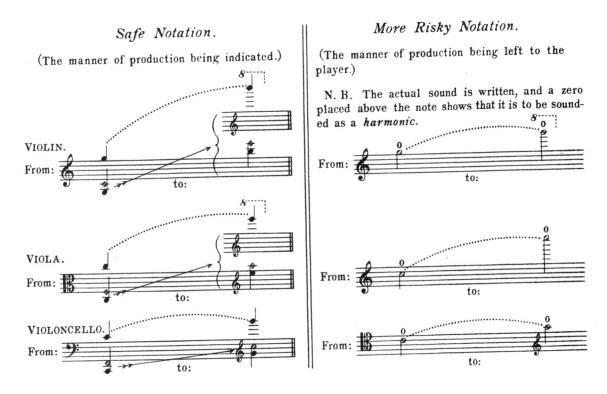

Safe Notation.

(The manner of production being indicated.)

More Risky Notation.

(The manner of production being left to the player.)

N. B. The actual sound is written, and a zero placed above the note shows that it is to be sounded as a *harmonic*.

VIOLIN.

VIOLA.

VIOLONCELLO.

DOUBLE-BASS.

As a fourth on this instrument constitutes too great a stretch for the fingers, Double-bass players do not make use of artificial harmonics; the only harmonics that may be written for them are the natural ones between the 2nd and 6th, 7th, or 8th upper partials (See list on Page 188.)

The only harmonics lower than those given above which the composer has at his disposal are the natural ones, i. e. the **2nd** and **3rd** upper partials.

(V. for the Violin P. **160**; for the Viola P. **174**; for the Violoncello P. **181**; for the Double-bass P. **188**.)

Remark: The 2nd upper partials of two neighboring strings may be safely used as double-stops on any one of the instruments of the String Quartet.

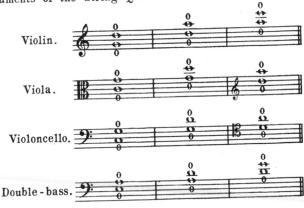

Double-Stops in Orchestral writing.

An interval played as a double-stop on two strings of one and the same instrument is heavier, and not so pure and flexible as when played by two different instruments.

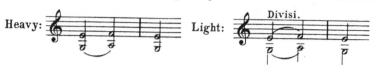

In *piano* passages, double-stops are not very flexible, not very well adapted for modulating purposes, and their truth of intonation is very doubtful. Double-stops are most frequently given to the Violas, in the heart of the orchestra, and in the best part of the instrument's compass. Two parts are also frequently written for the Violas, each playing double-stops.

* * * *

The paramount qualification necessary to a symphonic composer consists in knowing how to write for the Strings; if they are properly treated the rest is of secondary importance. To acquire this knowledge there is only one way, and that is to *read and listen,* to hear and mark. Supposing the student knows the standard compositions of the classic masters well enough to be able to write out from memory a given page of Beethoven, then let him study modern compositions, and consult the works of such musicians as the following:

In *Germany:*   Humperdinck, Richard Strauss, Max Reger, Hindemith.

In *Austria:*   Hugo Wolf, Goldmark, Bruckner, G. Mahler, A. Berg, Dohnanyi. Schoenberg

In *Italy:*   Puccini, Martucci, Leoncavallo, Mascagni, Wolff-Ferrari, Respighi, Malipiero.

In *Russia:*   Rimsky-Korsakow, Glazounow, Liadow, Borodine, Tchaikovsky, Stravinsky, Prokofief, Shostakovitch.

In *England:*   Mackenzie, Villiers-Stanford, Elgar, Vaughan Williams, Holst, Ireland, Delius, Bax, Bliss, Walton, Lambert, Moeran, Britten, Rubbra, Gordon Jacob, Malcolm Arnold, Alan Rawsthorne, Lennox Berkeley, Alan Bush, Humphrey

In *France:*   Berlioz, Bizet, Debussy, Ravel, Dukas, Fauré, Busser.   ⌊Searle.

In *America:*   Mac Dowell, Chadwick, Bloch, Copland, Roy Harris, Gershwin, Piston.

In *Norway & Sweden:*   Grieg, Sinding, Svendsen, Nielsen.

In *Czechoslovakia:*   Smetana, Dvorak, Novak, Martinů, Janaçék.

In *Spain:*   Falla, Turina.

In *Switzerland:*   Honneger, Frank Martin.

In *Finland:*   Sibelius, Palmgren.

and many others; nothing is more instructive than studying and comparing the methods of various composers, art being based upon observation rather than upon set formulæ.

Conclusion.

The primary object of this work having been to analyze and describe the technique of the instruments composing a modern orchestra, I have not been able to deal with the voice.

And indeed, would an analysis or description suffice for the treatment of such a subject? Is it from a method that the singer learns his craft?

Never a day passes without a musical composer consulting a professional on a Cor Anglais note, or on a Clarinet shake. How much more necessary it would be to go to the "shop o-ver the way" and ask advice of the singers!

The capabilities of the Cor Anglais and of the Clarinet can, at the worst, be studied up in a book, but the human voice is a far more complex instrument.

Singing must be learned by experience. Many composers perfectly well acquainted with the orchestra, know nothing of the art of writing for the voice. You will meet composers who do not so much as suspect that a Soprano must be treated differently from a Tenor, re-quiring the former to enunciate on *G, A,* and *B in alt,* and the latter to sing as low as is possible for a Soprano.

A composer if unable to sing himself, should at least know how others sing.

* * *

It was no part of my program to treat of the grouping of instruments, of balance and contrast, for let me repeat that the present book is no complete treatise on orchestration, but simply a manual intended to give some account of the progress made in instrument-making within the last fifty years.

Let us, however, summarize the most essential principles of our art:

(**1.**) Write your orchestral music so that each group can be heard without the others.

Just as an army comprises three arms, viz. Infantry, Cavalry, and Artillery, so the Or-chestra consists of Strings, Woodwind, and Brass.

Just as each of the three arms must be capable of action and self-defence independently of the other two, so must it be with the three groups of a symphonic orchestra. Imagine that at the first rehearsal the Woodwind will be read first, the Brass next, and the Strings last. Each group apart must give the sensation of complete harmony, with its *true* bass, and a fairly precise idea of the total effect.

(2.) Write in such a fashion that each musician may understand the part he plays in the orchestra.

The performers who are called upon to interpret your musical ideas should be able to judge at first sight whether you have intended their respective instruments to stand out conspicuously in the fore-ground, or to play a secondary but nevertheless tolerably important part, or whether you have meant them to keep entirely in the background. However difficult the work may be, it will immediately dawn on them, and they will do themselves justice in rendering it. The conductor will be able to concentrate his attention on the main movements, details will fall into line of themselves, the performers, dominated by the firm will of the composer, will spontaneously produce the necessary intensity of sound.

(3.) Change your orchestration when you change key.

It is evident that neither in Music nor in Painting any definite rules can be given as to when and how the various colors and different degrees of light and shade should be contrasted. When, it might be asked, should the Woodwind be substituted for the Strings?

This question would be of the same order as this other query: when should a modulation be made? These enquiries will always be unanswerable from the technical point of view.

Satirists would doubtless reply: "when nothing remains to be said."

However, this answer is only of a sentimental order. Is any other possible?

If common sense forbids us even to search for a rule, we may yet be allowed to make a comparison and draw a conclusion by analogy.

Modulating is like leaving one's home and setting out for India, China, or Japan, there to behold novel landscapes, under a sky of a different hue.

Now, it is logical that the same instinct which prompts us to modulate should likewise tell us to change our tone-color.

The two things go together; if we take one, we are immediately tempted to accept the other, but, of course, Art admits of no hard-and-fast rules.

(4.) Keep your instruments in the register where their tone is of best quality.

Avoid the extremely high notes. If, for a special effect, you are obliged to make use of them, do not do so for any length of time.

The lip-pressure required to produce the high notes of the Horn and Trumpet is so great that no player can bear the strain long. Let us take a lesson from a Brass Band: at the beginning of a piece each performer seems to be blowing harder than his neighbor, but after a while their enthusiasm abates in proportion to their diminishing strength, and, if the piece is at all long, hardly any volume of sound is left towards the end.

The great masters always wrote logically and clearly; they never lost sight of the practical means of execution.

APPENDIX
by
GORDON JACOB

FOREWORD

Some considerable time has now elapsed since the original publication of this work, yet, in spite of the many changes which have taken place during that period of ceaseless musical activity and constant experiment and development, the technique of orchestral instruments has remained for the most part fundamentally unaltered.

Where the latest practice and methods have been found to conflict with Widor's statements this has been pointed out, but the greater part of the Appendix has been devoted to the use of the various instruments by composers in recent times. No musical examples have been quoted, and the Appendix will be of little use unless the scores of the works of modern composers are studied carefully and in detail.

It is highly important that students should gradually build up for themselves a library of miniature scores. These are comparatively inexpensive, but if it is found impossible to afford to buy them they may now be borrowed from many public libraries. The study of whole scores is of infinitely greater value than that of the short extracts which are all that orchestration books have space to give, and the student who has not the enthusiasm, initiative and enterprise to dig for himself in the inexhaustible mine of printed scores will not go far.

In this connexion the list of composers to be found on p.196 will be found useful.

Ewell, Surrey
October 1945

CHAPTER I
(p. 11, Widor)

THE WOODWIND

The Flute

In addition to the composers whose works are recommended for study by Widor, the following should be noted by the student:

Rimsky-Korsakoff (e.g., *Scheherazade, Spanish Rhapsody*).

Debussy (e.g., *Prelude à l'apres midi d'un faune, Iberia*).

Ravel (e.g., *Daphnis et Chloe, Rhapsodie Espagnole*).

Stravinsky (e.g., *Fire Bird, Petrouchka, Octet for Wind Instruments, Sacre du Printemps*).

The modern French school, following the example of Fauré and Debussy, exploits the low notes of the flute to great effect. The bottom octave of the flute is somewhat deceptive in regard to power. When heard alone these notes are rich and full but they are very easily covered up by other instruments and therefore should be given the minimum of accompaniment. In passages for Wind alone it is often advisable to give the principal melodic line to the Oboe, the Flute being placed below it. If the reverse method is adopted the line given to the Oboe will stand out too clearly and the melody (on the Flute) will be obscured. If the Flute melody lies above the stave it can hold its own but, as Widor points out, the Flute is, more often than not, used to double a wind instrument or the violins in the octave above to give brightness and clarity. The Clarinet-Flute octave combination is a smoother sound than that of Oboe and Flute though the latter is often employed effectively.

The combination of Bassoon and Flute or of Clarinet and Flute two octaves apart is woody and pithy. The former was quite often employed by Mozart and Haydn, the latter is a more modern tone-colour and is best suited to rapidly moving figures. Mozart was also fond of the three-octave combination Bassoon-Violins-Flute.

Another effective combination is that of Bassoon and Flute in actual unison. This is, of course, very limited in range, as the compasses of the instruments only overlap for about an octave upwards from middle C.

The Piccolo

When a composer writes for two Flutes he usually employs two lines of score for them in order that the second Flute may interchange with Piccolo. When three Flutes are used the third player does this. This procedure is adopted in order to keep the best player for Flute solos and not to interefere with his embouchure. There is no reason however why both, or, in the case of three players, all the players should not change to Piccolo. Suitable occasions for this are rare, of course, and it should very seldom be necessary to use more than one Piccolo.

The Piccolo can be used as an upward extension of the Flute in a very high-pitched solo passage; the melody is handed on from Flute to Piccolo and back again, and skilful players can give the effect of the phrase being played by a single performer.

But it is in the tutti that the Piccolo is most useful. It imparts immense brilliance to a fully scored passage and adds bite to the highest registers of the violins.

In soft passages it can add a charming piquancy if used staccato in octaves with the Flute especially if the passage is such that pizzicato strings, and possibly Harp and Glockenspiel, can be associated with it.

The Piccolo is above all a virtuoso instrument. and rapid runs and trills form its natural element. It is however so high in pitch that it is rarely used undoubled at the octave below.

In the double octave above the Clarinet the Piccolo is of excellent effect in rapid and skittish passages, and it is very incisive at the double octave above the muted Trumpet. In *Kikimora* Liadov uses muted Trumpet, Xylophone and Piccolo together in strongly marked rhythmic groups of notes.

The Bass Flute

Widor was right in prophesying a future for the Bass Flute in G. Examples of its use can be found in Holst's *Planets*, Ravel's *Daphnis et Chloe* and Stravinsky's *Sacre du Printemps*; but that is, however, still a rarity and if a part is written for it, this must be cued in for Clarinet or Bassoon. This instrument has a marked individuality and should gradually establish itself more and more firmly in the orchestra. It is useful both as a solo instrument and in combination with other wood-wind instruments. Ravel and Stravinsky in the works mentioned above use it chiefly for solo work, but Holst discovered the chilly effect of three Flutes and a Bass Flute moving slowly about as a harmonic block of successive common chords.

The Bass Flute has the same written compass as the ordinary Flute, but sounds a fourth below. The composer therefore must write his Bass Flute a fourth higher than the sounds intended.

The Oboe

It is best to avoid altogether the two highest notes (F♯ and G) of this instrument. The best register is from about F above middle C to the B flat above the staff, but these limits must of course often be exceeded. Notes below the D above middle C are difficult to control and it is unwise to write them *piano* or *pianissimo*. Dvorak in the slow movement of his 'Cello concerto writes such notes, and Sibelius is rather given to doing the same, but the student is warned not to imitate these masters of orchestration in this respect though he may derive immense benefit in other ways through a study of their scores. Sibelius obtains a very characteristic and rather sombre tone-colour from Oboe and Clarinet in octaves, both fairly low in their registers.

A very striking use of the Oboe is to be found in the slow movement of Elgar's second symphony where it wanders about in triplet rhythm in complete contrast to the rest of the orchestra, its part being marked "molto rubato, quasi ad lib" (the passage is on pages 74 and 75 of the score). This highly poetical use of the Oboe bears the authentic stamp of genius.

Since Widor's book was first published great strides in Oboe technique have been made particularly in Great Britain owing to the example of Leon Goossens. Not only has the flexibility and power of execution extended in scope but the instrument has become in greater measure than before a vehicle of musical expression. The playing of Goossens and of his most gifted pupils has led British composers to write concertos and works of chamber music which exploit what is virtually the new art of Oboe-playing. Some of these works test the powers of even a Leon Goossens pretty severely but never unduly, and though solo works cannot be taken as models for orchestral writing they show what are the possibilities of the instrument in the hands of a great player. If Widor were now to rewrite his book he would certainly expunge the first sentence which appears under the head "Articulation" on page 21, though admittedly the Oboe cannot yet rival the Flute in agility.

The Oboe d'amore

A good many oboists now possess this instrument in addition to Oboe and Cor Anglais, and some modern composers have written parts for it e.g. Strauss in his *Sinfonia Domestica*, Ravel in his *Bolero*, etc.), but it is unsafe to use it unless one is making an orchestration for an orchestra in which it is known that the instrument is available. The tone, as Widor says, has great charm, lacking the heavy rather tragic quality of the Cor Anglais and at the same time being rather smoother and less pungent than the Oboe. The notation is the same as for Clarinet in A.

The Cor Anglais

All professional oboists can be relied upon to possess a Cor Anglais and, just as the second or third Flute player is often called upon to play Piccolo, so the second or third oboist can interchange with Cor Anglais. It is however preferable not to change about continually as the player has to have time to adapt himself to the change. In the case of small orchestras which only contain one Oboe-player these changes may be required fairly frequently but the orchestrator should do his utmost to avoid all but absolutely necessary changes. As a rule, where a work is scored for three oboists the third plays Cor Anglais throughout. The Cor Anglais, owing to its extremely prominent and characteristic *timbre*, is essentially a solo instrument. Its tone-colour is particularly suited to music of a melancholy cast, and in illustration of this one thinks immediately of Sibelius's *Swan of Tuonela* which is practically a solo throughout for Cor Anglais. In this magnificently sombre poem an extremely desolate and forlorn effect is produced by this means. Another locus classicus not mentioned by Widor is the slow movement of Dvorak's *New World* symphony. Here the solo lies within the compass of the Oboe, but, as it would lie rather low for that instrument, the Cor Anglais was chosen in order to obtain far better tone and a much greater degree of poetical beauty. The use of the Oboe would here resemble a rather raucous bagpipe whereas the Cor Anglais evokes an atmosphere of distance and mystery. Elgar, who as a rule prefers mixed tone colours to give the rich and opulent effects he loved, rather than the pure prime colours of solo instruments, uses the Cor Anglais combined in unison with Violas, 'Cellos, Clarinets and Horns, and well it helps to bring into prominence melodic lines in the tenor register of the orchestra. The American composer Aaron Copland has written an excellent short tone poem called *Quiet City* for Cor Anglais, Trumpet and Strings which is full of imaginative fantasy, and the English composer Ruth Gipps has provided the only example known to the writer of a quintet for Cor Anglais and Strings.

The Cor Anglais is above all a romantic and expressive instrument but, like the Oboe, its sharp biting staccato can be used on occasion for humorous or spiteful effects as Strauss, for instance, has shown in the *Critics* section of *Ein Heldenleben*. Almost any modern score will show effective instances of its use, and its unique character has earned for it a permanent place on the orchestral palette.

The Heckelphone

The Baritone Oboe mentioned by Widor is almost identical with the Heckelphone. This instrument is as rare as, or even rarer than the Bass Flute, but composers sometimes demand it, e.g., Holst in the *Planets* and Delius in his first *Dance Rhapsody*, both of which are scored for extra large orchestras. It probably has a future in the orchestra as its snarling tone is unique, but the composer who hopes for performances of his work will do well not to write an indispensable part for it.

The rarity of comparitively new instruments and the reluctance of composers to use them is sometimes put down to the conservatism of musicians, a quality more legendary than real. The true explanation is an economic one. Orchestral players naturally hesitate to sink capital in the purchase of an instrument which they will only be called upon to play once a year or less, and thus a vicious circle is set up: few instruments because few parts to play— few parts to play because few instruments. Can it be wondered at that it takes many years to establish a new instrument in the orchestra?

The Clarinet

Owing to recent improvements in Clarinet manufacture the old restrictions in regard to key have largely, if not entirely disappeared. Indeed the writer has been informed that in America the A Clarinet is almost unknown in all but large symphony orchestras. It is however still advisable to use as easy keys as possible for the sake of those who still possess older types of instruments or who are unpractised in playing in remoter keys. The difference in tone-colour and brilliance between the B flat and A Clarinets is entirely imaginary. The fact that Mozart and Brahms wrote for the A Clarinet in their quintets may have accounted for the idea that it has a more distinguished quality of tone than the B flat instrument, but actually there is more difference in tone between two different players on the same instrument than between the two instruments played by the same artist. In military bands the A Clarinet is never used and this fact too may be partly responsible for the idea that the B flat instrument is the more brilliant in tone because of the rather blatant style formerly cultivated in military bands owing to open-air conditions, and perhaps some lack of sensitivity as well. One hastens to add, in fairness to present-day military bandmasters and players, that nowadays a much higher standard of excellence in the matter of tone and musicianship exists than was formerly the case.

There is little more to add to Widor's excellent resumé of Clarinet technique except to mention a few of the works written specially for it in recent years: among these Stanford's *Clarinet Concerto* holds a prominent place and Arthur Bliss' *Quintet for Clarinet and Strings* is a work of great merit (Novello). Herbert Howells has also written a *Rhapsodic Quintet* which shows a keen realization of the possibilities of the medium (Stainer and Bell for the Carnegie Trust) and Arnold Bax's *Sonata with Piano* is of considerable interest.

It is needless to quote orchestral passages as these abound in every score. Scale-passages — especially chromatic scales — can be played with ease and great rapidity and everyone knows the effect of Clarinet arpeggios and the sweetness of expression of the medium register of the instrument, not to mention what Widor calls the Freischütz effect of the Chalumeau register.

The Bass Clarinet

The Bass Clarinet in A no longer exists, that in B flat being used in all keys. The second or third Clarinet player may be called upon to change to Bass Clarinet if so desired, but it is better not to change in the course of a movement unless it is quite unavoidable to do so.

This instrument is not solely a melodic one. It can form an admirable bass to the woodwind and with the double basses makes a strong enough support for wood-wind and strings *piano*. An extra key enables the low E flat to be produced (sounding D flat) so that the bottom note of the now discarded Bass Clarinet in A can be obtained. Widor votes for the F clef. The player however prefers the G clef as he can then read and finger the part as though he were playing on an ordinary Clarinet. We therefore beg leave to differ on this point. Scores in this country are nearly always printed with Bass Clarinet in the G clef.

The small Clarinet in E flat

Elgar used an E flat Clarinet in his symphonies to strengthen the flutes, while Strauss and a few others have also employed it, but it has not been generally absorbed into the orchestra.

The Bassoon

There is nothing to add to the excellent remarks of Widor on the subject of this instrument except perhaps to draw the student's attention to Elgar's and Sibelius's Bassoon parts. There are some excellent Bassoon solos in Elgar's *Falstaff* for instance, and Sibelius writes in a most telling way for it, often using two Bassoons in thirds or even seconds very low down in a way that looks peculiar on paper but comes out extraordinarily well in sound. It is a mistake to regard the Bassoon too much as a bass instrument— two Bassoons sustaining thirds in the medium tenor register for instance can give unobtrusive substance to an orchestral texture, and a Bassoon doubles almost any other instrument effectively in the octave or double octave below.

The Double Bassoon and Sarrusophone

In this country the Double Bassoon is of far more frequent appearance than the Sarrusophone. The modern instrument is fairly flexible and agile, and in the hands of a good player who has specialised in its use it is capable of a good deal more execution than Widor gives it credit for. Everyone must agree, however, with his strictures on the part written by Beethoven for this instrument in the choral symphony. Beethoven no doubt wrote 'col basso' in his score for page after page and gave it no further thought. This is a grim warning to the student to write nothing in his score without being fully conscious of its effect both on the audience and the staying power of the performer.

CHAPTER II
(p. 51, Widor)

THE BRASS

The Natural Horn

It is good training for the student to confine himself sometimes in his orchestration exercises to the use of the Natural Horn. This teaches him economy of means, a good foundation for effective horn writing (just as the study of strict counterpoint sows the seeds of good Free Contrapuntal writing). It also inculcates a healthy respect for the resourcefulness of the old masters. In doing this he should be very sparing in the use of stopped notes, just as they were.

The same remarks apply to the Natural Trumpet.

The Valve Horn

The present writer has not come across the across the ascending and descending Horns referred to on p.57 par.3, which in any case does not affect the attitude of the orchestrator very much. The system is probably entirely confined to instruments made by some particular French maker.

Widor's treatment of the Horn is very precise and illuminating and there is little to add to it except to draw attention to the great freedom and flexibility of modern Horn parts. Strauss, Elgar and Stravinsky, to mention but three orchestral masters, expect things from the Horns which would have made older composers' hair stand on end. But the Horn is not by nature a virtuoso instrument, and most of the time it is best employed in long holding-notes or in melodic phrases of a fairly vocal nature. Forsyth points out the effectiveness of cunningly constructed chromatic harmony for three or four muted Horns.

The German Horn has lately come to be used a good deal in this country rather than the French Horn. In some ways this is to be regretted as its wider bore takes off some of the noble poetic character of the instrument. It is, however, more certain in execution than the French Horn and is for this reason favoured by many players and some conductors. Sensitive, artistic playing can compensate in great measure for the naturally somewhat inferior tone of the German Instrument.

Shakes (p.61 par.8) It is not quite true to say that shakes on the horn are always performed by the lips and never by the valves, though the lip-shake is far more artistic in quiet solos and is of course always used in parts written for the old hand-horn. In modern scores, however, the student will find frequent examples of shakes which could not possibly be produced by the lips, but these come under the head of 'effects', being usually employed to add to the excitement of loud dramatic passages—"purple patches", in fact. Most major and minor valve-shakes are possible, especially between middle C and top G, the ones to be avoided being those which require more than one valve to be moved. German Horns are fitted with a fourth valve which puts them into the key of high B flat ("B flat alto"). This makes high notes easier to produce but need not be taken into consideration by the composer, the F transposition being consistently used throughout the compass in the written part. The player does the necessary re-transposition when he finds he wants to use the fourth valve.

The Valve Trumpet

The Trumpet in B flat is the one most used in this country, and composers are advised to write for it rather than for the Trumpet in C which lacks nobility and splendour of tone, though admittedly it is easier to produce top-notes on it. In any case, whether the composer writes for it or not his parts will be played on the B flat instrument.

With regard to Trumpet solos in the orchestra, no composer or orchestrator of any taste would give the Trumpet a sentimental melody to play except perhaps as a joke. Fanfare-like themes, of course, suit it best, or quiet melodic passages of neutral emotional significance or of a hymn-like nature. At all events a Trumpet melody should be dignified if meant to be taken seriously.

Mutes

Jazz has familiarised us with muted Trumpet effects. In this branch of music mutes of different shapes, sizes and materials are used, most of which have not yet invaded the orchestra. We have yet to witness during the course of a symphony concert the exhilarating sight of the Trumpet players holding their hats over the bells of their instruments!

The ordinary mute is used a great deal, however; perhaps over-used. It is a great mistake to use mutes on brass instruments merely to get a quiet effect as they alter the tone entirely, and soft "open" brass sounds splendid.

Muted Trumpets played *piano* blend admirably with the Oboe, and a three-Oboe effect may be obtained from an orchestra which only contains one, by combining it with two muted Trumpets. The low notes of the Flute also blend well with *pianissimo* muted Trumpets, especially if a fibre mute is used.

The *forte* and *fortissimo* of the muted Trumpet is very harsh and arresting, and dissonant chords for muted Trumpets and Trombones are of good dramatic effect. Soft staccato chords for full muted Brass are a legitimate comic device suitable for the satirical march themes and so on, chiefly to be found in film or radio incidental music.

The Cornet

We agree with Gevaert's remark quoted at the top of p.76. The Cornet has not proved its worth as an orchestral instrument, especially now that the B flat Trumpet has taken the place of the F Trumpet in the orchestra. The Cornet lacks distinction and is very little, if at all, more agile than the B flat Trumpet.

With regard to Widor's remark about the use of four Trumpets, one can only warn the student against extravagance. He will be wise to write for two only, or in a large symphonic work for three at the outside, if he wants conductors to look further into his score than the list of instruments required.

The Tenor Trombone

Widor's description of this instrument and its capabilities is very full and complete. With regard to pedal-notes, all are now available to a first-rate player, and certainly the A flat and G are perfectly practicable. But opportunities for their use are very rare and their sound is somewhat coarse. He does not mention mutes as applied to Trombones which now are an every-day occurrence. The effect on the tone is similar to that produced by the Trumpet mute. Most modern scores furnish illustrations of muted Trombones played both softly and loudly, especially those of Arnold Bax. Vaughan Williams uses soft muted Trombones in the slow movement of his *Symphony No. 4 in F minor* and loud ones in *Satan's Dance of Triumph* in *Job*. Elgar also used them quietly near the end of the slow movement of his *Symphony No. 1 in A flat* with magical effect. But, as with muted Trumpets, so with muted Trombones, the mute changes the actual tone of the instrument and should not be used with the intention of merely damping down the sound. The Trombones are capable of a true *pianissimo* without the use of mutes as Widor illustrates in his extract from *Parsifal* on p. 83, but it must be remembered that such *pianissimo* chords should be placed in the medium register.

One would emphasise the point made in par. 4, p. 80, about the lowest notes of the Tenor Trombone. Apart from the lack of strength and sustaining power, they are poor in musical quality even in the *piano* and *pianissimo*. They are much better on the Bass Trombone.

The Bass Trombone

The Bass Trombone used in this country is in G, not F. Therefore the table of positions given on p. 87 must be transposed up a tone, the bottom note of the 7th position being C♯ and the top note of the 1st position G.

Widor's recommendations as to its use are excellent, but one would add that the modern player can produce pedal notes in, at any rate, the first three positions, if required. Some instruments are fitted with special mechanism whereby all the semitones below bottom C♯ and fundamental G can be obtained. This is chiefly useful when no Tuba is available and essential low Tuba notes have to be 'cued in' for the Bass Trombone.

If the low C is urgently required on an instrument not fitted in this way, the player can push his slide out a fraction further than the 7th position and 'lip' the note flat, but there is some danger of the slide coming apart from the rest of the instrument unless plenty of time is given for careful adjustment.

The Trombone Glissando

The examples given in par. 10, p. 86, are certainly disastrously crude, but the glissando is now considered a legitimate musical effect though, of course, it should be used very seldom and then only under the guidance of impeccable taste. Care must be taken that the notes at the extreme ends of the glissando are not more than a diminished fifth apart and that the glissando can be executed without the player having to change the direction of the slide during its course. The tables of positions for Tenor and Bass Trombones can be consulted on this point. Glissandi where used are usually to be found at the end of movements where a great climax has been built up, their tearing effect adding the final touch of excitement (e.g. the final two pages of Ravel's *Bolero*).

The Tuba (p. 91 et seq. "SAXHORNS")

The Bass Tuba, as used now in our orchestras, is usually the Tuba in F (fundamental F below 'cello C, but capable of obtaining a few lower notes by means of combinations of its four valves). It closely resembles the "E flat Bass" of the military band, but is of course pitched a tone higher. Its part is not transposed.

The Tuba often acts as a "Double Bass" to the Brass section, that is to say it adds 16 foot tone by doubling the Bass Trombone in the sub-octave. Sometimes it is written in four-part harmony with the Trombones but it does not blend well with them except in *piano* and *pianissimo*.

Sibelius shews an acute realisation of the functions of the Tuba in the orchestra. He always writes a Tuba part differentiated from those of the Trombones though, of course, often in conjunction with them, and not infrequently makes the Tuba help the Double-basses, Bassoons, etc., to provide a firm bass to groupings of Strings, Woodwind and Horns while the rest of the heavy Brass is silent. Actually the Tuba in the *piano* and *pianissimo* makes a fine bass to the Horn quartet, but it should always be borne in mind that its tone becomes more obtrusive the higher it gets.

The Tuba is sometimes fitted with a fifth valve whose function is to correct faulty intonation when the other four valves are in operation; others are so constructed that the fourth valve itself overcomes such discrepancies by means of special mechanism.

The use of the Tuba as a solo instrument is rare, but examples exist from Wagner onwards. Apart from Wagner's Tuba-music for Fafner in the *Ring* there is the well-known opening to his *Faust* Overture, while further examples are to be found in Stravinsky's *Petrouchka* where the dancing bear walks across the stage, in Ravel's orchestration of Moussorgsky's *Bydlo* in the *Tableaux d'une Exposition* (both of these being high up in the instrument's compass) and in Arnold Bax's *Second Symphony* (slow movement) the instrument being muted in this case. Strauss also mutes the Tuba in *Don Quixote*.

The Tenor Tuba

This is the Euphonium of the military band, and in pitch and character it much resembles the Baritone Saxhorn in Bb (par. 7, p. 93, Widor). In the orchestra it is written in the treble clef, as shown in Widor's example, a ninth higher than the sounds required. In the military band its part is written in the bass clef and is not transposed.

The Tenor Tuba is occasionally used in works scored for very large orchestras, e.g. Holst's *Planets* where it is particularly effective in *Mars*, Bax's *Fourth Symphony*, Strauss' *Heldenleben*, etc. In Strauss' *Don Quixote* there is an important solo part for Tenor Tuba. This Tenor Tuba must be distinguished from the Wagner 'Tenor Tuben' in E flat used by him in the *Ring* (and later used similarly by Bruckner) as part of a special quartet of Tubas see par. 3, p. 91, and the musical example at the top of p. 97 where, incidentally, there is a misprint in the Contrabass-Tuba part; the final tied quaver should of course be G, not B flat).

Note on Brass-Band Notation
for Trombones and Tubas, etc.

In the Brass band the Tenor Trombone parts are written as transposing parts a ninth higher than the required pitch and in the treble clef, and the Euphonium the same, exactly as is the Tenor Tuba part in the orchestra. The Bass Trombone is written non-transposed in the Bass clef. The Tubas, or 'Basses' as they are called in the Brass band, are also written in the treble clef and transposed. Thus middle C for the E flat Bass represents in sound the E flat just below the bass staff, while for the B flat Bass it represents the B flat below the bass staff. In Brass band scores, in fact, the Bass Trombone is the only instrument which uses the bass clef and is not transposed. All the other instruments are in either B flat or E flat and use the treble clef exclusively, C representing B flat or E flat, as the case may be, at pitches which vary with the size and range of the instruments. For instance, middle C for the Soprano Cornet in E flat represents the E flat a minor third above, while for the Tenor Horn in E flat it sounds the E flat a major sixth below and for the E flat bass, As we have said, it sounds a major sixth plus an octave below. In the case of the B flat instruments middle C for the Cornets sounds B flat a tone below. for the Baritones, Euphonium and Tenor Trombones a ninth below and for the B flat Bass a ninth plus an octave below.

The reason for this apparently complicated system is that the fingering and technique of all the valve-brass instruments are practically identical, and so the musical notation is merely a symbol representing fingering and lip-pressure. With a little practice a player can thus change from one instrument to another without the mental effort of substituting a new set of symbols for those to which his reaction has become automatic through use.

In the *Military* band the orchestral notation is used for the Brass instruments except the Euphonium, whose part is written in the bass clef and at its true pitch.

CHAPTER III
(p. 98, Widor)

PERCUSSION INSTRUMENTS

The Kettle Drums (Timpani)

Widor gives a splendidly full account of these, to which it is not necessary to add very much.

With regard to limits of pitch (par. 4, p. 99, Widor) the low E flat is quite good in *piano* and *pianissimo*, while top G on the smallest drum is used by Elgar in the *Troyte* variation of the *Enigma* and by Walton in the last movement of his *B flat Symphony*. An early example of top F sharp is to be found in Mendelssohn's *Capriccio in B minor* for Pianoforte and Orchestra. But these high notes are certainly rather a strain on the drum-head and should only be used as a vital necessity.

The Machine-drums mentioned in par. 6, p. 100 have not yet come into general use, at any rate in this country, therefore Timpani parts should be written to be playable on the ordinary Drums unless alternative parts are provided.

The Sticks (par. 8, p. 101, Widor)

The choice of sticks is usually left to the performer though more attention might be paid to this subject by orchestrators. For radio-transmission it has been found that certain passages of a rhythmical nature come out more clearly if wooden-headed sticks are used. The Timpani sometimes tend to sound blurred and even to have a blurring effect on the rest of the orchestral ensemble in broadcast music, when ordinary soft sticks are used in a strongly marked rhythm.

We have often had occasion to mention Sibelius in these notes, and do not hesitate again to recommend the study of his scores in regard to his Timpani parts. To Sibelius each instrument of the orchestra has a strongly marked personality and is never used mechanically or perfunctorily. This will be found to be true in a very marked sense with regard to his use of the Timpani. But Sibelius is, of course, not alone in this, and any modern score will show the regard which composers pay to the Timpanist as a musician, and their appreciation of what he can do.

Percussion Instruments in general

Widor's remarks on these are full and complete, but there is one point which has to be made and that is the necessity for economy in the orchestra. In some scores one finds that four or five percussion-players are needed in addition to the Timpanist. This is perfectly feasible in the case of large works written by established composers and which can only be played by first-rate and fully-equipped symphony orchestras. But for works of a less ambitious type by composers not yet world-famous it is strongly urged that restraint should be used. At the most two players, apart from Timpani, should be demanded. But these two players can be made to change from instrument to instrument as required, and with a little skill can be used to produce all the colour and excitement required. Even one player can thus be used, provided that common sense is exercised in regard to the time allowed for the various changes. Indeed, in some small theatre orchestras there is only one player for Timpani and Percussion combined, yet so skilful is he that effect after effect can be provided by him. Economy in another sense is also to be urged on the orchestrator. Save up your effects and they will be all the more overpowering when they do arrive. Percussion is, of course, not only used loudly, as most of Widor's musical extracts show, and charming effects can be obtained by the tasteful use of these instruments, which add rhythm and sparkle to the lighter forms of music and impressiveness when used to add their weight to symphonic climaxes. In Widor's day percussion was not considered quite the thing in symphonic music, in fact he says he has never heard of a Side-drum being used in a symphony, but since then all these instruments have come to be regarded as integral parts of the orchestra for all styles of music, symphonic works by such composers as Elgar, Vaughan Williams, Bax and Bliss showing the use of many of them, especially Bass-Drum and Cymbals, Side-Drum, Triangle, Glockenspiel and Tambourine.

The XYLOPHONE has now reached a high state of virtuosity, a clever player being able to execute very rapid runs, repeated notes, glissandi and so on.

A percussion player is expected to be able to perform on every instrument except possibly the Celesta (which really hardly comes under the head of percussion) which is played by a pianist drawn, perhaps, from the ranks of the Violins.

If TUBULAR BELLS are used it is wisest to select notes for them to play from the scale of E flat major as they are for the most part built to that scale. Probably we have the "1812" Overture to thank for that. Bells tuned to notes outside that scale may be difficult to obtain and therefore should be avoided.

CHAPTER IV
(p. 125, Widor)

THE SAXOPHONES

The Alto Saxophone has been used with great effect by Vaughan Williams in Scene VI of *Job* to characterise the snivelling hypocrisy of Job's comforters, which it does admirably.

It also has an important solo part in Ravel's orchestration of Moussorgsky's *Tableaux d'une Exposition* (*Il Vecchio Castello*). Ravel uses three Saxophones in his *Bolero*, the Sopranino in F, the Soprano in B flat and the Tenor in B flat. Debussy wrote a Rhapsody for Saxophone and Orchestra and a few concertos and rhapsodies have been written for Sigurd Rascher, the well-known saxophonist, including one called *Saxo-rhapsody* by Eric Coates.

But, on the whole, serious composers have tended to fight shy of it, only using it on very rare and special occasions. The best of the family, as Widor says, is the Alto Saxophone in E flat (par. 4, p.126, Widor), but the Tenor in B flat is very good. The Baritone in E flat had a very full tone but seems to have fallen out of use to a large extent.

In certain small orchestras which are required to play both dance music and "straight" music some of the Woodwind players can usually "double" on Saxophones. Such orchestras often contain no Horns, and it has been found that essential Horn passages can be transferred to Alto or Tenor Saxophones with some degree of success. A Tenor Saxophone can also fill the place of a missing Trombone, for if it is placed between two Trombones in chords the blend is very good even in the *forte*. Widor correctly observes (par. 11, p.127) that the Saxophones tend to stand out from the rest of the orchestra and this has been the principal reason for their failing to establish themselves in it except as very occasional solo instruments. The trouble is that they have what might be called a "hybrid" tone which prevents them from fitting comfortably into the Wood-wind group, to which it would seem they ought to belong, and thus they upset conventional ideas about orchestration. Actually, of course, they form a distinct family, though their tone is capable to a considerable extent of combination with that of the heavy Brass section of the orchestra.

It is said that Sax tried to persuade Wagner to include Saxophones in his scores but that Wagner refused to have anything to do with them. He must have realised that they would not blend well with any of the normal Wood-wind instruments and groups, though he might have done interesting things with them if he had used a quartet of them, just as he did with his quartet of "Wagner-Tubas." Indeed it should be possible to use a *concertante* group of members of the Saxophone family contrasted with the rest of the orchestra. The writer is informed that in the United States, ensemble playing by Saxophones has been brought to a much higher degree of artistic finish than elsewhere, a trio or quartet practising together for perhaps two or three years until they all attain even the same rate of vibrato. There, also, tone production has been cultivated to such an extent that the Saxophone group can not only produce a fine *pianissimo* but in the *fortissimo* it can compete so successfully as almost to overpower the Trumpets and Trombones.

In America the playing of Jazz is taken as a serious branch of musical art, and this is bound to have repercussions on "straight" music in the future to a greater and greater extent, at any rate as regards orchestration.

The Harp (p.128, Widor)

French composers have always been great exponents of the Harp, and Widor's explanations and examples are excellent in every way. The *chromatic* Harp mentioned in par. 16, p.138, has still failed to find its way into the orchestra.

The scores of Debussy and Ravel's works are full of exquisite Harp-writing which well repay study.

One use of the Harp which is most effective is the doubling in unison, high up, of a moderately quick Wood-wind passage. A kind of icy cutting edge which is deliciously scintillating is given to the music.

The Organ

The reaction of most musicians to the Organ might be summarised in some such way as this: "Grand in Bach and the like; essentially a polyphonic instrument; good in music written by organists of imagination (such as Widor himself) who really understand the unique musical capabilities of the instrument and never let it degenerate into attempting to imitate the orchestra; regrettable in arrangements of orchestral pieces except perhaps from a purely virtuoso point of view in which musical satisfaction is replaced by the kind of breathless admiration one feels for the performances of the acrobat or prestidigitateur; to be avoided in combination with the orchestra except in old music which relies on a substratum of organ-tone, e.g. the church-music of Bach and his contemporaries."

Holst, feeling the weakness of the orchestral bass in sustaining long notes, used the pedal-board only in his *Hymn of Jesus*, and the shuddering effect of low pedal notes certainly adds something to the orchestra which cannot otherwise be obtained. Elgar, in the *Dream of Gerontius* holds on the minor third, G sharp and B, for a very long time, the Organ giving a perfectly uniform and unchanging tone-quality which no orchestral instruments could give (p. 187 of the score).

This is an excellent example both of imaginative genius and of the capacity of a composer to exploit a unique characteristic of an instrument. The unchanging and unchangeable minor third here suggests the mystery of eternity.

Thus, when used with real imagination by a truly poetical composer the Organ can take its place in the orchestra not as a competitor with it but as a means of expression. It should not be used simply to make more noise at a climax, and it should not be used at all unless a real and inescapable need for it is felt by the composer.

Before leaving this subject one might idly speculate on the invective which the Cinema Organ and its slippery-fingered practitioners would have drawn from our author!

CHAPTER V
(p.148, Widor)

THE STRINGS

The Violin
There is nothing to be added to Widor's admirable section on the Violin. The table of availiable double-stops and chords (pp.151-157, Widor) and the explanation of Harmonics (pp.158-161, Widor) are particularly of the utmost practical help to the non-violinist.

The Viola
Just as the technique and repertoire of the Oboe have been enlarged in this country by the superb playing of Leon Goossens and his pupils, so have those of the Viola by that of Lionel Tertis and of others who have either been his pupils or have been spurred on by his example, e.g. Bernard Shore and William Primrose. Not only have concertos and sonatas for the Viola been produced in fair quantity, the most distinguished being that of William Walton, but the Viola section of the String orchestra has received a greater amount of attention and appreciation from composers than it formerly enjoyed. Up to a little time ago the *Sinfonia concertante* of Mozart, Berlioz's *Harold in Italy*, and, to a less extent, Strauss' *Don Quixote* were more or less isolated examples of the use of the Viola as a solo instrument, but of late solo passages for Viola have become a common ingredient of orchestral works and much technical and musical ability has been required of orchestral violists. Vaughan Williams has always shown a predilection for the Violas and for Viola solos in his works from the *London Symphony* to *Flos Campi* and his Viola-writing is always grateful to play and to hear. As Widor says (par.3,p.166) the outer strings are the best, the most characteristic and unique in sound being the fourth (C) string. The middle strings have a veiled, romantically mysterious quality and the top string produces a tone somewhat allied to the Oboe. The unison of Violas, Oboes and Cor Anglais is very telling, while that of Violas and Clarinets, especially in the low register, is rich in the extreme. Bassoons may be added to this, and they add still further richness and roundness of tone.

The compass given by Widor (par.1 p.166) is still to be recommended for orchestral Violas though good solo players can reach G or even A above the top C he gives as the upward limit. Extreme high notes have not, naturally, as good a tone as the same notes on the Violin, being rather thin and pinched in effect.

Divisi passages for Violas and Cellos in medium register have a lovely quality which might be described as idealised Organ tone, and Violas divided into three or four parts give a tone-colour of great beauty and expressiveness (Sibelius *Tapiola* Full Score, p.7 et seq., and p.33 et seq.).

The Violoncello
Notation (par.17, p.182, Widor). The notation in the G clef is now invariably written at the true pitch.

The Violoncello in the orchestra (par. 18, p.182, Widor). It is a little misleading to give the impression that the 'Cello is usually employed independently of the Double-bass and that "the Double-bass is usually left to bear unsupported the enormous weight of the harmonic mass," especially when in the very next sentence we are told that the Double-bass alone "seems dull and devoid of tonal precision." The facts are that the 'Cellos can support a good deal of weight above and still give a clear, strong bass, that more than half the time they still share the bass line with the Double-basses, and that when the 'Cellos are playing a tenor part the Bassoons, Bass Clarinet or some such instruments have to be used in conjunction with the Double-basses unless the music is very quiet and has a simple bass line, otherwise there is insufficient support for the harmony.

Passages for Violoncelli divisi are sometimes written. A very well known instance of this occurs at the beginning of Rossini's overture to *William Tell,* and Wagner uses the effect in the *Ring*. Sibelius's *Tapiola* also contains an example (p.32, Full Score also shows the use of harmonics for Violas, 'Cellos and Double-basses).

The Double-Bass

Quality of the Strings (par. 6, p.186, Widor). The top string cannot really be called "as intensely expressive as a 'Cello string," though virtuosi can admittedly obtain a certain amount of expressiveness by the use of vibrato. The tone is somewhat dull and lacks variety, as anyone who has attended a Double-bass recital must admit, but the skill and artistry of present-day players is beyond question.

The Mute

The Double-bass can be muted, and frequently is, but the mute must be sufficienty heavy to damp the vibrations of the bridge. Conductors should see that their bass players are provided with really efficient mutes.

String Effects

A well known effect not mentioned by Widor is the *ponticello tremolo*. This, when executed *pianissimo*, produces a mysterious rustling effect which is frequently used in music of a dramatic character.

The opposite of *sul ponticello* is *sul tasto* or *sur la touche*. A *pianissimo* tremolo executed in this way is so feathery and light as to be barely audible, espocially if the mute is used at the same time.

The indication for plucking strings near the sounding-board of the Harp is *sur la table*.

Table of Instrumental Compasses
(p. 192, Widor)

The following corrections should be made in this:

Bass Clarinet   Tuned in B flat only, but can obtain low C sharp.

Double Bassoon   Most instruments can now descend to B flat.

Horn   Ignore "Ascending and Descending Horns."
Compass of the Horn is from the B natural given as the lowest note of the "Descending Horn" to the F given as the highest note of the "Ascending Horn."

Trumpet   Nowadays tuned in B flat, not C. Do not use the A Trumpet which is a modification of the B flat (by the addition of a longer shank) and has imperfect intonation.
The D Trumpet is often used now for Bach and Handel parts, and sometimes for very high modern parts.
The B flat Trumpet may be taken up to D if properly approached.

Cornet à Pistons   Advisable not to use it in the orchestra.

Bass Trombone   Compass from C sharp to G, a tone higher than that given in the Table.

Tuba   Can descend to E flat or D. Should not be taken above about D or E flat above middle C.

Tenor Tuba   Rarely used. Tuned in B flat. Compass from E below Bass staff to B flat above middle C. Part written a ninth higher, in treble (G) clef.

Kettle-drums   Lowest drum can descend to E flat, and the highest ascend to G, but F to F, as given in the Table, is the normal compass for the drums.

CONCLUSION
(p.197, Widor)

The following suggestions are added to Widor's four paragraphs devoted to the principals of scoring:

5. Make sure that you can recognise infallibly the sound of every instrument in every part of its compass.

6. If you are a student at one of the big schools of music, attend all orchestral rehearsals and listen carefully to the various ways in which instruments and groups are combined. Listen score in hand if possible, and go over the work mentally afterwards with the score while the sound is still fresh in your memory.

7. Make friends with orchestral players, and get them to talk "shop" to you and show you their instruments. If you hear orchestral players talking "shop" together, keep quiet and listen to them.

8. Before actually starting to write a score, rule out the bar lines of the entire work and put in the clefs before you write a note. You can then proceed unhampered by the irksome demands of manual labour. Put clefs and key-signatures on every page.

9. Do not necessarily start writing your score on the first page and plough straight on, but put in what you are sure you want anywhere in the course of the work, even if it is only a few notes sprinkled here and there. It is assumed that a short score of the work has first been made.

10. If there are several climaxes in the work, but one supreme one, score this first, and lay it out so as to get the maximum sonority. You can then see to it that this big moment is not overshadowed by others.

11. See that you do not use the Horns incessantly. There is rather a temptation to do this to ensure fulness of tone in the middle of the orchestra. Give them all the rests you can. The same injunction applies to the Oboes.

12. If a Wind-instrument is to have an important and lengthy solo passage arrange for it to have some bars rest beforehand so that the player can begin his solo unfatigued.

13. Avoid constantly giving Wind and Strings identical passages in unison. If the character of the music allows it, devise brilliant passage work for Strings at your climaxes while Wind and Brass play longish notes on which they can get plenty of tone.

14. Do not overwork the Percussion department. The effect of percussion is in inverse proportion to its use. It is a good plan to fill in the percussion parts after the whole of the rest of the score has been completed. Do not change the tuning of your Timpani for the sake of one note or so and then change them back to the original tuning.

15. If you want performances of your works, neither employ instruments not in general use, nor an outsize orchestra. If you use the less common instruments, cue their essential parts in for instruments which are sure to be there.

16. Mark all bowing for Strings and phrasing for Wind with the greatest care. Be very careful, too, to put in all expression-marks, and see especially that all entries of instruments have dynamic indications. Do not put in your p's and f's mechanically all down the page. It is often necessary to mark the Brass, for instance, at a lower dynamic level than the Wood-wind or Strings or both, to get a good balance.

17. Do not write any notes in the score that are not really wanted, just for the sake of giving an instrument something to do. Every note in your score must have purpose.

18. Avoid doing what Delius did in his *Song before Sunrise,* to the second Oboe. It has only two notes or so to play in the whole work, and they are *pianissimo* low C's, or some such thing. Leave out an instrument altogether rather than treat it like that.

19. Do not over-use the muted Brass. Realise the fine effect of full Brass *piano* or *pianissimo,* comfortably placed, without mutes.

20. Do not write a passage in an unassuming work which is so difficult that only a very exceptional player can perform it. In all things show a sense of proportion.

21. Remember that the orchestra is a collection of human beings, not a vast machine. Try to please the players by showing that you understand the peculiar genius of each instrument. You will then gain their approbation and co-operation, which will carry your work a long way towards success.

∴ Manuscript Orchestral Parts

Composers are not always affluent and may prefer to copy their own parts for economic reasons. In any case students should be urged to do so if there is a chance of their work being performed or run through, as they are then made to realise more fully what they have written for each player.

∴ The following hints are therefore appended:

i) Write large clear notes and do not cramp space.

ii) Make sure that rehearsal letters or numbers occur every twenty bars or so. Place these letters or numbers at points where fresh entries take place, or a change of mood or colour first makes its appearance.

iii) Put clef and key-signature at the beginning of every line.

iv) Write pairs of instruments (2 Flutes, 2 Oboes, etc.) on the same sheet on two bracketed staves.

v) See that the Wind parts are so arranged that a few bars rest is allowed for turning over. This ought to be obvious, but is sometimes neglected by beginners with very trying results. The same thing should be done, if possible, in String parts, but it is not quite so vital, as two players share a desk and are playing identical notes. In very small orchestras, however, there may be only one Viola, Cello and/or Bass player, in which case rests must of course be allowed for turning over, as in Wind and Percussion parts.

vi) When an instrument has a long rest it is very easy for the player to miscount his bars and come in in the wrong place. To ensure against this cues are inserted in the part. A cue should be placed a few bars before the entry of the instrument which is resting and should consist of three or four bars which the player is likely to hear. A prominent phrase is chosen and against it is put the name of the instrument playing it. Cues are usually needed in Brass and Percussion parts which have prolonged rests. If a transposing part is given as a cue it should be written at its full pitch, but if the resting instrument's part is a transposing one the cues are transposed accordingly. For instance, a Horn passage given as a cue for a Trombone will be written at its sounded ("concert") pitch, whereas an Oboe passage given as a cue to a Clarinet will be transposed as though it were a Clarinet passage in B flat or A as the case may be. Cues should be written in small notes, or different coloured ink, with a rest clearly shown in each bar for the silent instrument.

vii) Cues given of passages for instruments which may be missing are written into the parts of other instruments in just the same way as the other kind of cue described in the foregoing paragraph, the name of the instrument for which such a passage was originally written being given with the cue.

viii) In a rest the number of bars is given, but if rehearsal-letters or changes of time-signature appear— and the latter are sometimes of frequent occurrence in a modern work— the number of bars' rest is broken up accordingly.

If any doubt is felt in the matter of writing out good orchestral parts a set of parts should be obtained (either **MS.** or printed, or, better, both) and carefully examined. A bad, amateurish set of parts, unclean and illegible, will antagonise an orchestra at once, and will naturally interfere with the smooth running of a piece. The composer is therefore wise who regards this matter of parts as one of prime importance.

Dover Orchestral Scores

Bach, Johann Sebastian, COMPLETE CONCERTI FOR SOLO KEYBOARD AND ORCHESTRA IN FULL SCORE. Bach's seven complete concerti for solo keyboard and orchestra in full score from the authoritative Bach-Gesellschaft edition. 206pp. 9 x 12. 24929-8

Bach, Johann Sebastian, THE SIX BRANDENBURG CONCERTOS AND THE FOUR ORCHESTRAL SUITES IN FULL SCORE. Complete standard Bach-Gesellschaft editions in large, clear format. Study score. 273pp. 9 x 12. 23376-6

Bach, Johann Sebastian, THE THREE VIOLIN CONCERTI IN FULL SCORE. Concerto in A Minor, BWV 1041; Concerto in E Major, BWV 1042; and Concerto for Two Violins in D Minor, BWV 1043. Bach-Gesellschaft editions. 64pp. 9⅜ x 12¼. 25124-1

Beethoven, Ludwig van, COMPLETE PIANO CONCERTOS IN FULL SCORE. Complete scores of five great Beethoven piano concertos, with all cadenzas as he wrote them, reproduced from authoritative Breitkopf & Härtel edition. New Table of Contents. 384pp. 9⅜ x 12¼. 24563-2

Beethoven, Ludwig van, SIX GREAT OVERTURES IN FULL SCORE. Six staples of the orchestral repertoire from authoritative Breitkopf & Härtel edition. *Leonore Overtures,* Nos. 1–3; Overtures to *Coriolanus, Egmont, Fidelio.* 288pp. 9 x 12. 24789-9

Beethoven, Ludwig van, SYMPHONIES NOS. 1, 2, 3, AND 4 IN FULL SCORE. Republication of H. Litolff edition. 272pp. 9 x 12. 26033-X

Beethoven, Ludwig van, SYMPHONIES NOS. 5, 6 AND 7 IN FULL SCORE, Ludwig van Beethoven. Republication of H. Litolff edition. 272pp. 9 x 12. 26034-8

Beethoven, Ludwig van, SYMPHONIES NOS. 8 AND 9 IN FULL SCORE. Republication of H. Litolff edition. 256pp. 9 x 12. 26035-6

Beethoven, Ludwig van; Mendelssohn, Felix; and Tchaikovsky, Peter Ilyitch, GREAT ROMANTIC VIOLIN CONCERTI IN FULL SCORE. The Beethoven Op. 61, Mendelssohn Op. 64 and Tchaikovsky Op. 35 concertos reprinted from Breitkopf & Härtel editions. 224pp. 9 x 12. 24989-1

Brahms, Johannes, COMPLETE CONCERTI IN FULL SCORE. Piano Concertos Nos. 1 and 2; Violin Concerto, Op. 77; Concerto for Violin and Cello, Op. 102. Definitive Breitkopf & Härtel edition. 352pp. 9⅜ x 12¼. 24170-X

Brahms, Johannes, COMPLETE SYMPHONIES. Full orchestral scores in one volume. No. 1 in C Minor, Op. 68; No. 2 in D Major, Op. 73; No. 3 in F Major, Op. 90; and No. 4 in E Minor, Op. 98. Reproduced from definitive Vienna Gesellschaft der Musikfreunde edition. Study score. 344pp. 9 x 12. 23053-8

Brahms, Johannes, THREE ORCHESTRAL WORKS IN FULL SCORE: Academic Festival Overture, Tragic Overture and Variations on a Theme by Joseph Haydn. Reproduced from the authoritative Breitkopf & Härtel edition three of Brahms's great orchestral favorites. Editor's commentary in German and English. 112pp. 9⅜ x 12¼. 24637-X

Chopin, Frédéric, THE PIANO CONCERTOS IN FULL SCORE. The authoritative Breitkopf & Härtel full-score edition in one volume; Piano Concertos No. 1 in E Minor and No. 2 in F Minor. 176pp. 9 x 12. 25835-1

Corelli, Arcangelo, COMPLETE CONCERTI GROSSI IN FULL SCORE. All 12 concerti in the famous late nineteenth-century edition prepared by violinist Joseph Joachim and musicologist Friedrich Chrysander. 240pp. 8⅜ x 11¼. 25606-5

Debussy, Claude, THREE GREAT ORCHESTRAL WORKS IN FULL SCORE. Three of the Impressionist's most-recorded, most-performed favorites: *Prélude à l'Après-midi d'un Faune, Nocturnes,* and *La Mer.* Reprinted from early French editions. 279pp. 9 x 12. 24441-5

Dvořák, Antonín, SERENADE NO. 1, OP. 22, AND SERENADE NO. 2, OP. 44, IN FULL SCORE. Two works typified by elegance of form, intense harmony, rhythmic variety, and uninhibited emotionalism. 96pp. 9 x 12. 41895-2

Dvořák, Antonín, SYMPHONY NO. 8 IN G MAJOR, OP. 88, SYMPHONY NO. 9 IN E MINOR, OP. 95 ("NEW WORLD") IN FULL SCORE. Two celebrated symphonies by the great Czech composer, the Eighth and the immensely popular Ninth, "From the New World," in one volume. 272pp. 9 x 12. 24749-X

Elgar, Edward, CELLO CONCERTO IN E MINOR, OP. 85, IN FULL SCORE. A tour de force for any cellist, this frequently performed work is widely regarded as an elegy for a lost world. Melodic and evocative, it exhibits a remarkable scope, ranging from tragic passion to buoyant optimism. Reproduced from an authoritative source. 112pp. 8⅜ x 11. 41896-0

Franck, César, SYMPHONY IN D MINOR IN FULL SCORE. Superb, authoritative edition of Franck's only symphony, an often-performed and recorded masterwork of late French romantic style. 160pp. 9 x 12. 25373-2

Handel, George Frideric, COMPLETE CONCERTI GROSSI IN FULL SCORE. Monumental Opus 6 Concerti Grossi, Opus 3 and "Alexander's Feast" Concerti Grossi—19 in all—reproduced from the most authoritative edition. 258pp. 9⅜ x 12¼. 24187-4

Handel, George Frideric, GREAT ORGAN CONCERTI, OPP. 4 & 7, IN FULL SCORE. 12 organ concerti composed by the great Baroque master are reproduced in full score from the Deutsche Handelgesellschaft edition. 138pp. 9⅜ x 12¼. 24462-8

Handel, George Frideric, WATER MUSIC AND MUSIC FOR THE ROYAL FIREWORKS IN FULL SCORE. Full scores of two of the most popular Baroque orchestral works performed today—reprinted from the definitive Deutsche Handelgesellschaft edition. Total of 96pp. 8¼ x 11. 25070-9

Haydn, Joseph, SYMPHONIES 88–92 IN FULL SCORE: The Haydn Society Edition. Full score of symphonies Nos. 88 through 92. Large, readable noteheads, ample margins for fingerings, etc., and extensive Editor's Commentary. 304pp. 9 x 12. (Available in U.S. only) 24445-8

Liszt, Franz, THE PIANO CONCERTI IN FULL SCORE. Here in one volume are Piano Concerto No. 1 in E-flat Major and Piano Concerto No. 2 in A Major—among the most studied, recorded, and performed of all works for piano and orchestra. 144pp. 9 x 12. 25221-3

Mahler, Gustav, DAS LIED VON DER ERDE IN FULL SCORE. Mahler's masterpiece, a fusion of song and symphony, reprinted from the original 1912 Universal Edition. English translations of song texts. 160pp. 9 x 12. 25657-X

Mahler, Gustav, SYMPHONIES NOS. 1 AND 2 IN FULL SCORE. Unabridged, authoritative Austrian editions of Symphony No. 1 in D Major ("Titan") and Symphony No. 2 in C Minor ("Resurrection"). 384pp. 8¼ x 11. 25473-9

Mahler, Gustav, SYMPHONIES NOS. 3 AND 4 IN FULL SCORE. Two brilliantly contrasting masterworks—one scored for a massive ensemble, the other for small orchestra and soloist—reprinted from authoritative Viennese editions. 368pp. 9⅜ x 12¼. 26166-2

Dover Orchestral Scores

Mahler, Gustav, SYMPHONY NO. 8 IN FULL SCORE. Authoritative edition of massive, complex "Symphony of a Thousand." Scored for orchestra, eight solo voices, double chorus, boys' choir and organ. Reprint of Izdatel'stvo "Muzyka," Moscow, edition. Translation of texts. 272pp. 9⅜ x 12¼. 26022-4

Mendelssohn, Felix, MAJOR ORCHESTRAL WORKS IN FULL SCORE. Considered to be Mendelssohn's finest orchestral works, here in one volume are the complete *Midsummer Night's Dream; Hebrides Overture; Calm Sea and Prosperous Voyage Overture;* Symphony No. 3 in A ("Scottish"); and Symphony No. 4 in A ("Italian"). Breitkopf & Härtel edition. Study score. 406pp. 9 x 12. 23184-4

Mozart, Wolfgang Amadeus, CONCERTI FOR WIND INSTRUMENTS IN FULL SCORE. Exceptional volume contains ten pieces for orchestra and wind instruments and includes some of Mozart's finest, most popular music. 272pp. 9⅜ x 12¼. 25228-0

Mozart, Wolfgang Amadeus, LATER SYMPHONIES. Full orchestral scores to last symphonies (Nos. 35–41) reproduced from definitive Breitkopf & Härtel Complete Works edition. Study score. 285pp. 9 x 12. 23052-X

Mozart, Wolfgang Amadeus, PIANO CONCERTOS NOS. 11–16 IN FULL SCORE. Authoritative Breitkopf & Härtel edition of six staples of the concerto repertoire, including Mozart's cadenzas for Nos. 12–16. 256pp. 9⅜ x 12¼. 25468-2

Mozart, Wolfgang Amadeus, PIANO CONCERTOS NOS. 17–22 IN FULL SCORE. Six complete piano concertos in full score, with Mozart's own cadenzas for Nos. 17–19. Breitkopf & Härtel edition. Study score. 370pp. 9⅜ x 12¼. 23599-8

Mozart, Wolfgang Amadeus, PIANO CONCERTOS NOS. 23–27 IN FULL SCORE. Mozart's last five piano concertos in full score, plus cadenzas for Nos. 23 and 27, and the Concert Rondo in D Major, K.382. Breitkopf & Härtel edition. Study score. 310pp. 9⅜ x 12¼. 23600-5

Mozart, Wolfgang Amadeus, 17 DIVERTIMENTI FOR VARIOUS INSTRUMENTS. Sparkling pieces of great vitality and brilliance from 1771 to 1779; consecutively numbered from 1 to 17. Reproduced from definitive Breitkopf & Härtel Complete Works edition. Study score. 241pp. 9⅜ x 12¼. 23862-8

Mozart, Wolfgang Amadeus, THE VIOLIN CONCERTI AND THE SINFONIA CONCERTANTE, K.364, IN FULL SCORE. All five violin concerti and famed double concerto reproduced from authoritative Breitkopf & Härtel Complete Works Edition. 208pp. 9⅜ x 12¼. 25169-1

Ravel, Maurice, DAPHNIS AND CHLOE IN FULL SCORE. Definitive full-score edition of Ravel's rich musical setting of a Greek fable by Longus is reprinted here from the original French edition. 320pp. 9⅜ x 12¼. (Not available in France or Germany) 25826-2

Ravel, Maurice, LE TOMBEAU DE COUPERIN and VALSES NOBLES ET SENTIMENTALES IN FULL SCORE. *Le Tombeau de Couperin* consists of "Prelude," "Forlane," "Menuet," and "Rigaudon"; the uninterrupted 8 waltzes of *Valses Nobles et Sentimentales* abound with lilting rhythms and unexpected harmonic subtleties. 144pp. 9⅜ x 12¼. (Not available in France or Germany) 41898-7

Ravel, Maurice, RAPSODIE ESPAGNOLE, MOTHER GOOSE and PAVANE FOR A DEAD PRINCESS IN FULL SCORE. Full authoritative scores of 3 enormously popular works by the great French composer, each rich in orchestral settings. 160pp. 9⅜ x 12¼. 41899-5

Schubert, Franz, FOUR SYMPHONIES IN FULL SCORE. Schubert's four most popular symphonies: No. 4 in C Minor ("Tragic"); No. 5 in B-flat Major; No. 8 in B Minor ("Unfinished"); and No. 9 in C Major ("Great"). Breitkopf & Härtel edition. Study score. 261pp. 9⅜ x 12¼. 23681-1

Schubert, Franz, SYMPHONY NO. 3 IN D MAJOR AND SYMPHONY NO. 6 IN C MAJOR IN FULL SCORE. The former is scored for 12 wind instruments and timpani; the latter is known as "The Little Symphony in C" to distinguish it from Symphony No. 9, "The Great Symphony in C." Authoritative editions. 128pp. 9⅜ x 12¼. 42134-1

Schumann, Robert, COMPLETE SYMPHONIES IN FULL SCORE. No. 1 in B-flat Major, Op. 38 ("Spring"); No. 2 in C Major, Op. 61; No. 3 in E-flat Major, Op. 97 ("Rhenish"); and No. 4 in D Minor, Op. 120. Breitkopf & Härtel editions. Study score. 416pp. 9⅜ x 12¼. 24013-4

Schumann, Robert, GREAT WORKS FOR PIANO AND ORCHESTRA IN FULL SCORE. Collection of three superb pieces for piano and orchestra, including the popular Piano Concerto in A Minor. Breitkopf & Härtel edition. 183pp. 9⅜ x 12¼. 24340-0

Strauss, Johann, Jr., THE GREAT WALTZES IN FULL SCORE. Complete scores of eight melodic masterpieces: "The Beautiful Blue Danube," "Emperor Waltz," "Tales of the Vienna Woods," "Wiener Blut," and four more. Authoritative editions. 336pp. 8⅜ x 11¼. 26009-7

Strauss, Richard, TONE POEMS, SERIES I: DON JUAN, TOD UND VERKLARUNG, and DON QUIXOTE IN FULL SCORE. Three of the most often performed and recorded works in entire orchestral repertoire, reproduced in full score from original editions. 286pp. 9⅜ x 12¼. (Available in U.S. only) 23754-0

Strauss, Richard, TONE POEMS, SERIES II: TILL EULENSPIEGELS LUSTIGE STREICHE, "ALSO SPRACH ZARATHUSTRA," and EIN HELDENLEBEN IN FULL SCORE. Three important orchestral works, including very popular *Till Eulenspiegel's Merry Pranks,* reproduced in full score from original editions. Study score. 315pp. 9⅜ x 12¼. (Available in U.S. only) 23755-9

Stravinsky, Igor, THE FIREBIRD IN FULL SCORE (Original 1910 Version). Inexpensive edition of modern masterpiece, renowned for brilliant orchestration, glowing color. Authoritative Russian edition. 176pp. 9⅜ x 12¼. (Available in U.S. only) 25535-2

Stravinsky, Igor, PETRUSHKA IN FULL SCORE: Original Version. Full-score edition of Stravinsky's masterful score for the great Ballets Russes 1911 production of *Petrushka.* 160pp. 9⅜ x 12¼. (Available in U.S. only) 25680-4

Stravinsky, Igor, THE RITE OF SPRING IN FULL SCORE. Full-score edition of most famous musical work of the 20th century, created as a ballet score for Diaghilev's Ballets Russes. 176pp. 9⅜ x 12¼. (Available in U.S. only) 25857-2

Tchaikovsky, Peter Ilyitch, FOURTH, FIFTH AND SIXTH SYMPHONIES IN FULL SCORE. Complete orchestral scores of Symphony No. 4 in F Minor, Op. 36; Symphony No. 5 in E Minor, Op. 64; Symphony No. 6 in B Minor, "Pathetique," Op. 74. Study score. Breitkopf & Härtel editions. 480pp. 9⅜ x 12¼. 23861-X

Tchaikovsky, Peter Ilyitch, NUTCRACKER SUITE IN FULL SCORE. Among the most popular ballet pieces ever created; available in a complete, inexpensive, high-quality score to study and enjoy. 128pp. 9 x 12. 25379-1

Tchaikovsky, Peter Ilyitch, ROMEO AND JULIET OVERTURE AND CAPRICCIO ITALIEN IN FULL SCORE. Two of Russian master's most popular compositions. From authoritative Russian edition; new translation of Russian footnotes. 208pp. 8⅜ x 11½. 25217-5

von Weber, Carl Maria, GREAT OVERTURES IN FULL SCORE. Overtures to *Oberon, Der Freischutz, Euryanthe* and *Preciosa* reprinted from authoritative Breitkopf & Härtel editions. 112pp. 9 x 12. 25225-6

*Available from your music dealer or write for **free** Music Catalog to*
Dover Publications, Inc., Dept. MUBI, 31 East 2nd Street, Mineola, NY 11501
*Visit us online at **www.doverpublications.com***